Australian Universities

A Conversation about Public Good

PUBLIC AND SOCIAL POLICY SERIES

Gaby Ramia, Series Editor

The Public and Social Policy series publishes books that pose challenging questions about policy from national, comparative and international perspectives. The series explores policy design, implementation and evaluation; the politics of policy making; and analyses of particular areas of public and social policy.

Australian social attitudes IV: the age of insecurity
Ed. Shaun Wilson and Markus Hadler

Australian universities: a conversation about public good
Ed. Julia Horne and Matthew A.M. Thomas

Buying and selling the poor: inside Australia's privatised welfare-to-work market
Siobhan O'Sullivan, Michael McGann and Mark Considine

Globalisation, the state and regional Australia
Amanda Walsh

Markets, rights and power in Australian social policy
Ed. Gabrielle Meagher and Susan Goodwin

One planet, one health
Ed. Merrilyn Walton

Quit smoking weapons of mass distraction
Simon Chapman

Risking together: how finance is dominating everyday life in Australia
Dick Bryan and Mike Rafferty

Wind turbine syndrome: a communicated disease
Simon Chapman and Fiona Crichton

Australian Universities

A Conversation about Public Good

Edited by Julia Horne and
Matthew A.M. Thomas

SYDNEY UNIVERSITY PRESS

First published by Sydney University Press

Sydney University Press
Fisher Library F03
University of Sydney NSW 2006
Australia
sup.info@sydney.edu.au
sydneyuniversitypress.com.au

A catalogue record for this book is available from the National Library of Australia.

ISBN 9781761540301 hardback
ISBN 9781743328712 epub
ISBN 9781743328804 pdf

Cover design by Miguel Yamin.

We acknowledge the traditional owners of the lands on which Sydney University Press is located, the Gadigal people of the Eora Nation, and we pay our respects to the knowledge embedded forever within the Aboriginal Custodianship of Country.

Contents

List of Abbreviations ix

List of Tables xi

List of Figures xiii

(Re)starting the conversation 1
Julia Horne and Matthew A.M. Thomas

Part 1 Reimagining Australian universities 15

1 The *One Sydney, Many People* story 17
Lisa Jackson Pulver with Peta Greenfield

2 One million livelihoods 29
Susan Goodwin and Ariadne Vromen

3 Why are Australian universities so large? 41
Glyn Davis

4 Reform for what purposes? 55
Ren-Hao Xu

Part 2 Reconsidering students 65

5 When do we answer the call for cultural change? 67
Jennifer Barrett, Lisa Jackson Pulver, Peta Greenfield and Michelle Dickson

6 Beyond "access" and "affordability" 87
Samantha McMahon and Valerie Harwood

7 International students in Australia since the early 1900s 103
Julia Horne

8 International students: During, before and after 119
Gaby Ramia

Part 3 Rethinking structures 131

9 Who should pay for university? 133
Gareth Bryant

10 Fees and HECS and the politics of access to university 151
Gwilym Croucher

11 The 2020 Job-ready Graduates Package and what it means for students 163
Tim Payne

12 Twenty years of research in Australia's universities and implications for the future 177
Alan Pettigrew

Part 4 Revisiting the public good 197

13 Let us have more scientists, and more humanists 199
Michael A. Goodman

14 Building a university culture fit for purpose 215
Tim Soutphommasane and Stephanie Wood

15 Teaching and learning at Australian universities in uncertain times 229
Matthew A.M. Thomas, John Iromea, Remy Low, Victoria Rawlings and Susan Banki

16 Universities, their publics, and climate change 241
Tamson Pietsch

Continuing the conversation 251
Julia Horne and Matthew A.M. Thomas

Contributors 255

List of Abbreviations

ADFA	Australian Defence Force Academy
ALP	Australian Labor Party
ARC	Australian Research Council
CGS	Commonwealth Grant Scheme
Coalition	The Liberal-National Coalition is an alliance of two political parties, the Liberal Party of Australia and the National Party of Australia. It forms one of the two major groupings in Australian federal politics.
CRC	Cooperative Research Centre
CRTS	Commonwealth Reconstruction Training Scheme
EEA	European Economic Area
ERA	Excellence in Research for Australia program
ESOS	Education Services for Overseas Students Framework
FTE	Full-time Equivalent
Go8	Group of Eight
GUF	General University Funds on Research
HECS	Higher Education Contribution Scheme
HELP	Higher Education Loans Program

HEPP	Higher Education Participation and Partnerships
IRLSAF	Indigenous, Regional and Low SES Attainment Fund
JRG	Job-ready Graduates Higher Education Reform Package
ISFEE	International Student Fee Income
LCP	Liberal Country Party
LNP	Liberal/National Party
MRFF	Medical Research Future Fund
NSW	New South Wales
OECD	Organisation for Economic and Co-operation and Development
QILT	Quality Indicators for Learning and Teaching
RBG	Research Block Grant
SDGs	Sustainable Development Goals
TAP	Tertiary Access Payment
TEAS	Tertiary Education Allowance Scheme
UNSW	University of New South Wales
VET	Vocational Education and Training

List of Tables

Table 2.1 Changes in the age of familial independence for accessing university student income support. 34

Table 12.1 Changes in Research Block Grant categories. 183

Table 12.2 Percentage of female Research-only and Teaching and Research staff by academic level. 187

Table 12.3 Total International Student Fee Income. 190

List of Figures

Figure 5.1 National domestic enrolments in higher education 2003–19. 72

Figure 5.2 National tertiary attainment – Aboriginal and Torres Strait Islander students. 79

Figure 6.1 Diagrammatic pedagogies: mapping possibilities for outreach. 97

Figure 12.1a Distribution of RBG allocations in 2001. 180

Figure 12.1b Distribution of RBG allocations in 2020. 181

Figure 12.2 General University Funds as a percentage of total expenditure on research in 2018. 189

Figure 12.3 Total ISFEE vs Total GUF by group. 191

(Re)starting the conversation

Julia Horne and Matthew A.M. Thomas

The importance of conversation

One evening in May 2020, not long after the initial lockdown restrictions were eased, several of us gathered in a colleague's house in Sydney for convivial conversation over dinner. We caught up on each other's lockdown lives, revelled in the stories of zoom indiscretions, and despaired at the havoc wreaked by COVID-19 in the rest of the world. Our discussion then turned to the federal government's newly legislated JobKeeper program which had become a gatekeeper of sorts of what jobs to "keep" through direct financial support and what, the implication was, to abandon amidst the unknown and uncertain future economic forces. Chefs, waitresses, maître d's – keep. Musicians, entertainers, actors – [thinking pause] – abandon. Shop assistants, office workers, construction workers – definitely keep. University casuals – [no pause] – abandon. Staff who work at private universities, colleges and clubs – keep. Staff at public universities – definitely abandon. Or at least, that's how it felt.

"We need UniKeeper!" quipped one of the colleagues. She was right: the unfortunate revelation was that private universities and colleges were eligible for JobKeeper, whereas public universities were not. Universities were increasingly expected to find alternative sources of funding for teaching and research to supplement the fast-declining government sources. This occurred even as other employees working at public institutions – including politicians – were not under threat of losing their jobs.

A few months later, the Commonwealth Parliament of Australia passed the Job-ready Graduates Package, condemned by sociologist Raewyn Connell as "the most miserable excuse for a higher education policy in the eighty years that such documents have been written in Australia".[1] A further revelation was that it resulted in private higher education institutions now receiving almost the same proportion of government funding as public universities, even though the former do not conduct research. Yet research, a required mission of public universities, is very expensive and the gap between government research funding and the real costs of research had been growing ever wider over the last 30 years, requiring universities themselves to supplement the shortfall from their teaching revenues. There was something clearly not right.

Furthermore, according to reliable senior university sources from across the sector, the Morrison government's conversational mode was becoming increasingly hostile to universities, a combative attitude, many claimed, with little if any common ground. Government ministers and their advisers seemed no longer inclined to listen, let alone converse with universities about their future.

It is true that in 2020 and 2021 important funding was allotted to struggling rural universities, many of which were shedding staff at a great rate to combat the significant effects of declining revenue. There was also a one-off $1 billion emergency rescue package announced to support ongoing research threatened by diminished external income, especially international student fee income. And there was desperately needed increased support for Aboriginal and Torres Strait Islander students.

But the bigger point remains: over the last decade governments stopped making time to constructively discuss the place of public universities in Australian higher education, not amongst themselves, nor through organised consultation with universities, nor with the public. Furthermore, there is now a serious divergence between current government funding policy and the question of how to sustainably fund the central missions of teaching and research for present and future generations of Australians. Indeed, many of us in universities have grown to accept a lack of interest by governments in the broader question of sustaining public universities as a vital public resource for Australia, its peoples, and the means for significant global engagement. Instead, in the period up until the 2022 federal election, many universities endured government sniping and suspicion over their activities: academic relations with China are now effectively legislated to make them almost not worth the effort despite important collaborative work in fields such as medical science; broad and mostly wild accusations about universities suppressing "free speech" are ubiquitous; and, perhaps most repugnant of all, a sustained attack on the humanities and the social sciences arose, even though many of its disciplines are the foundation of the university tradition and immensely relevant for modern day employment, seemingly the only concern of current governments.

In sum, there was no longer a conversational common ground between universities and the Commonwealth government that was both consultative and constructive. The new Labor government went to the 2022 election on a policy of a "universities accord".[2] Time will tell what that means for the future and the nature of conversations to be had. As the chapters in this book show, discussing and finding "common ground" could lead to some of the most exciting and creative thinking about universities in decades.

How did we get here?

For the first 140 years of universities in Australia, there were many robust debates and much action around reform within and between universities and governments, with generally constructive outcomes.[3] From their foundation in 1850, the "public" ownership of universities in Australia has meant a continued – and often contested – discussion about their place in society. The first Australian universities were established in the 19th century by colonial governments as self-governing, non-collegiate, public institutions, largely non-residential, gently secular, and upholding access based on academic merit by examination rather than on one's religious beliefs (as was then the practice in the Anglo-speaking world). And by the late 19th century, they were comprehensive rather than specialist with a wide range of professional courses.[4] In 1914, Australia had six universities, all public institutions, one in each state with a national total of 4,274 students and 330 academic staff. From the mid-1940s until 1988, the number of universities in Australia grew from 6 to 19, an average of three new universities per decade. Student enrolment rose from 11,675 in 1943 to 28,792 in 1953, and to 181,483 in 1986. Over the same period, the percentage of female student enrolments rose to 47 per cent of total enrolments.[5] The expansion was due to federal Labor and Coalition governments both recognising the importance of higher education to Australia's social and economic development. Various Commonwealth financial arrangements over the four decades from 1943 sought to provide assistance to students (including research students) to study at universities. And significantly, there was a Commonwealth assurance of sufficient funding to modernise the ageing and ailing infrastructure of universities and to employ more staff for the increased student cohort.[6]

The last major higher education reforms in Australia began in 1988, and we still live with them. Called the Dawkins reforms, they sought to build on the existing structure of Australian universities in order to create a mass university system which aimed to reach across class, culture and society to admit students regardless of wealth or educational advantage. The number of universities increased from 19 to 38 in a span of just several years. Enormous transformation and disruption followed in the wake of these reforms. To name just a few: an exponential rise in the numbers of students and staff; major changes to Commonwealth funding arrangements to universities for teaching, research and public accountability; and a new Australian-designed tuition fee structure to help pay for the expanded system without overburdening students. Government policy was also implemented to reinvent international students as an export market by allowing universities to charge them full fees.[7]

In short, the Australian Commonwealth's *Higher Education Funding Act* (1988) – the formal name for the Dawkins reforms – ushered in a new era of higher education in Australia. A once diversified sector of higher education comprising many institutions of varying size and different missions was now called a "unified system" of universities with very little diversity between them.[8] In 1989, there were 73 higher education institutions, some with comprehensive offerings (19 universities), others with specialist and niche offerings such as music conservatoriums and art schools along with teaching, nursing, physiotherapy, agricultural and technology colleges. By 1992 there were only 38 higher education institutions, all universities, some spread across the cities and the metropolitan hinterland, and others in the rural regions, offering much the same comprehensive degree offerings.[9]

The reforms were to become the defining education policy of the Australian Labor Party during its 13 years (1983–96) in government. The changes were substantial, especially for the smaller specialist colleges, many of which had fewer than 1,000 students. Enforced by a heavy fiscal hand, any institution without 8,000 equivalent full-time students by the designated date would not receive the promised public funding. Small was no longer viable as specialist colleges and rural universities scrambled to find suitable partners with which to "amalgamate", the term used at the time to describe the frenetic activity of structural reorganisation. In their "amalgamated" forms, many universities were hastily created in a short period of time with new missions as comprehensive higher education and research institutions.[10] Nor were some of the long-established universities fully prepared for this new higher education system. Australia's oldest university, for example – the University of Sydney – now had five additional faculties formed as a consequence of incorporating an art school, teacher's college, nursing college, conservatorium of music, and college of applied health sciences (with such disciplines as physiotherapy and speech therapy).[11]

Nonetheless, 38 universities welcomed the next generation of university students in this now massified system. Over more than three decades between 1992 and 2018, university student numbers soared from 559,365 to 1,562,520, an increase of almost 300 per cent, but the number of public universities remained about the same. The 2018 figures represent some of the highest participation rates of school leavers in the world, and at least 30 per cent higher than the often-compared higher education landscape in the United Kingdom.[12] The reforms also allowed for the establishment of private higher education institutions, initially private universities, such as Bond University, and in recent years, a growing number of much smaller private institutions such as the Christian Alphacrucis College.

Until 1987 all universities in Australia were public institutions largely funded by the public purse. Even now the university system is still almost entirely public: out of 42 universities in Australia, 37 were created by acts of Australian parliaments and are – by an enormous margin of 90 per cent and more – the largest supplier of higher education in Australia.[13]

It is within this context that Dawkins and the Labor government introduced these profound changes to the organisation of higher education in Australia over a period of four years. These Labor reforms remain the essential foundation of the higher education system in Australia to this day.

Universities and the public good

Yet it is not just "public" ownership and financing that matter. At their core, higher education institutions are – or should be – focused on supporting and enhancing the public good. Of course, arriving at a shared definition of "public good" would itself be an exercise in democratic engagement, but in what follows we briefly highlight several elements of the public good that we consider essential in transforming higher education in the future.

First, we believe the good of the public is served when universities help educate its citizenry. We use the verb "educate" here intentionally – in lieu of the more instrumental "train" – to imply that this process is one of broad significance. No matter the discipline, universities help cultivate critical thinking, ethics, creativity, social dispositions, and new ways of seeing, thinking and being within the world. Institutions are best when they educate, guide and develop students as whole people, not simply future employees. The good of the public is therefore enhanced when its citizens emerge from universities with deeper understandings of the complex ways in which the world works, and how we as humans are situated collectively and relationally within it.[14]

Second, we believe the good of the public is served when universities advance knowledge. Pursuing and discovering new knowledge is vital to the future of humanity. It enables us to understand our bodies and live healthier lives; reconsider social and political relations; prevent deforestation and climate atrocity; build infrastructures that reduce poverty; appreciate beauty, in all its forms; and so, so much more. Universities – typically replete with highly educated knowledge seekers and producers – are well positioned to conduct these activities, all of which have immense benefits for the public.

Third, we believe the good of the public is served when universities are in communities, and communities are in universities; where a reciprocal and symbiotic relationship exists. Whilst the ivory tower metaphor persists, the truth is that universities have never been more engaged with communities, but we also know that more and stronger efforts are necessary. Universities are best when they engage directly with their publics and nourish relationships with communities; when they act as members of civil society and use their resources to benefit other societal institutions; and when they are open to the public, perceived as a shared and local site for robust discussion and debate.[15]

Whilst these public goods may seem lofty – and a far cry from the highly corporatised iterations currently operating in Australia – we think they are essential to developing a strong and meaningful future for universities. Supporting and enhancing the public good must be at the heart of a public university, and our hope is that this volume helps readers to reimagine, reconsider, rethink and revisit what universities were, are and could be.

The collection

This volume, we hope, will advance the conversation. After that first post-lockdown dinner in 2020, we decided to host a series of seven webinars to help engage and shape constructive conversations about universities, facilitated under the banner of the long-running Sydney-based seminar series, "History of University Life". The underlying theme of the 2020–21 seminar was the importance of public universities in uncertain times. The series focused on the past, present and future of universities to understand the here and now of higher education and why universities are important to our individual and, crucially, collective wellbeing. It was clear from the series that people inside and outside universities felt strongly enough to participate in a conversation about the future; there was much to say.

The conversations were held live online – we could do little else in pandemic times. We asked experts from a range of disciplines to speak for ten minutes each on a particular aspect of university life, after which we threw the conversation open to our online audiences who participated rigorously with polite gusto. The webinars were promoted on Twitter and through various university and organisational channels, then subsequently posted to YouTube and Vimeo, ultimately reaching an audience of over 1,400 people across Australia and beyond.

This volume is inspired by over a decade of seminars hosted by "History of University Life" but more directly originated in these original webinars produced and disseminated during the evolving and uncertain times of the COVID-19 global pandemic. The negative effects of the pandemic were far-reaching, not least for the higher education sector. Yet one of its less negative impacts was the space created to broadly reflect upon how the systems and structures that shape our work, lives, education, and more, were designed and functioning. Despite all of its terror, the pandemic compelled many of us to reconsider who we were, who we wanted to be, and how we might get there. Higher education, as one of the most influential social institutions, also seemed ripe for reconsideration.

In what follows we argue for a constructive conversation about the "best" higher education reform that will serve the Australian people *in all their diversity*. We shy away from using the phrase "in the national interest" because the phrase is not precise, and is often used lazily to justify policy decisions. There are weaknesses in the current system, and identifying and understanding these will, we hope, lead to more complex and promising policy approaches to higher education. To name some of the system weaknesses discussed in this collection:

- Educational disadvantage in Australia often begins in school and is still a major barrier to full university participation amongst culturally diverse young Australians.

- Universities are still foreign places for many Aboriginal and Torres Strait Islander peoples and, despite some progress, the challenge remains to overturn this state of affairs.
- There continues to be a lack of policy recognition that diversity at our universities, perhaps most importantly amongst university students, simultaneously increases Australia's social, cultural and economic wellbeing.
- The financing of the sector tends to be pursued exclusively in narrow fiscal terms when it should be considered in broader terms to understand the social impacts.
- The mythology around scale – that the bigger a university is, the better – no longer necessarily serves the best interests of higher education in Australia.
- Funding for research and major infrastructure is expected to come from non-government sources (for example, international student fees and philanthropy).
- Universities as "fit for purpose" requires institutional agility to change internal cultures (including those that underpin pedagogy) as well as the ability to be first responders, as it were, to crises that face humanity, not the least of which is climate change. This is expected despite considerable regulatory and pecuniary restrictions that often hamper the necessary agility.
- And finally, an approach to policymaking and reform that in the past two decades has advanced the short term rather than nurturing more enduring gains. The approach has often been politically partisan and ideologically driven, rather than wide-ranging, consultative, inclusive and imaginative.

Indeed, universities are far from perfect structures and, no doubt, there is much specific internal reform required to make these large organisations – some of the largest universities in the world – operate both efficiently and humanely.

In this introductory chapter, we've sought to lay the foundation for a broader conversation about higher education in Australia, but the real "conversational" work occurs in the chapters that follow. For example, the still too low rate of Aboriginal and Torres Strait Islander participation is simply not good enough despite more than three decades since the publication of A Fair Chance for All, the 1990

Commonwealth discussion paper on equity.[16] As that publication stated, equity in higher education will only be achieved "by changing the balance of the student population to reflect more closely the composition of society as a whole".[17] The discussion paper identified Aboriginal and Torres Strait Islander peoples as one of the six main groups experiencing educational disadvantage, and they remain so, as Jennifer Barrett, Lisa Jackson Pulver, Peta Greenfield and Michelle Dickson explain in their joint contribution.

Young people from low socio-economic backgrounds are another group still suffering disadvantage. Susan Goodwin and Ariadne Vromen argue for a new approach to student assistance to help break the vicious cycle of young people's educational disadvantage, while Samantha McMahon and Valerie Harwood explore what young people actually say about universities for clues on how to help make universities more accessible. Meanwhile, in two nicely paired contributions, Gwilym Croucher explains the equity principles that underlay the original Higher Education Contribution Scheme (HECS) introduced by the Hawke Labor government; and Tim Payne provides a careful analysis of the Job-ready Graduates Package, the major reform initiative of the Morrison Coalition government, discussed briefly above.

Tim Soutphommasane and Stephanie Wood argue for "good culture" strategically implemented, to create a sense of trust and collective purpose. Indigenous strategy, argues Lisa Jackson Pulver (with Peta Greenfield), is not only about improving educational or professional opportunities for Aboriginal and Torres Strait Islander peoples, but also creating a sense of place and engagement infused with Indigenous insight for the benefit of everyone who studies or works at a university. Gaby Ramia tackles the worrying trend that sees international students in economic terms rather than as social beings, while Julia Horne examines the history of international students in Australia – all the way back to the early 1900s – for relevant lessons for the present. Matthew Thomas brings together three reflections about the pedagogical transition to online teaching during the pandemic, and the lessons for the culture of learning, lest we simply go back to "business as usual" without thinking critically about what teaching and learning is and could be. And Tamson Pietsch offers the concepts of "publics" and "social contract" as a way for universities to respond to the future, especially around the global challenge of climate change.

Gareth Bryant argues for a nuanced analysis of the current "logics" of university funding in order to plan for the present and future. Alan Pettigrew identifies patterns of research funding over the last 20 years to understand the present government funding conundrum. But while the question of how higher education is funded has consumed government policymakers since the 1980s, other contributors remind us this question should not be the only one on the reform agenda. Not since the Dawkins reforms in 1988 have governments built new universities despite a prior 140 years of history in doing so. Instead, the implied policy is that existing universities simply expand, which Glyn Davis explains is neither sustainable nor especially desirable. Ren-Hao Xu takes as his critical starting point the very idea of "reform" in order to compare approaches between Australia and Taiwan, while Michael Goodman looks back at two key historical moments of Commonwealth government intervention in the 1940s and 1950s, which, despite sometimes rocky periods, largely opened constructive dialogue between universities and the Commonwealth.

Overall, our aim with this collection is to understand both the historical and present constraints in the current system as well as to offer some possible ways forward, or at a minimum, some vital questions to consider. The choice of topics was not intended to be comprehensive – other potential editors would probably focus on different areas. We have, however, selected 16 contributions that offer achievable – and exciting – goals for the future of higher education in Australia.

Our collective hope is that the book might be read by policymakers, university strategists, students, and all of us interested in public higher education in Australia. We hope that future discussions might be conducted constructively, ideally through wide consultation that includes members of the public and, crucially, universities themselves. Together, the collection provides a backwards glance to past policies and public commitments and a sense of purpose for the future. And above all, we hope the book helps governments of all persuasions to (re)start the conversation.

Notes

1 Connell, Raewyn (2022). Remaking universities: notes from the sidelines of catastrophe. *Griffith Review 75 – Learning Curves*, 11–17.
2 Horne, Julia (2022). A new accord: restoring good relations between government and universities. *Australian Book Review* July (444): 26–27.
3 Horne, Julia (2020). Mass education and university reform in late twentieth century Australia. *British Journal of Educational Studies* 68(5): 671–90.
4 Horne, Julia and Geoffrey Sherington (2012). *Sydney: the making of a public university*. Melbourne: The Miegunyah Press; Selleck, R.J.W. (2004). *The shop: the University of Melbourne 1850–1939*. Melbourne: Melbourne University Press; Turney, Clifford, Ursula Bygott and Peter Chippendale (1990). *Australia's first: a history of the University of Sydney 1850–1939*, vol. 1. Sydney: Hale & Iremonger.
5 Figures are from Commonwealth Year Books: Commonwealth Statistician (1916). *Official Year Book of the Commonwealth of Australia*, Melbourne: Commonwealth Bureau of Census and Statistics 9: 815; Commonwealth Statistician (1944–45). *Official Year Book of the Commonwealth of Australia*, Canberra: Commonwealth Bureau of Census and Statistics 36: 197; Commonwealth Statistician (1955). *Official Year Book of the Commonwealth of Australia*, Canberra: Commonwealth Bureau of Census and Statistics 41: 420; Australian Statistician (1980). *Year Book Australia*, Canberra: Australian Bureau of Statistics 64: 285; Australian Statistician (1988). *Year Book Australia*, Australian Bureau of Statistics 71: 429.
6 Horne, Julia and Geoffrey Sherington (2013a). Dominion legacies: the Australian experience. In Deryck Schreuder, ed. *Universities for a new world: making a global network in international higher education 1913–2013*. California: Sage Publications; Forsyth, H. (2014). *A history of the modern Australian university*. Sydney: NewSouth; Macintyre, Stuart (2015). *Australia's boldest experiment*. Sydney: NewSouth; Croucher, Gwilym and James Waghorne (2020). *Australian universities: a history of common cause*. Sydney: UNSW Press.
7 Macintyre, Stuart, André Brett and Gwilym Croucher (2017). *No end of a lesson? Australia's unified national system of higher education*. Melbourne: Melbourne University Press.
8 Marginson, Simon (2016). *Higher education and the common good*. Melbourne: Melbourne University Publishing.
9 Davis, Glyn (2017). *The Australian idea of a university*. Melbourne: Melbourne University Press; Marginson, Simon (2016). *Higher education and the common good*. Melbourne: Melbourne University Publishing.
10 Mackinnon, Alison (2016). *A new kid on the block: the University of South Australia in the unified national system*. Melbourne: Melbourne University Press; Hogan, Terry (2016). *Coming of age: Griffith University in the unified national system*. Melbourne: Melbourne University Press.

11 Horne, Julia and Stephen Garton (2017). *Preserving the past: the University of Sydney and the unified national system of higher education 1987–96.* Melbourne: Melbourne University Press; Brett, André, Gwilym Croucher and Stuart Macintyre (2016). *Life after Dawkins: the University of Melbourne in the unified national system of higher education.* Melbourne: Melbourne University Press.

12 Department of Education Students Dataset 2019.

13 Department of Education Students Dataset 2018. The remaining five comprise three private Australian universities and two international universities (University of Notre Dame and Carnegie Mellon University).

14 Thomas, Matthew A.M. and Susan Banki (2021). Toward a framework for assessing the "global" and "citizen" in global citizenship education in Australia and beyond. *Discourse: Studies in the Cultural Politics of Education* 42(5): 732–48.

15 Connell, Raewyn (2019). *The good university: what universities actually do and why it's time for radical change.* London: Zed Books.

16 For historical assessments of the report, see Macintyre et al. (2017), *No end of a lesson?*, 113–19; Horne (2020), Mass education and university reform in late twentieth century Australia, 683–86.

17 Department of Employment, Education and Training (1990). *A Fair Chance for All: National and Institutional Planning for Equity in Higher Education: A Discussion Paper.* Canberra: Australian Government Publishing Service, 8. The six groups were Aboriginal and Torres Strait Islander peoples, women, students from non-English speaking backgrounds, students from rural and remote areas, students from low socio-economic groups, and students with disabilities.

Part 1

Reimagining Australian universities

1

The *One Sydney, Many People* story

Lisa Jackson Pulver with Peta Greenfield

> Ngyini ngalawangun mari budjari Gadinurada.
> *We meet together on the very beautiful Gadi Country.*

Indigenous Strategies are now familiar across the higher education sector, but they are a very recent phenomenon. What they represent and how they express aspiration is unique to each university. While most sit in intricate relationships with other strategies both internal and external to the home institution there are some that do not. For those that do, they become a tangible expression of the way that higher education seeks to serve the public and continues to evolve in accordance with community expectations. This includes expectations of nurturing Aboriginal and Torres Strait Islander students and staff to explore the best in themselves, building culturally safe campuses for all members of the tertiary community, and ensuring that generations coming through our doors receive a world-class education to help them pursue their own goals. With these complexities in mind, one of the great strengths of Indigenous Strategies is that they allow us to centre higher learning in a specific place: on Country. Each Indigenous Strategy is as unique as the Country or Countries that it serves. Here, I reflect on the experience of creating the University of Sydney's new *One Sydney, Many People* Strategy, 2021–24, to explore what it means for a university like ours to have connection to Country.

The *One Sydney, Many People* Strategy takes a whole-of-university approach to "valuing, respecting and celebrating Aboriginal and Torres Strait Islander people's knowledges and cultures".[1] The Strategy is the culmination of work within the university, ongoing collaboration with local community, and is supported in its development by an External Advisory Group of distinguished and respected Aboriginal and Torres Strait Islander peoples. *One Sydney, Many People* builds upon the work of the university's first Indigenous Peoples' Strategy, *Wingara Mura – Bunga Barrabugu*, 2012–16 ([WMBB] Thinking path to make tomorrow)[2] and acknowledges both the achievements and the challenges it faced along the way. *One Sydney, Many People* is born from the work conducted under the *Unfinished Business* Action Plan 2020 – a plan that concluded the work of WMBB – and from extensive collegial and community engagement.

Strategies such as this are seen by the university and the community as a formal document of intent. Behind this Strategy stands a vision for the University of Sydney that is focused on building and supporting cadres of culturally engaged students and staff. The key to growing cultural engagement is understanding. I invite you to open the *One Sydney, Many People* Strategy with me and we'll go on a bit of a tour together.

Language is the heart of culture – and it connects us to place – to Country

The first words of the Strategy are "Ngyini ngalawangun mari budjari Gadinurada" (We meet together on the very beautiful Gadi Country). The Gadi language is at the heart of the lands of the university's first campuses in Camperdown and Darlington. It is fitting that the language of the Gadigal opens this Strategy. First, it is an act of respect to the traditional custodians of this place which has been the site of learning and knowledge exchange for over 60,000 years. Second, this phrase is an encouragement to become more familiar with the language of this place; you can include this phrase or others offered by the local people in your area in your own Acknowledgement of Country.

Indigenous languages were rarely acknowledged or truly understood by non-Aboriginal people for some time. In the last 200 years in particular, some did not think these languages were important or were assumed to be diminished and gone. We are really fortunate that that is not the case for all languages – with the work of noted Aboriginal linguist Jakelin Troy and others on the language of this place, we are in a position to make a concerted attempt to include appropriate Gadi language in our everyday practice.[3] The university is really starting to understand and own its role *on* this land, to really consider its responsibilities to its own belonging here and to its obligations into the future. How we describe our environment, what we call things, and the proper use of Australian language – which in this area is the Gadi Gal (people of the Gadi) language – is very much a part of that.

The progression of Indigenous languages into the normal ebb and flow of university days is a step towards embracing the full breadth of who we are as an Australian University. Indigenous languages are part of the Australian lexicon. One story I remember – from long ago – is that we speak the way we do with our accent because of the influence, contribution and engagement of Aboriginal people from the earliest days of the colony. Our distinctive Australian accent is a legacy of the comingled influences of local languages with English, Scots, Irish and Welsh sounds. At the same time, this land started to change considerably because of the consequences of the colonial endeavour: Aboriginal people were removed from their families, people moved from – or were forced away from – their ancestral lands, with many forbidden from continuing cultural practices, language was suppressed. Even so, there is a resilience in language. And what is really exciting is that these languages remain and continue to be reclaimed, revitalised, documented, shared and used. Gadi language is front and centre of this Strategy, and we all have the opportunity to understand it, to learn from it, to cherish it and to speak it.

Sometimes, people ask the question of how they can start to engage culturally on this land. One of the easiest ways is to be thoughtful and genuine in our practice of Acknowledgement of Country. There is an extended and heartfelt Acknowledgement of Country on page three of the *One Sydney, Many People* Strategy that offers recognition for the many lands that the university operates upon. Each of these lands is unique, each carrying embedded knowledges of traditional custodians, and each with ways of being and doing that have the capacity to centre our research and focus our pursuit of higher learning with respect. There are also the generative benefits from performing an Acknowledgement of Country. When done from your own personal gratitude for the lands you live and work on, the Acknowledgement not only demonstrates respect for the history of learning that is the legacy of Aboriginal peoples' care for Country, it opens the space to be present, to reflect on *this* moment in time, and to take stock of this amazing place that we each call home.

Anyone can perform an Acknowledgement of Country. Nearly all of us are visitors to this country, so we must Acknowledge Country – a practice that reminds us of the unique inheritance we partake in. An Acknowledgement differs from a Welcome to Country, which is performed by cultural custodians and Elders on their own Country.

In 2008, Aunty Matilda House illustrated the significance of Welcome to Country and drew attention to the key concepts that galvanise us when we offer Acknowledgement of Country. This occurred in Parliament House, the day before Prime Minister Rudd gave the National Apology to the Stolen Generations on behalf of the Commonwealth of Australia.

People were waiting in the marble area just inside the doors. Aunty Matilda and many Aboriginal Elders from other places, along with both Houses of Parliament, and many, many, many others were anticipating something important. Aunty Matilda House got up on the podium and started her part of the Welcome to Country ceremony. She started to talk and told us that the Welcome is not a bit of entertainment for our pleasure. This smoking, the clap sticks, the singing, the dancing is what we've been doing for a long, long, long, long time. She went on to share that in her Welcome to Country, she's not just welcoming people to the event of the day, as important as it is. She said words to the effect of, No matter where you come from, no matter whether you arrived yesterday, or a hundred years ago, or 230-odd years ago or longer, that you are on *this* Country, Ngunnawal land. And that you have got rights and obligations and responsibilities to this place and to each other.

This is my interpretation of what I heard that special day. We have such a diverse Australian community and we all belong here. Many Australians cannot simply "go back home" – they have no idea of where that is now; they have no connection, no language, no culture of those places. For some, their nations no longer exist or are not safe for them. And many Australian people are from multi-ethnic backgrounds.

The message I got from Aunty Matilda that day is this: the onus is on each and every one of us to understand what it means to belong *here*, to understand the language, to know the history – the good bits and the terrible – to be courageous, and to own it. And we've each got a responsibility to pass that belonging to future generations, whether our ancestry here stretches back thousands of generations or just a few, or whether we are the very first in our family to call this land home.

Simply put – we all belong here. We all have rights, obligations and responsibilities.

For us all to Acknowledge Country is a step in the right direction. It is putting Country at the forefront of what you do and offering that recognition as a part of your responsibility to Country. When I reflect on what Aunty Matilda said in 2008, it has stayed with me. It touched me deeply and helped me understand my own drive to help others get away from simply putting Aboriginal Welcomes to the side, stuffed in a silo for use whenever there is a special occasion. We are Australians and it is time we openly listen, embrace and understand that there are ways of knowing and doing that are central to Aboriginal world views and accept these in the way we go about our daily work and lives. These are what truly makes Australia special.

Thinking about your respectful relationship to the lands on which you live and work and acknowledging that is the first step. Building personal reflection into your Acknowledgement of Country will ensure this practice takes on a life of its own and meaning through your use of it.

The development of *Yanhambabirra Burambabirra Yalbailinya* (Come, Share and Learn)

One of the most distinctive features of the *One Sydney, Many People* Strategy when you start to go through the document is the striking artwork by Luke Penrith, *Yanhambabirra Burambabirra Yalbailinya* (Come, Share and Learn). Luke Penrith is a contemporary artist with connections to the Wiradjuri, Wotjobaluk, the Yuin and the Gumbaynggirr Nation.

An important part of the vision for this piece is the journey of the university and our desire to consciously engage with our Australian environment. When we talk about being culturally engaged, part of that is the deep understanding that when you sit in a lecture theatre, tutorial room, studio, or chemistry lab, or any other room at the university, there is nowhere else in the world where you could be other than here in Australia. It is illustrative to compare where we are on this journey with that of our near neighbour Aotearoa New Zealand. When you enter a university or government space in Aotearoa New Zealand, you know exactly where you are. And while we're not the same as our brothers and sisters across the ditch, there are important principles at play. In their spaces, in their language, in their history, people, businesses and organisations know where they are and how they fit in. And if they do forget – there are clear Treaty reparations that can be activated.

And yet so often in Australia, we can walk through familiar places and forget that we are on this ancient land. That is not okay. This university was founded in the geography of this land and Luke's artwork is about drawing inspiration from Gadigal language and lands and brings the vision of the university to life in a way that engages with the long history of this land as a place of learning. It tells us to never forget.

The picture depicts a rich story of knowledge, community, growth of aspiration, and of journeying. In the centre of the artwork is a Gadi tree (of the Xanthorrhoea genus). This tree is emblematic of the unique identity of this place. There are 29 different species of the Gadi in the world and all those species are here in Australia. When you see a Gadi tree, you *know* that you are in Australia. The Gadi is a term specific to this place, the land of the Gadigal, and the species has different names across the nation. There is a great potency in the choice to place the Gadi at the centre of this artwork. It anchors us, the viewers, to Gadigal country and reminds us that all the learning and knowledge exchange that happens here at the university is embedded in Gadigal land. This artwork is also a nod to the first official seal of the University of Sydney – based on a drawing by artist Marshall Claxton.

This was but one of the stories we shared with Luke when he was planning his artwork. In the 1850s an artist had just arrived in Sydney when he saw a competition for someone to create a design for this new aspirational university in the colonial land. I imagine he looked around the site and noticed a number of things, specifically the many different kinds of flora throughout the site under the southern skies. I presume he was thoughtful in this process – he did something quite amazing. His entry to the competition was Lady Learning sitting upon a stone plinth putting a laurel wreath upon the head of a kneeling scholar. Up in the sky was the Southern Cross and in the background was a Gadi tree. The artist was Marshall Claxton, and his entry – with some adaptations – went on to become the first identifiable seal of this university. When you look at that seal, there's no mistake about which hemisphere you're in and whose land you're on. We're so fortunate to see the continuation of the Gadi tree legacy on our Camperdown and Darlington campuses today with some of the Gadi around here predating the university. We suspect some Gadi even predate the arrival of those first colonists who envisioned a new home for themselves.

It is fitting that the Gadi tree is the central image of Luke's painting. When you look closer, the significance of the Gadi tree is strengthened; in the middle of the Gadi tree is a heart. This is an acknowledgement that our university is located in the heart of Gadigal country. This ancient heart of the land continues to beat today. When we say, "Yi Dya, Yi Gwugu", *Always Was, Always Will Be*, it is a reminder that Aboriginal people have been here for more than 60,000 years, through all the changes that have come in that time from adapting to a land that was shaping itself, a climate known for extremes through to navigating unimaginable natural disasters.[4] That is most extraordinary: these cultures have continued – and thrived – all that time and there's nowhere else on earth where that is the case. There is something profound about the heartbeat that continues on, and this is part of what Luke captures by placing the beating heart at the centre of the Gadi tree.

The painting starts from the Gadi with the heart at the centre and we can see, rippling out from that, four strands which connect to the four strong pillars in our Strategy. First, we have Nguragaingun *Culture and Community*, then Eora *People*, Ngara *Education and Research*, and finally Pemulian *Environment*. Each of these extends from the heart of the Gadi, which reflects how these four pillars were developed through extensive collaboration with people from across the university. To take one example, let's consider Pemulian in more detail.

The pillar of Pemulian "Environment"

Pemulian translates roughly as "a sense of place" and captures the idea of truly *knowing* a place. For example, the meaning associated with a place where a grandchild dances a story from the old people; the feeling a parent has when they hear their child sing songs in Gadigal language; that sense of knowledge when you walk through a strand of trees and say, "I can eat that berry," or "I know that plant would be really good medicine if I ever suffered a burn." Pemulian captures all those ideas about deeply knowing a place in the centre of your heart and knowing your connections in that place.

This pillar came about because many people wanted to know how they can walk through the university and have conversations about this place facilitated by the environment itself. This desire was evident in many of the 3,000 individual pieces of feedback that we received about what should be in our strategy. Basically, people asked, "How can we easily have conversations about place that are meaningful and respectful to the history of this land?"

One way to work towards answering this request is to implement a dual naming program across our campuses so we can all understand how Aboriginal people described the features and the places that our university now inhabits. We will be able to describe with Aboriginal words the different types of water that flow through the campus or describe the different aspects of the sky or the gentle undulations of the land or the shape or purpose of the geographic characteristics such as the kangaroo ground, the ceremonial areas or the gathering sites. This is something we're working towards and involves thinking about the physical environment as a whole including the built environment and the lands on which the buildings sit. To this end, it will allow consideration of how we can pay proper tribute to the Aboriginal history of this place, of this space, and of the opportunity it has given to generations of scholars and the Australian community.

Pemulian also goes beyond the physical; it is a way of engaging with the spiritual environment. A question I often ask is, what does it mean to be on a place that has always been a place of culture, a place of learning, a place of life transitions? I think it goes beyond the physical manifestation of the environment; it is really about *how* people belong. The big question that builds from this is how do we empower people in their sense of responsibility to this place? Aboriginal people have been responsible to this land for the past 60,000 years. How do we build that deep connection for everyone who is part of our university community for the next 50, 100, 1,000 or 60,000 years?

Pemulian gets to the heart of truly understanding where we are. And this expands out from The Apology in 2008. One of the really critical things that The Apology achieved was to underline the end of the history wars. Before 2008 there were people saying, "No, the removal of children did not happen", or "the land was not stolen" or "Cook discovered Australia". But in that moment of The Apology, we finally acknowledged – as a nation – the painful truth of that history and its effect on so many of us. That moment of The Apology was significant, in part, because it opened the way for people to seek out more truths about Aboriginal matters on this land. As part of the Strategy, Pemulian carries that hope for truth. We have a great opportunity to decide how it is we want to be into the future. For the university, that means embracing the fact that, as a place of higher education and of learning, people come here because they want a quality education on a land that has always been a place of knowledge exchange.

There are many places of higher learning in the international environment so to come here is a decision to have a uniquely *Australian* education. Part of that education has to be imbued with how it is we *are* on Country. To make that choice is also to take on a sense of belonging to this place, to take on a sense of responsibility to this place which is only possible through acknowledging that while there is great hope and opportunity here, it is only the truths we are willing to face about our past that will shape things to come. We cannot shy away from the fact that we are dealing with a lot of critical and pressing issues. Responsibility to the environment matters. We are dealing with terrible drought, awful fires, smoke encasing our cities, a pandemic with waves of illness and an unknown post infection sequela, floods, increasing water and mosquito-borne disease, widening inequalities, challenges with water resources, gas mining that is threatening our ability to practise sustainable farming and much more. Aboriginal and Torres Strait Islander sciences have got a lot to contribute when it comes to addressing these challenges from traditional practices of back-burning and water conservation methods to sustainable fishing methods. There's so much that can be learnt from the people of this land. It is vital that Aboriginal and Torres Strait Islander peoples are not excluded from these conversations as our future utterly depends on them. The call to action in Pemulian is that without discussion of environment our universities are losing one of the few remaining opportunities to lead research that can help save the world.

Each of the pillars of the Strategy offers this kind of depth. The goals set out in *One Sydney, Many People* under each pillar are practical, robust, and give us all a real opportunity to think about where we've been, how we are now, and what we want to strive for together.

The power of the visitors' circles

When we look further out towards the edges of Luke's painting you can see two additional large circles, one in the top left corner and one in the bottom right. These are two strong visitors' circles. The visitor circle in the top left represents those people who know where they're going; they have a sense of confidence about what they are doing. You might interpret them as our graduates. They're on a journey and they're very happy and strong. They know something of the history of this land, they know their role in history, and they have a sense of how they want to be in the future. They radiate with the understanding that Australia should be embraced, warts and all, as the great nation that it is, to move forward so that no one is excluded.

Then there are others who are on a different journey. They are represented as the visitor circle in the bottom right corner. These visitors are people who are still discovering what it is to be Australian, what it is to belong here. These visitors may be new students or students who are progressing in their learning, unsure but curious. When Luke was sharing this part of the painting with me it reminded me of when I was running a program of Public Health with a stream in Indigenous Health. Most of the students were international students and first-generation Australians. I asked them, "What are you doing here?" I expected to be overwhelmed with students who were fourth, fifth, sixth, seventh generation Australian. And the international and first-generation students said, "We came from a place that had a strong culture." Many of them wanted to learn about Aboriginal ways so they could take that knowledge and understanding back home to share with their families. The first-generation Australians were also keen to embrace the culture of this land, to build their cultural understanding of the place they now called home. When I asked a couple of the others in the room, "What's your story – why are you here?", they said, "Well, it's about time we learned something about this place." They took inspiration from those new arrivals to this land about what is culture. Australia has a strong, living, enduring culture and it is a culture that is changing. It is a culture that embraces many different things, but we always have that heartbeat of the first cultures. So, the visitor's circle in the lower corner represents those possibilities for learning culture, and building that appreciation for the culture that is calling us all home.

Luke's artwork does a fantastic job of bringing the aspirations of the *One Sydney, Many People* Strategy to life. If you are part of the University of Sydney, you are bound to encounter elements of this stunning painting whether online or on campus as we work together on the long-term goals outlined in the Strategy. I encourage you to reflect on your journey so far on this great land we today call Australia. Whether you are connected with the University of Sydney or another institution, we all benefit from thinking about our relationship to place, how we belong, and what our rights, obligations and responsibilities are to this beautiful land we call home.

Notes

1 The University of Sydney (2021). *One Sydney, Many People: Strategy 2021–2024*, 2. https://bit.ly/3Obu08o.
2 The University of Sydney (2012). *Wingara Mura – Bunga Barrabugu: The University of Sydney Aboriginal and Torres Strait Islander Integrated Strategy.*
3 Troy, Jakelin (1994). *The Sydney language.* Canberra: Panther Publishing and Printing.
4 With thanks to Cameron Davison for his support as a Gadi Language expert for confirming the spelling and pronunciation of the phrase "Yi Dya, Yi Gwugu".

2

One million livelihoods

Granting social citizenship to Australian university students

Susan Goodwin and Ariadne Vromen

The COVID-19 pandemic produced a crisis for Australian universities, one that was made increasingly visible to the public through increased media and policy attention. Higher education, we were told, was the fourth largest export industry in the country. The loss of international students endangered not just the universities themselves, but the entire economy. The sudden attention to universities as central pillars of the economy led to intense public debate about the way they were managed, their business model, and their public purpose.

But the pandemic impacted not only university management and university staff, but also the lives of university students. University students all over Australia, many living far from home, encountered the loss of their face-to-face education, and for many, also their livelihoods. In March 2020, when the pandemic hit, there were around 1.4 million students enrolled in Australian universities. Of these, one million were domestic students. To put these numbers in perspective, at the same time there were just under four million school students across all age groups in Australia.

These 1.4 million students were hyper-exposed to the economic shock of the pandemic. At the time, around four in five undergraduate students – 82 per cent – were in paid work, primarily in precarious, casual work. In *Coming of Age in a Crisis*, Shirley Jackson found that many industries that employ young workers, notably fast food, hospitality, retail and the arts, shrunk or closed completely during 2020.[1]

For many in the community, it came as a surprise that not even domestic or "Australian" university students could turn to the social safety net in their time of need. There seemed to be a misconception in the broader Australian community that university students who lost their jobs would have access to government benefits. This is not the case. In fact, only one third of university students regularly receive any form of government student income support, meaning that two thirds rely wholly on private sources of income to support themselves while studying, generally through employment income or parental support.[2] In Australia, taking government subsidies for tuition fees out of the equation, going to university is now by and large a *privately funded exercise.*

In this chapter, we challenge the premise and correlated assumptions that getting a university education should be privately funded, and argue instead that all Australian university students should be afforded social rights through the provision of universally applied student income support while studying. The social democratic case proposed here is a provocation to expand the "publicness" of higher education beyond the costs of tuition, but it is also a provocation to expand the recognition of the "citizenness" of young people, beyond the rights to drink and vote.

Central to this argument is the notion of "youth welfare citizenship", which focuses on the social rights of young people. The arbitrary ways in which social and economic rights to independence are currently defined in student income support policy challenge the misconception that young people share the same social rights as other (adult) citizens. We use the concept of "youth citizenship" in relation to university students to emphasise the specific ways in which their status as citizens is currently limited. Moreover, the call for expanding student income support should be applicable to *all* higher education students, regardless of age or circumstances.

Our call is not a new one. It has been raised in numerous government inquiries into universities and the social security system over the decades.[3] During the pandemic, university students put access to social rights on the political agenda. In late 2020, the National Union of Students mounted the Change the Age campaign – a petition calling on government to lower the age that young people could apply for income support as independent citizens down from 22 to 18.

In Australia, as elsewhere, there has been a mass expansion of higher education over the last 30 years.[4] This expansion can be linked to fundamental transformations in the labour market. The shift to what is often referred to as a post-industrial society, characterised by a "knowledge-based economy", has increased demand for educated workers and for specialised skills. In turn, occupational training previously provided in the workplace, such as nursing, policing, some fields of engineering and so on, has been integrated into higher education systems, and many more occupations now require tertiary level qualifications.

With these economic changes it is no longer the norm when entering the labour market to gain secure work or "standard employment" after the end of compulsory schooling. To avoid underemployment or unemployment, many now undertake some form of training or higher education. While further study is frequently presented as a "choice", in fact to establish their futures and economic security, young people are increasingly compelled to engage with the education system.

The extension of education and the disappearance of traditional post-school youth jobs has produced the problem of how to finance this period. Put simply, a lot of young people do not have enough income because they are in further education, are unemployed, or are underemployed during the void between compulsory school education and secure employment. For young people, this period of transition is also contingent on income support policies, and it is the arrangement of these policies that can make or break – or support or deny – what Tom Chevalier calls " youth welfare citizenship".[5]

A brief history of student income support in Australia

Living allowances funded by the Commonwealth government for university students have been available since 1943, when the Commonwealth Financial Assistance scheme was introduced. The scheme was largely only available to students under the age of 21, the voting age at the time, and all living allowances were subject to a family means test.

In 1951, the Menzies government established the Commonwealth Scholarship scheme. While tuition fees, which were awarded competitively on academic merit, were paid without a means test, living allowances were subject to familial means-testing. Living allowances were paid at two rates – the "living at home" rate and the "living away from home" rate.

The expansion of Commonwealth Scholarships to a small number of "mature age" students, aged 25 to 30, in 1951, introduced the concept of "independent" students by providing living allowances to older students without a parental means test. Mature age students were not expected to be supported by their parents.

In 1956, another category of adults was exempted from the parental means test – married students. While being married rendered university students independent of their parents, a spousal means test was applied, meaning that for the purposes of a university living allowance there was an expectation of spousal support. Both expectations of parental and spousal support operate to "familialise" social citizenship rights: individuals do not accrue rights to public support simply as individuals. These two forms of familialisation have continued through to the present day, albeit with some tinkering with the details of the *age* of independence from parents and the definitions of what is counted as a spousal relationship. Indeed, as discussed above, it is the apparent arbitrariness of the formulations of dependency that provokes cause to question the fundamental principles at stake in the extensions of financial dependency and responsibility in Australia.

In 1969, the Aboriginal Study Grants Scheme was introduced as part of the Commonwealth government's special measures for "Aboriginal Advancement". This scheme, which has continued with various adjustments, is known as ABSTUDY. Whilst it remains a separate scheme specifically for Aboriginal and Torres Strait Islander students, from 2000 ABSTUDY was reformed so that it mirrored benefits payable to non-Indigenous students, including the same age cut-offs for parental means testing.[6]

In 1973 the Whitlam government abolished university fees and introduced the Tertiary Education Assistance Scheme (TEAS). With the abolition of university fees, the competitive nature of the earlier scholarship schemes was removed. Any full-time student could apply for TEAS; however, it was subject to parental income testing for students under 25. In 1987, the Hawke Labor government replaced TEAS with a new payment for all students called Austudy. The Keating-led Labor government that followed Hawke reduced the age of independence for Austudy to 23 in 1994, and down again to 22 in 1995.

In 1998, under the Howard Coalition government, student income support was moved from the education portfolio to the social security system, ostensibly as an efficiency drive, and a new payment, Youth Allowance, was introduced. This payment was for young people in education *and* those who were unemployed, newly casting student income support as a welfare payment. The age of independence for student support was raised back up to 25.

The provision of student income support through the social security system has been maintained through to the present, and current students apply for income support payments through Centrelink. Symbolically and practically, the transfer of responsibility for student income support to Centrelink has meant that student living allowances have shifted from being a grant to foster university education access and completion to being seen as a welfare payment: with all of the restrictive reporting obligations and monitoring and, we add, stigma and poverty, that go with "being on Centrelink".

In 2010, the Gillard Labor government reduced the age of independence to 24, then down to 23 in 2011, and down to 22 in 2012. The age of independence has remained at 22 since this time across both Labor and LNP governments. Currently there are, confusingly, three living allowances available to university students – Youth Allowance, for 18–24-year-olds, paid at dependent and independent rates, ABSTUDY, for Indigenous students, paid at dependent and independent rates, and Austudy, for students over the age of 25, paid at the independent rate. Table 2.1 shows bipartisan practices of tinkering with the age of "independence" and limiting access to student income support.

Beyond attaining a specific age, a second way in which Australian university students are able to establish themselves as being independent has been by demonstrating that they have been financially

Table 2.1 Changes in the age of familial independence for accessing university student income support.

Year	Prime Minister/ Political Party	Age of familial independence
1951	Menzies (LCP)	25
1975	Whitlam (ALP)	25
1994	Keating (ALP)	23
1995	Keating (ALP)	22
1998	Howard (LNP)	25
2010	Gillard (ALP)	24
2011	Gillard (ALP)	23
2012	Gillard (ALP)	22

self-supporting by meeting strict workforce participation criteria. The principle being applied here is that the assumed financial dependency on parents can be shown to be severed through sustained labour market participation. As with changes in the biological age definition, there have been many changes in the workforce participation criteria that are applied. However, the most significant way in which young people's citizenship has been attenuated through student income support policies has been by enforcing the idea of ongoing parental dependency.

The case for student social citizenship

From a social democratic perspective, the degree to which social policy enables individuals to uphold a socially acceptable standard of living *independently of family relationships*, is a key concern. However, welfare and income support arrangements can treat young people as either adult citizens (as individuals) or as children (as dependants).

In France, for example, social policies are highly *familialised*, meaning their purpose is to help families take care of their children without providing any direct support to the children themselves, and "youth" is treated as an extended "childhood". University students up to the age of 25 are fundamentally seen as "social minors", or "dependants" who rely on their parents' support, and do not have access to income support in their own right. In turn, there are explicit legal obligations on parents to take care of their children until they find stable employment.[7]

On the other hand, social citizenship is *individualised* when young people are conceived of as adults. Subsequently, parents are no longer assumed to support their children, even when they pursue their studies, once they reach 18. In this approach, young people in higher education benefit from universal support, without taking into account parental income. In Nordic countries, for example, student grants are paid directly to young people at the age of 18 (including those students still in secondary school). There is no parental means test, although student grants are paid at different rates for those living at home with parents and those living away from home.

Australian social policy *familialises* young people. As demonstrated above, parental means tests for student incomes have been applied since the very first living allowances for students were introduced in 1943, and are currently applied up to the age of 22, thereby treating young people as children. However, there is no legal obligation on parents to provide young people with financial support. Instead, the notion that parents will continue, and are obligated to, support their offspring beyond 18 and the extension of dependency through to university has become a normative expectation shaped by policy.

One obvious problem with the denial of youth welfare citizenship is that it assumes parents are not only able but are also willing to support their adult children by contributing to their living and education expenses. However, the evidence does not support this assumption, and student income policies have been revised and amended to try and deal with the plethora of situations where parental support is absent. Currently, young people who are orphans, in state care, are refugees without parents in the country or who can prove a permanent breakdown in their parental relationship may be considered to be independent for the purposes of Youth Allowance. Yet these are all considered exceptional circumstances. The norms of youth dependence, parental presence and parental responsibility for financial support are retained.

Further, the biological ages set by policymakers are imposed upon the whole population, regardless of differences between different population groups, standardising dependence and independence for all. In submissions to a 2005 Senate Committee inquiry into student incomes, Aboriginal student organisations and advocates questioned the appropriateness of the age of independence for Indigenous students.[8] Citing evidence that the age of independence in the Indigenous population in Australia is significantly skewed to a younger age than the non-Indigenous population, it was argued that the age threshold was inconsistent with Indigenous youth population density. It has also been argued that Indigenous young people assume social and financial independence at a much earlier age than non-Indigenous people, and that the policy misalignment contributes to student, family and community hardship. In 2011, the National Tertiary Education Union (NTEU) recommended that "all Indigenous students studying at university (including students enrolled in enabling courses) be classified as being Independent for the purposes of ABSTUDY" to support Indigenous student access to higher education.[9]

For all Australian university students, it is the *mix* between available sources of income from the state, the labour market and the family that determines their standard of living. Here we explore the differences in how this mix is structured for young people from lower, intermediate and upper socio-economic backgrounds.

For those university students from low-income families who *are* eligible for Youth Allowance, they still need to supplement their student payments with income from largely precarious, casual paid work in order to secure their livelihoods. This is because the rate of Youth Allowance is well below the Henderson Poverty Line and because the low parental income threshold for Youth Allowance means that financial support from the family is limited. In addition to the burden of having to "earn and learn", receiving financial support through the social security system subjects these students to its compliance and monitoring regimes, including regular auditing of income and family relationship status. A universal student income would diminish the need for costly and punitive forms of monitoring through existing bureaucratic mechanisms.

For university students from intermediate socio-economic backgrounds such as from families of average income workers – or the so-called "squeezed middle" – *not* being eligible for Youth Allowance requires them to undertake enough paid work to compensate for the pressure their forced dependency places on family resources. For both groups of students, their choices – if and when they go to university, where they go to university, what courses they enrol in, where they live, who they live with, and how they balance paid work and study – are extremely constrained. To manage financially, they may have to defer all or part of their studies (or drop out) and consequently their choice of courses or universities may be limited. A requirement to work long hours to survive while enrolled at university will have a significant impact on the duration and success of their studies. This treacherous balancing act will only be exacerbated for some students by provisions in the 2020 Job-ready Graduates Package that will penalise those who take too long to complete their studies.

These young Australians from lower income backgrounds are concerned about their educational and working futures; they worry about social mobility and equality. As is shown in the chapter by McMahon and Harwood in this volume, they find it hard to imagine that they have an equal right to university education, as citizens. Other research with young people shows that their options and choices remain highly structured even though they may describe their life decisions as individualised and their own to make.[10]

For university students from upper socio-economic backgrounds, being expected to finance their university studies from a pool of family resources is also problematic. It is problematic *culturally* because it promotes and reinforces an ideal of parents providing for their children well into adulthood, when in fact it is only the very few that can afford to fully fund their offspring through university. In economically divided societies like Australia, the familialisation of young people as normal and desirable inevitably produces distinctions: between parents who can and cannot support university students, and between university students who do or do not have to work. It is problematic *politically*, because, as with all young people, it denies these young people their social citizenship rights.

The parental means test is often touted as a bulwark against "middle class welfare" and a way to reduce public expenditure on university education. But the denial of youth welfare citizenship, even to university students from wealthy families, will not address the greater problem of growing income and educational inequality in Australia. Indeed, positioning *all* young people as independent adults at the age of 18 could break the nexus that encourages the flow of intrafamilial transmissions of wealth and privilege, and the current scenario that makes going to university harder for some and easier for elite others.

Conclusion: granting student social citizenship for the public good

Universities provide an avenue for individual social mobility and collective social, economic and political progress. Further education provides individuals with opportunities to build their capabilities and can be the pathway to secure employment. Higher education is also a public good, providing the knowledge, explanations, strategic ideas and accurate information required for social and technological change. In addition, universities have become a key site for participation in society and social inclusion. In turn, both the individual and social costs of exclusion from further education are profound and long lasting. While the current meritocratic framing of a university education tends to reinforce individual responsibility for life trajectories, the public good lens shifts the focus to what we owe university students and to what they are entitled.

To conclude, we suggest that reforming higher education in a social democratic direction involves a major reframing of Australia's social welfare system. As the National Union of Students argued almost two decades ago, "Tinkering at the edges of what is essentially a mean and narrowly based system will not do much to address the overall problems of educational inequality."[11] Remaking universities for the public good involves de-privatising university educations at the level of livelihoods as well. On the basis of the youth citizenship argument, parental means testing of anyone over the age of 18 should be discarded – in democratic countries political and social citizenship rights at the age of independence should align. Arguments for a Universal Basic Income in Australia also provide new ways of thinking about how student income support could be reformed in order to achieve youth citizenship.

Indeed, the case presented here goes beyond provisions for "university students", as youth welfare citizenship pertains to the rights of *all* young people in the period of transition between compulsory education and employment. Investment in supporting student livelihoods while they access further education needs to be seen less as an individual or family investment, but as a social investment: universal student income support is required to support national and global economic and social development. In this sense, while our argument here pertains to university students, it could apply equally to students in all forms of post-school education and training, and, potentially, to students enrolled in Australian universities who come from other nations. This is one significant way in which we can re-angle the social democratic ideal: that access to a university education should be truly fair and meritocratic, and its provision delivers a collective, public good.

Notes

1 Universities Australia (2019). Submission to the Senate Inquiry into the adequacy of Newstart and related payments; Jackson, Shirley (2020). *Coming of age in a crisis: young workers, COVID-19 and the youth guarantee. A per capita discussion paper.*
2 Universities Australia, Newstart and related payments.
3 Previous Inquiries: 2005 Senate Employment, Workplace Relations and Education References Committee: Student income support; 2011 Department of Education, Employment and Workplace Relations: Review of student income support reforms; 2019 Senate Standing Committee on Community Affairs: Adequacy of Newstart and related payments and alternative mechanisms to determine the level of income support payments in Australia.
4 Antonucci, Lorenza (2018). Not all experiences of precarious work lead to precarity: the case study of young people at university and their welfare mixes. *Journal of Youth Studies* 21(7): 888–904.
5 Chevalier, Tom (2016). Varieties of youth welfare citizenship: towards a two-dimension typology. *Journal of European Social Policy* 26(1): 3–19.

6 Bills Digest No. 19 2000–01 Indigenous Education (Targeted Assistance) Bill 2000. https://www.aph.gov.au/Parliamentary_Business/Bills_Legislation/bd/bd0001/01bd019.

7 Tom Chevalier and Bruno Palier explain that the centrality of family obligations towards its members is expressed in the French civil code regulation concerning the obligation of support ("obligation alimentaire"). Chevalier, Tom and Bruno Palier (2014). The dualisation of social policies towards young people in France: between familism and activation. In *Young People and Social Policy in Europe*, 189–209. London: Palgrave Macmillan.

8 Commonwealth of Australia (2005). The Senate Employment, Workplace Relations and Education References Committee: Student income support.

9 NTEU (2011). Submission to Department of Education, Employment and Workplace Relations, Review of student income support reforms, 11.

10 Vromen, Ariadne, Brian D. Loader and Michael A. Xenos (2015). Beyond lifestyle politics in a time of crisis?: comparing young peoples' issue agendas and views on inequality. *Policy Studies* 36(6): 532–49; Donovan, Felix (2018). Living class in a 'meritocratic' Australia: the burdens of class and choice on young people's end-of-school transitions. *Journal of Sociology* 54(3): 396–411.

11 Commonwealth of Australia (2005). The Senate Employment, Workplace Relations and Education References Committee: Student income support, 59.

3

Why are Australian universities so large?

Glyn Davis

> It is "time for universities to consider their economic model".
>
> Prime Minister Scott Morrison (2021)[1]

Australian public universities do not choose their economic model. Key settings are determined by the federal government, led by the prime minister. Those decisions, embedded in federal policy, constrain options. So if we want to understand a surprising characteristic of Australia's public universities – their large student enrolment – we must look not to choices by individual universities, but to Canberra.

Many current politicians enrolled in tertiary study in the 1980s at a time when going to university was still a minority choice. Only 7.9 per cent of Australians held tertiary qualifications. Just one in four undergraduates was female.

They joined a tertiary system still shaped by policy decisions from the Whitlam and Fraser governments – free study for students but in a system squeezed by a long slow decline in funding per student. The ratio of staff to students was drifting upwards, one of many economies imposed on universities to restrain the overall cost of tertiary education. The education minister of the day controlled the number of Australians enrolled at each institution. Only 8 per cent of students were drawn from overseas.

There were 19 universities, and most largely operated on a single campus, offering only a handful of college places and little amenity for students outside teaching hours. The university relied on Canberra for funding – typically 90 per cent or more of operating revenue for an Australian public university came from the Commonwealth.

Yet soon there was a pivotal moment for Australian tertiary education. In 1990, under Minister for Employment, Education and Training John Dawkins, the system was marked by mergers, the reintroduction of student fees (offset by a deferred loans system), the first significant growth in fee-paying international students, and a massive expansion of domestic enrolments.

Over the next 30 years the number of Australians with tertiary qualifications would increase more than threefold. At the peak of demand, just before COVID-19 closed international travel, Australian universities taught some 1.4 million students, including 400,000 international students.

Yet the number of Australian universities would not keep pace with this growth in student demand. In 1994 there were 36 public universities and one private institution in Australia. Nearly two decades later there are still only 37 public with three small private universities and two international universities. Though enrolments have risen sharply over more than a generation, the number of providers is little changed.

This contrasts with earlier decades, when new universities were created to deal with growth in the system. Our capital cities added a second new university or more, while regional towns also became centres of higher learning. UNSW (founded 1949) was part of a second wave of institutions, Macquarie (founded 1964) part of a third, the University of Technology Sydney (founded 1988) part of a fourth – and for the moment final – wave.

This practice of accommodating growth by creating new universities largely ended in the early 1990s. Instead, additional students were placed on an existing campus, making them expand each year. As a consequence, the typical Australian public university is large by global standards.

In 1973, University of California Berkeley Professor of Educational Sociology Martin Trow speculated about the future of higher education.

He noted three possible organisational phases – traditional elite universities, which cater for up to 15 per cent of the population, a mass education system which educates up to half of the young people and, finally, universal participation involving new types of education providers.

Trow suggested any progression across this spectrum would necessarily change the characteristics of universities. A move from elite to mass education, as Australia has undertaken, would see the public rationale for participation shift from shaping the mind to transmitting skills. Trow predicted, accurately, a mass system would combine merit and equity programs to broaden access. He argued that system growth would require institutions to become more comprehensive, to develop a wider array of programs and standards, and more complex administrative arrangements. This would involve "formerly academics who now are clearly full-time university administrators" while "below them there is a large and growing bureaucratic staff".[2]

In his original analysis, Trow implied that small and elite institutions would grow only modestly and strive to retain their elite status. Hence mass participation would be accommodated in newly established large institutions. This future did not unfold quite as expected, at least in Australia. In the absence of long-established privileged private institutions, the nation's research-intensive public universities did not stay small. On the contrary, they are now among the largest universities not just in Australia, but globally. The differences within the system, reflected in part in institutional scale, have not materialised. Instead, every university became a much larger version of itself.

The shift to large-scale institutions

Movement from elite to mass provision can be described in many ways. Much analysis stresses the policy ideas which animate government to fund more places. Such accounts emphasise an economic logic for more higher education. Business and the professions need skills, the health system demands high levels of training, as does school education, and developments in technology stress the importance of research and innovation.

Once prime ministers spoke of Australian universities providing "the indispensable intellectual foundation for the liberal ideal of human freedom to flourish".[3] Now government policy statements inevitably focus on the economic benefits of public investment, and link education to employment; in 2020 federal Education Minister Dan Tehan called his legislation *Job-ready Graduates* – and used the measure to cut funding to arts and other subjects perceived by the minister as less worthy of public subsidy.

Ministers rarely discuss the consequences of massive growth within universities to service the economy. These include greater management control and more precarious employment for many academic and professional staff. There are claims an economic logic has pervaded decision processes within the institution, for example through closing smaller courses in favour of cost-efficient large-scale teaching. Changes during the COVID-19 lockdown included a shift to online provision and the cancellation of many building programs providing lecture theatres and staff offices. These changes likely presage a more fundamental shift towards even lower-cost education provision.

This volume canvasses the rich debates around the purpose of higher education, and the implications for universities when politicians translate their understanding into legislation and policy. In this context I explore a single variable: the scale of higher education institutions. What does it mean when almost every Australian public university, triples in student numbers within a few decades? For changes in the scale of an institution, I will suggest, shape much about character and culture. They also reflect limited choices for universities – that elusive new "economic model" the then Prime Minister Scott Morrison was keen institutions consider.

Despite the importance of scale, its consequences are not much included in accounts of change in public organisations. At best, the small scholarly literature on scale and universities focuses on correlations between size and research outcomes.[4]

Yet growth introduces complexity, and Australian universities become difficult to compare with their smaller international counterparts. As Gavin Moodie reports in his extensive analysis of universities, the average size of a Russell Group university in the United Kingdom is 17,867 undergraduate and postgraduate students. In contrast, the average enrolment of a U15 institution in Canada is 38,888 students, while members of the elite Association of American Universities enrol on average 36,103 students.[5]

In Australia, the five largest Group of Eight universities educate an average 64,328 students. This is nearly four times larger than equivalent universities in the United Kingdom, and nearly twice as large as comparable institutions in the United States.

The Australian averages disguise some huge individual institutions – on the latest available figures Monash enrols 86,753 students and RMIT 94,933. These are extraordinarily large public universities by global standards.

A single institutional snapshot illustrates the sheer size of an Australian university. Over the past three decades, student numbers at the University of Sydney grew by 122 per cent, academic staff by 89 per cent and professional staff by 55 per cent. For domestic enrolments, the University of Sydney went from 27,674 to 61,309 students. Even more remarkable is the 1,677 per cent increase in international enrolments. At the same time federal government funding fell by 60 per cent as a share of overall income, replaced by student income and philanthropy.

So over 30 years the University of Sydney has become larger and more privately funded. Like the rest of the sector, the University of Sydney depends heavily on income from international students. Even in good times it must grow continuously to maintain operations, since government funding has long been indexed at a rate less than inflation.

Scale shapes the experience of those who study or work in Australian higher education. It influences the sense of belonging, staff satisfaction surveys, complaints about reporting overload, and distance between staff and management. Scale requires administrative routines, sophisticated student systems and constant building projects to provide space, services and security commensurate with a mid-sized city. On any working day during semester the University of Sydney campus hosts more people than the entire population of Tamworth, a large inland city, while the Parkville campus of the University of Melbourne is in effect the fifth largest city in the state of Victoria.

Like cities, universities begin to look and behave the same because they must tackle similar challenges, balance the same competing demands. Scale equals complexity, and complexity imposes intricacy and technical requirements not demanded of smaller organisations.

Scale and character

The huge growth in enrolments reflects an important underlying economic reality. Even as governments grew the number of student places, they constrained per student expenditure. This created a dilemma for public universities, which faced static or diminishing funding for each student enrolled. To endure, institutions turned to the only available other source of income. From a handful of fee-paying international students in 1989, universities began recruiting across the region.

By 2020, nearly one in every four students on campus was a fee-paying international student. Their fees allowed the overall system to operate despite inadequate Commonwealth support. By then the average Australian public university derived nearly half its income from student fees – 23.5 per cent from international students and 18.8 per cent from domestic students.[6] Since many domestic student fees barely cover costs, universities rely heavily on international students to fund capital expansion and staff hires.

The inescapable cost of relying on international revenue is an ever-expanding student body. With no new universities created, existing public universities grow rapidly. Inevitably this affects internal university dynamics. International income is concentrated in business-related qualifications such as commerce, finance and management degrees. There were around 60,000 international students studying business qualifications across Australia in 2001, and more than 200,000 by 2017.[7]

A heavy concentration of income from a handful of disciplines creates challenges about how money is allocated within a university. Some faculties generate revenue, others impose costs. Expensive scientific and medical research – essential for global ranking success, in turn the basis of student recruitment – occurs in faculties which struggle to cover their overheads. Collegial decision making is stretched when some faculties produce surplus income while others consume the returns.

Investing in research, suggests a European analysis, is the price of a "proper" higher education actor like a university.[8] To support this activity, every Australian public university has developed a complicated system of internal cross-subsidies, taxing profitable courses to ensure inadequately funded programs and research can endure. The more complex the organisational mission, the more administrative staff and systems are required to manage operations, and the more arcane but urgent the argument about where student revenue should flow.

Comparative studies of scale and universities are not common, daunted perhaps by differences in national models and the problems of measurement. Only a handful of studies offer a view on scale as a variable. One German study finds – unsurprisingly – that smaller institutions are more agile, responsive and innovative; the authors speculate that "the relatively higher administrative overheads of larger universities become an organisational liability in times of rapid institutional change".[9]

A study from the United Kingdom concludes both the smallest and the largest institutions are most likely to expand their central administration relative to the number of academics.[10]

This U-shaped distribution is not entirely convincing. It is true that small institutions must still meet all the regulatory and reporting requirements imposed by governments, and therefore will have higher administrative costs. But the evidence from Australia points to substantial efficiencies achieved in both academic and professional staff areas regardless of scale, whether measured as research outputs or costs per student.

Of course, achieving more with less does not make for a happy, congenial workplace.

For students, large universities mean studying in less than intimate institutions, often with a student cohort spread across several regional and suburban campuses. This is true for staff as well. The merger of previously separate institutions means academic and professional staff often travel between sites. The possibility of calling by a nearby office to sort out an issue with a colleague or share a class is made more testing by distance. Urban housing prices mean few staff can afford to live near inner-city campuses.

Scale has affected who works on campus. Overall employment opportunities have grown as more students enrol, but the composition of the workforce has shifted. Universities rely on student income, with its inherent fluctuations and seasonal work flow. The increased use of contract and casual appointments reflects this pattern.

Australian universities are now marked by more casual staff appointments, contributing around 23 per cent of effective full-time staff, up from 15 per cent a generation earlier.[11] A “precariat” marks much contemporary higher education. Tenuous annual employment contracts have become a stressful expectation for many academics, particularly those in commerce and health science faculties with numerous international enrolments and large first year classes. The dramatic contraction which followed the onset of the pandemic in 2020 left some 17,000 academic and general staff without employment.[12]

Alongside the precariat are many doctoral graduates who aspire to university teaching and research roles but cannot find a place in the system. This reflects a mismatch between doctoral places and workforce recruitment. Not every research graduate aspires to academic positions, but many do. The number of academic positions in Australia has roughly doubled so far this century but the number of doctoral graduates has increased nearly seven-fold.[13]

Hence new doctoral graduates now compete against bigger pools of qualified applicants, and against more lateral appointments as universities recruit directly from the professions. Access to many qualified graduates make it easier for universities to rely on casual employees rather than employ expensive permanent staff. The result is a smaller tenured core and a large insecure periphery.

Operations at scale require many additional non-academic skills. Universities must install and run large data infrastructure, build and manage facilities, develop expertise in philanthropy, handle communications and expand student services. Here the evidence runs against popular perception. Much commentary on universities takes for granted that the number of administrators has increased dramatically. The data suggest otherwise. Universities have grown their academic and non-academic staff evenly and broadly in ratio with overall growth in student numbers. The ratio between academic and professional staff has changed little over the decades, despite the growing administrative demands imposed by complexity.

Larger universities may produce less satisfied employees, but this is impossible to measure without reliable and comparable data. The few available studies do not enable disaggregation by institutional size.

The nearest proxy – student satisfaction – has a loose correlation with organisational size, though the differences across all Australian public universities are modest.[14] It would hardly surprise if the happiest students study in small and specialised institutions with a strong sense of cohort. Many people prefer intimate communities with shared purposes and outlook, and smaller universities in general have higher levels of student satisfaction than larger universities. The same is likely true for staff.

Scale and the Australian university

For those working in higher education, larger institutions require huge buildings on an often crowded campus, detailed reporting requirements, and management of large classes. The common complaint across the contemporary university is little time for quality teaching, research or providing support to students.

Are there alternatives? Once Australia dealt with increased demand for places by creating new universities. Governments stopped doing so to save money. In the United Kingdom, there are still small institutions for those students and staff who value a more intimate setting. Likewise, the Canadian and American systems are marked by choice, including universities which primarily teach undergraduates. These would not be accredited under Australian law. While the number of universities remains constrained, and research is a legal requirement for university status, an Australian public university is necessarily a large institution.

Yet looking ahead, population growth means 100,000 or more additional domestic undergraduates are expected to join the system over the next decade.[15] Either Australia accommodates these new students in existing institutions or it creates alternatives.

This could be a moment of innovation – a time for new institutions that take advantage of pedagogical technologies to widen participation, a chance to experiment with graduate apprenticeships, trial novel aggregations of disciplines, teach in multiple languages, pursue knowledge of institutional governance. We can learn from the success of online learning during the pandemic, and encourage ranking systems which do more than measure research but place at least equal value on teaching quality.

There are few signs such prospects presently interest the wider public. Yet two risks might encourage policymakers to consider carefully current policy settings.

First is the funding model. By withdrawing public funding, government has deeded the nation a university sector that relies heavily on the families of Asia. The pandemic has exposed the risk. Many universities now face serious debt, further research funding cuts and, in time, falling global rankings. We are yet to see a public university go bankrupt in Australia, but the possibility looms.

Of course, government could address this by raising public investment. Alas, the government's 2020 legislation package simply accelerates the trend to lower per-student funding, with an overall cut of 8.3 per cent to student funding over the next three years.

The second risk is less immediate but still likely. There are many potential disruptions to higher education, particularly from private providers in Silicon Valley keen to provide online alternatives to traditional degree education. So far, public universities have proved alert to the threat and skilled at innovation. But in a large organisation, management attention is stretched and enmeshed. Time to react is limited. New ways of working require investment.

Just as an ecosystem dominated by one species is vulnerable to sudden environmental change, so a challenge from new technology will affect the entire Australian tertiary system in similar ways. A system with more varied institutions, some large and others small, some comprehensive and others specialist, commuter or residential, may have more scope for experimentation and rapid evolution.

Faced with these challenges, the federal government has suggested universities bear some responsibility for their own difficulties. Senators have criticised universities for relying on international students, particularly those from China – though they do not condemn other local industries even more dependent on Chinese income, from agriculture to tourism. The same senators offer no view on how universities should maintain quality and standards now the international student market has contracted.

Instead, sometime Education Minister Alan Tudge (2021) suggested that COVID-19 presents a "unique opportunity to reassess university business models".[16] Amid huge losses inflicted by the pandemic, then Prime Minister Morrison told *7:30*: "I think we should remember, these are very large organisations with billion dollar reserves and they've got multi-million CEOs and they're making decisions about how they're running their own organisations."[17] The Morrison government declined to allow public universities to join the JobKeeper scheme to support employees, but extended that privilege to most Australian businesses and charities, including private universities and colleges. Yet then Prime Minister Morrison's own academic specialisation in economic geography should have equipped him to appreciate the problem of scale.[18]

As argued in this chapter, the shape of Australian universities is the consequence of federal higher education policy. The decision to stop creating new universities led, inevitably, to sustained growth. The reliance on international students, likewise, is a response to restricted Commonwealth funding. Key variables for university strategy are controlled by Canberra – how much a university can charge domestic students, how many domestic undergraduates it can enrol, whether the borders will be open to international students. The Commonwealth directs most research funding, a further crucial variable in shaping universities.

If there is a different business model available, political leaders should articulate this with clarity. They have not been able to do so, precisely because the Australian public university is, above all, shaped by choices made in Canberra. There is no alternative economic model under current policy settings. Mr Morrison's injunction was not a meaningful insight about choice, but government deflecting blame about the consequences of its decisions.

As a student, the former prime minister lived through the decisions which created the now familiar Australian public university. As a policymaker he reinforced the path dependency which makes universities reliant on Commonwealth money. There can be no new economic model while Canberra sets these rules.

Some Australian universities will soon enrol 100,000 students. Such an institution will be barely recognisable as a scholarly community, a conversation among students and academics, a place where professional staff hope to know each class and support learning. Scale already shapes much that happens at the Australian public university; we might hope it is not the only choice.

Notes

1 Morrison, Scott (2021). Prime minister tells universities to fix their funding model. *Research Professional News*, 17 February. https://bit.ly/3o467Vx. This analysis of higher education policy was presented to an October 2018 seminar at the University of Sydney, and updated in 2021.
2 Trow, Martin (1973). Problems in the transition from elite to mass higher education. Berkeley: Carnegie Commission on Higher Education. https://eric.ed.gov/?id=ED091983.
3 Robert Menzies, quoted in Davis, Glyn (2020). Universities and the liberal imagination. *Meanjin* 79(4): 216–23.
4 Leydesdorff, Loet, Lutz Bornmann and John Mingers (2018). Statistical significance and effect sizes of differences among research universities at the level of nations and worldwide based on the Leiden rankings. Working Paper. https://arxiv.org/abs/1710.11020.
5 Moodie, Gavin (2014). How different are higher education institutions in the UK, US and Australia? The significance of government involvement. *Higher Education Quarterly* 69(1).
6 Universities Australia (2019). *Higher Education: Facts and Figures, July 2019.* https://www.universitiesaustralia.edu.au/wp-content/uploads/2019/08/190716-Facts-and-Figures-2019-Final-v2.pdf.
7 Department of Education and Training (2018). Selected Higher Education Statistics – 2018, Canberra. https://bit.ly/3PbC3D9.
8 Baltaru, Roxana-Diana. and Yasemin Nuhoglu Soysal (2018). Administrators in higher education: organizational expansion in a transforming institution. *Higher Education* 76: 213–29.
9 Schubert, Torben and Guoliang Yang (2016). Institutional change and the optimal size of universities. *Scientometrics* 108: 1129–53.
10 Andrews, Rhys and George A. Boyne (2014). Task complexity, organizational size, and administrative intensity: the case of UK universities. *Public Administration* 92(3): 656–72.

11 Norton, Andrew and Ittima Cherastudtham (2018). *Mapping Australian higher education*. Melbourne: Grattan Institute. https://grattan.edu.au/wp-content/uploads/2018/09/907-Mapping-Australian-higher-education-2018.pdf, 38.
12 Universities Australia (2021). "17,000 uni jobs lost to COVID-19," Media release, 3 February 2021. https://bit.ly/3PgDEYI.
13 Norton and Cherastudtham, *Mapping Australian higher education*, 42.
14 Quality Indicators for Learning and Teaching [QILT] (2019). *2018 Student Experience Survey. National Report*. Canberra: Department of Education.
15 Norton, Andrew (2019). "Enrolments flatlining: Australian unis' financial strife in three charts." *Conversation,* 7 November 2019. https://theconversation.com/enrolments-flatlining-australian-unis-financial-strife-in-three-charts-126342.
16 Tudge, Alan. Getting more for Australia from our university research. Media release, 26 February 2021. https://ministers.dese.gov.au/tudge/getting-more-australia-our-university-research.
17 "Prime Minister Scott Morrison on JobKeeper, hotel quarantine and COVIDSafe". *ABC 7.30*, 22 July 2020. https://www.abc.net.au/7.30/prime-minister-scott-morrison-on-jobkeeper,-hotel/12478890.
18 A point made in an excellent anonymous commentary on the draft chapter, so thanks to the reviewer.

4

Reform for what purposes?

Higher education enrolment in Taiwan and implications for Australia

Ren-Hao Xu

Introduction

Understanding the history of higher education reforms is vital for inquiring into what and how particular social dynamics – such as the tension between the publicly and privately subsidised higher education funding systems – have emerged, and what can be learned from the past for the present. This chapter therefore considers Taiwanese higher education to provide an historical-comparative perspective on enrolment-related reform for Australia. In short, Taiwan enlarged its higher education system through the growth of private providers, which created study opportunities for many students who had previously been excluded. Despite this success, reliance on private providers has caused a significant issue for policymakers following demographic shifts that have reduced demand for university study, requiring the closure of private universities and affecting the quality of education.

Rather than slipping into the (arguably worthwhile) debate about whether university systems should be attached to social welfare or subsidised by the private sector, this chapter examines the change in public policies concerning university enrolment through Taiwan's history of higher education reforms. It focuses primarily on enrolment-related policies, which represent a fundamental idea regarding "higher education for whom". Undoubtedly, the higher education systems of Australia and Taiwan differ in important ways. Nevertheless, an historical-comparative perspective enables us to "recontextualise" local practices from foreign stories, establishing an alternative and critical understanding of reforms.[1]

Taiwan is an interesting case for Australia's policymakers for several reasons. First and foremost, both countries experienced reforms in similar timeframes: Australia's well-known Dawkins reforms and Bradley Review occurred in the late 1980s to early 1990s, and 2008, respectively; in Taiwan, the 410 Civic Education Reform (410 教育改革) happened in the early 1990s, and the Enrolment Regulations in 2008. Moreover, as population characteristics play a key role in enrolment-related reforms, these two countries are of similar population: 25.7 million in Australia; 23.8 million in Taiwan.[2] Last, both central governments are decisive in determining the volume of university places.[3] These conditions suggest the trajectory of enrolment-related reforms in Taiwan may enable Australian policymakers to reimagine alternatives for their higher education.

The worldwide rise of enrolment-related reforms

Enrolment-related reforms can be understood as mechanisms that governments use in an attempt to achieve greater – or more focused – student participation.[4] For instance, universities around the world were small and provided limited admissions for young men (and some women) of the affluent classes in the early 20th century. At that time, enrolment-related policies tended to control university provisions on a very small scale because demand (and access) was weak. Since the mid-1960s, however, higher education enrolment was increasingly assumed to be correlated with economic growth.[5] Many countries and international organisations, such as the World Bank, therefore concluded they must make policy decisions to widen student participation in universities, further linking university graduates with the workforce.[6] The growth trend in student enrolment has been further pushed by governments while the role of the university in the knowledge-based economy – the key engine of knowledge production and knowledge transmission – was specifically highlighted by the Organisation for Economic Co-operation and Development (OECD) in 1996.[7] Worldwide, enrolment-related policies have since been accelerated to enhance the numbers of places across the disciplines of science, technology, engineering and mathematics towards meeting the needs of a knowledge-based economy. Over time, the function of enrolment-related reforms or policies has been changing along with the social dynamics in closely meeting varied national priorities.[8]

Behind the higher education system in Taiwan

Around the world, Taiwan has one of the highest proportions of the population with university degrees: in 2019, approximately 70 per cent of those aged 25–34 held a bachelor's degree.[9] Moreover, Taiwan has a dual (public-private) highly differentiated system where the recent domestic undergraduate student enrolment was 1.24 million, spread across 126 universities comprised of 44 publicly and 82 privately-owned institutions, with the majority of domestic students (approximately 69 per cent) enrolled in the latter sector.[10] As such, the provision of university places is largely driven by privately-owned universities.

But how did Taiwan achieve such high enrolment in its higher education system? The answer goes back to the 410 Civic Education Reform of 1994, which was pushed by various civil education groups from below. Before implementation of the reform, the supply of university places was extensively regulated by the bureaucratic Ministry of Education for the planned national economy.[11] Economic activities of Taiwan were primarily undertaken by the primary and secondary sectors of industries; for instance, farming and textile production. The provision of university education was largely determined by this style of economy, with the majority of higher education providers prior to the 1990s operating as specialised junior colleges providing vocationally oriented programs.[12] This type of higher education institution was similar to Australia's Colleges of Advanced Education that provided a more vocational nature of courses than universities from 1967 until the early 1990s.[13] The Taiwanese centrally planned system led to many courses in the public universities being oversubscribed due to an excessively competitive university entrance examination. This narrow gate to university education oriented all the learning activities towards preparation for the entrance examination, resulting in a phenomenon wherein thousands of students commonly paid for private tutoring after school hours to ensure successful selection. Such limited educational opportunity was criticised by various stakeholders, including university teachers, student teachers, and parents, eventually igniting the movement in 1994. Due to the 410 Civic Education Movement that pressured the Kuomintang government, the restriction on university places was finally lifted.[14] Based on the recommendations made by an independent panel outside the Ministry of Education, the Kuomintang government released a large-scale educational reform agenda, including the deregulation of university-place allocation in 1996.[15] Within a decade, the number of universities increased from 23 to 75 and enrolment rose from 625,929 to 944,977.[16]

However, as Connell notes, privatisation of higher education often occurred along with systematic expansion in many parts of the world.[17] Taiwan is a prime example. The reforms both opened doors to welcome students into universities across the nation, and at the same time largely removed the restrictions on the private sector. In order to have enough university places, the main policy approach – institutional upgrade – allowed nearly all the specialised junior colleges to be upgraded to university status. That is to say, private universities have always had a presence in Taiwanese higher education, but have seen particular growth since the 1990s. By extensively upgrading the colleges, the number of universities spiked from 24 in 1994 to 147 in 2008.[18] One consequence of this upgrade-oriented policy was the number of private universities overtook the public sector, and more than half of the students enrolled in non-government-funded places.

There is one essential turning point to note in this story, however. This enrolment-related reform did not consider any long-term demographic changes towards population decline. The expanded higher education capacity did not match population growth rates, as Taiwan's overall 18-year-old population plunged from 395,000 in 1983 to 249,000 in 2020.[19] This declining student population gravely impacted the massified higher education system, resulting in many universities, in particular those in the private sector, experiencing a shortage of students, and even closing their doors.[20] Given that these universities suffered from the lack of student revenue, they expunged hundreds of jobs, including permanent staff positions. Yet, university staff and students' anger along with their protests successfully influenced the government to respond to the severe imbalance between higher education provision and the student population.[21] Since 2008, a hard cap has been imposed to displace expansion-driven enrolment policies, in which the volume of university places was capped at the 2008 level with the negotiation between the universities and government being closed.[22]

Moreover, the government unveiled a suite of assessment criteria as its method to review the number of student enrolments. Under this review mechanism, the previously granted numbers of places at a university would be cut by the government due to a decline in student enrolment. The imposed assessment criteria created a competition mechanism where the universities needed to fulfil the volume of registered places by attracting enough students to enrol; otherwise, they could be downsized due to the unmet target. However, this competitive game barely affected the publicly owned universities because they have been largely subsidised by the state's expenditure, enabling them to consistently strengthen their research and teaching goals. Additionally, their longstanding tradition of having a highly academic reputation ensured stronger demand from students. These conditions advantaged public universities because private universities relied on tuition fees as their main revenue and as a result overlooked some quality assurance requirements during student selection to survive. In sum, what private universities faced and their responses have further deteriorated the quality of the higher education system in Taiwan.

Changes in public and private universities

Pausing for a moment on the issues behind the higher education reform in Taiwan, it's necessary to discuss the enrolment-related reforms. The policy approach the government adopted to widen university access in the early 1990s established the landscape of a privately oriented higher education system in Taiwan. The enlargement of university provision was accomplished by the institutional upgrade or transformation of specialised junior colleges to meet the requirements of the 410 Civic Educational Reform.[23] Yet, these specialised junior colleges were primarily owned by the private sector. Hence, while the higher education system was massified, privatisation inevitably increased markedly.

It is worth connecting the enrolment policies in Australia here. As stated earlier, there was also an institutional reconstruction in Australia throughout the late 1980s to the mid-1990s. Although the governments of both Taiwan and Australia largely unified the different types of higher education institutions into a university format as a major element of their reconstruction, a significant difference was that the upgraded colleges in Australia were publicly owned whereas in Taiwan it was opposite. As such, in the case of Taiwan, those upgraded colleges later received less government funding in comparison with the public universities as both sectors were challenged by significant demographic shifts.

The privatisation of higher education in Taiwan – largely derived from the policy approach of institutional upgrades – led to two outcomes. First, in the case of Taiwan, a fairer higher education system emerged along with massification. Indeed, the enrolment reform based on the tenet of universal educational opportunities has broken the longstanding tradition that university was reserved only for those students from upper socio-economic backgrounds. Thousands of Taiwanese students became the first in their families to attend university due to the expansion-driven enrolment reforms of 1994. However, as mentioned earlier, the majority of these students studied in privately owned universities as evidenced by enrolment in the public sector which dropped from 42 per cent in 1994 to 31.65 per cent in 2006.[24] Furthermore, access to public and private universities has been distributed unevenly. For instance, according to his case study, Luoh argues that the probability of becoming a National Taiwan University student for an 18-year-old in Taipei City is approximately 3 per cent, while for the same cohort in Ta-An District, one of the wealthiest suburbs of Taipei City, it is 6.10 per cent, and in Taitung County it's a mere 0.19 per cent, as this is one of the most disadvantaged areas in Taiwan.[25] It is also evident that the average household income has a significant effect on "public university access".[26] In other words, those socially and geographically disadvantaged students paid higher tuition fees and received less government subsidisation, as compared with the upper socio-economic background students who have had greater opportunities for public university admission. Second, over time, what can be seen is a bizarre outcome in Taiwan. Due to the impact of student shortages, many private universities have been forced to shut down. This trend suggests that those socially disadvantaged students who enrolled in the private sector now not only need to pay double the cost of tuition, compared with the public sector, but also suffer from the declining quality of university education. In other words, these students in private universities are paying more money for a lower quality education.

What can Australia learn from Taiwan?

So what exactly can Australia learn from the history of enrolment policies in Taiwan? The case of Taiwan shows how its higher education enrolment has been largely rearranged by privatisation-driven massification and demographic shifts towards student population decline. In the first instance, and ignoring the issue of privatisation, Taiwan's story highlights that students, and the country as a whole, gained social and material benefits from massification. This massified higher education system has conjoined with other social policies to strengthen a robust and democratic society by extending the opportunities to enrol at universities. The desire to accelerate higher education expansion as the privileged pathway to professional work has also established a highly-skilled workforce in a global knowledge-based economy.

The main point, however, concerns the enrolment-related reforms. In expanding the system through the transformation of private specialised junior colleges into private universities, without considering potential demographic shifts and imbalanced public university access, the government produced a new type of inequality. A privatisation-driven massification merely widened university access superficially. Missing was an analysis of how the social and material resources were distributed as a result of enrolment-related policies. In Taiwan's case, university access and higher education enrolment manifested in the inequitable perpetuation of socio-economic classes, which was worsened by the privatisation. This massification of higher education was no longer a social betterment to widen educational opportunities but turned out to be a social problem that all of society needed to pay for; dealing with the closure of private universities, the deterioration of university quality, and most importantly, increased educational inequality.

Undoubtedly, the main lesson that Australia can learn is that the development of enrolment-related reform could cause unintended consequences if rushed and not carefully designed. Again, the higher education developments of Australia and Taiwan are certainly not identical. Nevertheless, Taiwan's experience provides a critical lens for Australia to recontextualise its reform policies. That is, Australia's reform – as designed to maximise economic competitiveness in and through higher education – should be kept in perspective and balanced with other programs.

In May 2022, the Australian Labor Party defeated the Liberal-National Coalition and formed a new government. Based on its election promises, Labor has planned to deliver up to 20,000 extra student places over two years in response to demands from the job market.[27] Yet, balancing the offered places to address skills shortfalls and achieving equitable access to university remains challenging in Australia. The dominant narrative that higher education has the purpose of job preparation and can lead individuals and society to be prosperous and efficient in the name of entrepreneurship should be put aside. Above all, the history of enrolment-related reforms is just one example of how higher education can affect social settings, leading to greater economic wealth and equality when consistently supported by state policy.

Notes

1 Steiner-Khamsi, Gita (2012). Understanding policy borrowing and lending: building comparative policy studies. In Gita Steiner-Khamsi and Florian Waldow, eds. *World YearBook of Education 2012: Policy borrowing and lending in education*, 1–18. London: Routledge.
2 Australian Bureau of Statistics (2021). National population. https://www.abs.gov.au/statistics/people/population/national-state-and-territory-population/latest-release; National Statistics Taiwan (2021). Total population. https://eng.stat.gov.tw/point.asp?index=9.
3 Chan, Sheng-Ju, Chia-Yu Yang and Hsiu-Hsi Liu (2018). Taiwanese struggle in university governance reforms: the case of incorporation. In Shin Jung Cheol ed. *Higher education governance in East Asia*, 73–88. Singapore: Springer; Marginson, Simon (1997). Investment in the self: the government of student financing in Australia. *Studies in Higher Education* 22(2): 119–31.
4 Altbach, Philip (2007). *Tradition and transition: the international imperative in higher education*. Rotterdam: Sense Publishers; Marginson, Simon (2018). High participation systems (HPS) of higher education. In Brendan Cantwell, Simon Marginson and Anna Smolentseva, eds. *High participation systems of higher education*, 1–44. Oxford: Oxford University Press.
5 Becker, Gary S. (1964). *Human capital: a theoretical and empirical analysis, with special reference to education*. Chicago: University of Chicago Press.
6 Welch, Anthony (2021). *Private higher education in East and Southeast Asia: growth, challenges, implications*. Paris: UNESCO.
7 Clarke, Thomas (2001). The knowledge economy. *Education & Training* 43(4/5): 189–96; OECD (1996). The knowledge-based economy. Paris: OECD Publishing.
8 Altbach, Philip (2007). *Tradition and transition: the international imperative in higher education*.
9 Taiwan Ministry of Education (2021). *International comparison of education statistical indicators*. Taipei: TMOE.
10 Taiwan Ministry of Education (2019). *International comparison of education statistical indicators 2018 edition*. Taipei: TMOE.
11 Law, Wing-Wah (2002). Education reform in Taiwan: a search for a 'national' identity through democratisation and Taiwanisation. *Compare* 32(1): 61–81.
12 Wang, Ru-Jer (2003). From elitism to mass higher education in Taiwan: the problems faced. *Higher Education* 46: 261–87.
13 Forsyth, Hannah (2014). *A history of the modern Australian university*. Sydney: NewSouth Publishing.
14 Law, Wing-Wah. Education reform in Taiwan.
15 The Executive Yuan (1996). *The review of education reform: the final report*. Taipei: The Executive Yuan.
16 Taiwan Ministry of Education (2001). *White paper: higher education policy*. Taipei: TMOE.

17 Connell, Raewyn (2019). *The good university: what universities actually do and why it's time for radical change*. London: Zed Books.
18 Taiwan Ministry of Education (2019). *International comparison of education statistical indicators 2018 edition.*
19 Taiwan Ministry of Education (2017a). The conditional standard of developmental enrolments and resources for tertiary education 20170714. Taipei: Taiwan Ministry of Education; National Development Council (2021). Population projection. https://bit.ly/3AR9tCM.
20 Welch, Anthony (2021). *Private higher education in East and Southeast Asia: growth, challenges, implications.*
21 Taiwan Ministry of Education (2017b). *The information sheet for the conditional standard of developmental enrolments and resources for tertiary education 2017*. Taipei: TMOE.
22 Taiwan Ministry of Education (2009). *The conditional standard of developmental enrolments and resources for tertiary education 20090611.* Taipei: TMOE.
23 Wang, Ru-Jer (2003). From elitism to mass higher education in Taiwan: the problems faced.
24 Taiwan Ministry of Education (2019). *International comparison of education statistical indicators 2018 edition*. Taipei: TMOE.
25 Luoh, Ming-Ching (2002). Who are NTU students? – differences across ethnic and gender groups and urban/rural discrepancy. *Taiwan Economic Review* 30(1): 113–47.
26 Shen, Hui-Chih and Ming-Jen Lin (2019). Education opportunity inequality across income in Taiwan. *Taiwan Economic Review* 47(3): 393–453.
27 Australian Labor Party (2022). *Your education: Supporting schools, TAFEs and universities* https://www.alp.org.au/policies/your-education.

Part 2

Reconsidering students

5

When do we answer the call for cultural change?

Aboriginal and Torres Strait Islander students and higher education

Jennifer Barrett, Lisa Jackson Pulver, Peta Greenfield and Michelle Dickson

How do you change a culture? What aspects should stay and which should go? Who determines what change is needed? How do you manage the dynamic nature of change in light of the need for the centrality of Aboriginal and Torres Strait Islander world views in Australian culture? These questions lie at the heart of thinking about the history of Aboriginal and Torres Strait Islander students in higher education. What does success really look like for universities and their constituencies on Country that was never ceded, never sold, and for which there has never been a treaty? The challenges faced and the achievements attained by Aboriginal and Torres Strait Islander students are influenced by university and government culture and policies as well as broader contextual factors. This Country has always been diverse with hundreds of languages spoken, signed, sung and danced by her first peoples. This means that culture looks and feels different depending on the place. Positive cultural change that deeply reflects people and place is only possible through working constructively together. To understand where we need to head, we need to see, hear and know clearly the path already walked.

This chapter covers policy history from the late 1960s through to today. We use a variety of phrasing when it comes to Aboriginal and Torres Strait Islander peoples and a number of reasons for this. In some cases, the phrasing reflects the historical contexts of source texts. In other cases, the phrasing reflects the fact that there are a variety of ways of expressing identity and the preference remains open.[1]

The path walked so far

The history of Aboriginal and Torres Strait Islander students in higher education can be difficult to trace. Not widely known, but understood through oral histories, are the stories of scholars in the postwar period of the 20th century. For example, we know that well over 5,000 Aboriginal and Torres Strait Islander peoples served in the armed forces of the First and Second World Wars alone. Scores more have served in more recent conflicts and peace-keeping operations including Korea, Vietnam, the Gulf Conflicts, and disaster relief across the globe. But how many of these veterans and service people returned home to educational opportunities that were afforded to others attending the same operational environments? From what little we know of Aboriginal and Torres Strait Islander returning service people, there remains valuable work to be done in recovering the full history of scholars in this area. One story we do know relates to the University of Sydney and an Aboriginal returned World War Two serviceman who studied under the Commonwealth Reconstruction and Training Scheme (CRTS). There are likely to be others as well. Like most records available at the time, there were few ways to identify and record people's backgrounds, particularly since this scheme did not require a formal matriculation from school. As a consequence, the CRTS scheme provided opportunities to returned servicemen and women to higher education who may otherwise have missed out.

Some names of our early Aboriginal academic scholars are recorded in various newspapers and student publications. Irwin Lewis, a Yamatji man, enrolled in an Arts degree at the University of Western Australia in 1957; Margaret Williams, a Malera Bundjalung and Gumbaynggirr woman, began her university journey at the University of Queensland in 1957. She went on to be the first known Aboriginal woman to graduate from an Australian university, attaining a diploma from the University of Melbourne in 1959; Geoffrey Penny, a Noongar man, matriculated to university in 1957. Charles Perkins, an Arrente and Kalkadoon man, and

Peter Gary Williams, a Gumbaynggirr and Mullumbimby man, enrolled in Arts at the University of Sydney, with Perkins completing his degree in 1966. It was the 1970s before more Aboriginal students gained entry, and 1980 when Worimi man Bill Jonas graduated with a PhD, the first identified Aboriginal person to attain that significant qualification. Australia's first university was established in 1850 yet there is a gap of over a century between the establishment of higher education in this country and the enrolment of students who could formally and openly identify as Aboriginal and Torres Strait Islander. Added to this is the fact that Torres Strait Islander peoples were rendered almost invisible through their conflation with Aboriginal people for many years. The recognition of Torres Strait Islander peoples does not come through in policy documentation until the late 1980s. This speaks volumes to the legacy of Australian colonialism.

The fact that we know the names of some of these students is striking. It emphasises how rare these scholars were in the public mindset. These early scholars stand in living memory and are evidence of the history that we need to hold close as we consider how the 21st century university sector can support student success.

How do you change a culture of exclusion? First comes acts of inclusion. Grassroots movements developed in the 1950s to support Aboriginal students to attain tertiary qualifications. The first was Abschol – a student-led charitable fund set up in 1951 at the University of Melbourne. It was officially endorsed by the National Union of Australian University Students (NUAUS) in 1953. The purpose of Abschol was to provide scholarships for Aboriginal students to fund their tertiary education. The scheme gradually gained momentum through the 1960s.[2] Irwin Lewis (UWA), Margaret Williams (UQ, later MU), and Geoffrey Penny (UWA) were each a recipient of an Abschol award. It is notable that the early successes of Aboriginal students at university were supported by the fruits of student activism. Over time, Abschol became increasingly political as student activists understood that scholarships offered to support tertiary level studies were not going to be enough without land rights, improvement in living conditions, access to educational opportunities in primary and secondary schooling, constitutional recognition, full rights of citizenship, and having Aboriginal and Torres Strait Islander peoples involved in decision-making processes that affected their lives.[3]

Tracing the history of Aboriginal and Torres Strait Islander students in higher education is marred by a range of factors including inconsistent data keeping, accessibility issues, government departmental changes leading to data loss, and the fact that students may choose to identify variably depending on a range of social, personal and political factors. For instance, the accessible longitudinal data for higher education between 1949–2000 does not report on Aboriginal and Torres Strait Islander students at all.[4] While the absence of evidence is not evidence of absence, when attempting to trace this history, obstacles arise that are tantamount to erasure.

Understanding the context of education at every level is fundamental to appreciating how the higher education space appears to Aboriginal and Torres Strait Islander students today. Secondary schooling is the obvious pathway into higher education, yet the exclusion of Aboriginal and Torres Strait Islander students from educational opportunities throughout the 19th and 20th centuries is significant.[5] Of the few who were permitted to continue to high school, many did not complete the upper years that were required to gain university entrance. Up until the 1970s many were forced into systems of control that masqueraded as education but were in reality coercive and traumatic experiences of familial separation. The complexities of intergenerational trauma are at play when thinking about the experience of Aboriginal and Torres Strait Islander students in higher education. The referendum in 1967 was instrumental in ensuring the right to education for Aboriginal and Torres Strait Islander peoples and led to modest government initiatives to support students at primary and secondary level, including the establishment of ABSTUDY in 1969. Further progress was made, at least in New South Wales, that removed the right of school principals to exclude Aboriginal and Torres Strait Islander students from education in 1972.[6] The change in policies in the late 1960s and 1970s were the first steps away from the exclusionary model.

The university sector changed slowly. The introduction of non-degree courses such as the Aboriginal Teachers' Aide program was a significant step in supporting self-determination. Vera Byno, a teachers' aide at Weilmoringle School, noted in 1973: "I think the kids like it because they can get on better with an Aboriginal teacher."[7]

Programs of this kind were in place throughout Australia by 1975 and supported through a variety of means including provision of education by universities. The model that gained popularity in the 1980s was centres for Aboriginal education – these continue to be a feature of university campuses today. With these supports in place, the enrolment of Aboriginal and Torres Strait Islander students at university increased as a percentage of domestic enrolments from 0.78 per cent in 1990 rising to 1.39 per cent in 2003 (see additional data in Figure 5.1).[8] The rise in student enrolments happened in tandem with government reporting with recommendations that focused on working together with Aboriginal and Torres Strait Islander peoples to reach shared decisions about the provision of education.

These centres were the result of choices made by institutions which have since set the conditions for cultural change. This is not to suggest that the work is done. Culture is dynamic and some decisions are reckoned with differently in hindsight. Nevertheless, what is learned along the way is significant for the decisions we make about the future. Supporting students in ways that are culturally appropriate is pivotal to the question of institutional culture and reflects the inclusivity of higher education as a whole.

As higher education shifted their practices, changes also emerged at a federal level. By the late 1980s, the federal Labor Party built on the landmark educational reforms of the short-lived Whitlam government a decade earlier and sought to expand higher education attainments for underrepresented cohorts including women and Aboriginal and Torres Strait Islander students. The focus on equity was a watershed moment for higher education. The government data on Aboriginal and Torres Strait Islander students provided in Dawkins' 1987 *Higher Education: A policy statement* (the White Paper) was stark: "In 1987 there were almost 2000 Aboriginal students enrolled in higher education, more than double the number enrolled in 1984."[9] The same paper put the overall number of students in higher education in excess of 400,000. These figures suggest that Aboriginal and Torres Strait Islander students made up about 0.5 per cent of students in higher education in the late 1980s.[10] With a clear aim of ensuring equity in outcomes as a measure of building national identity and success, Dawkins' White Paper led to

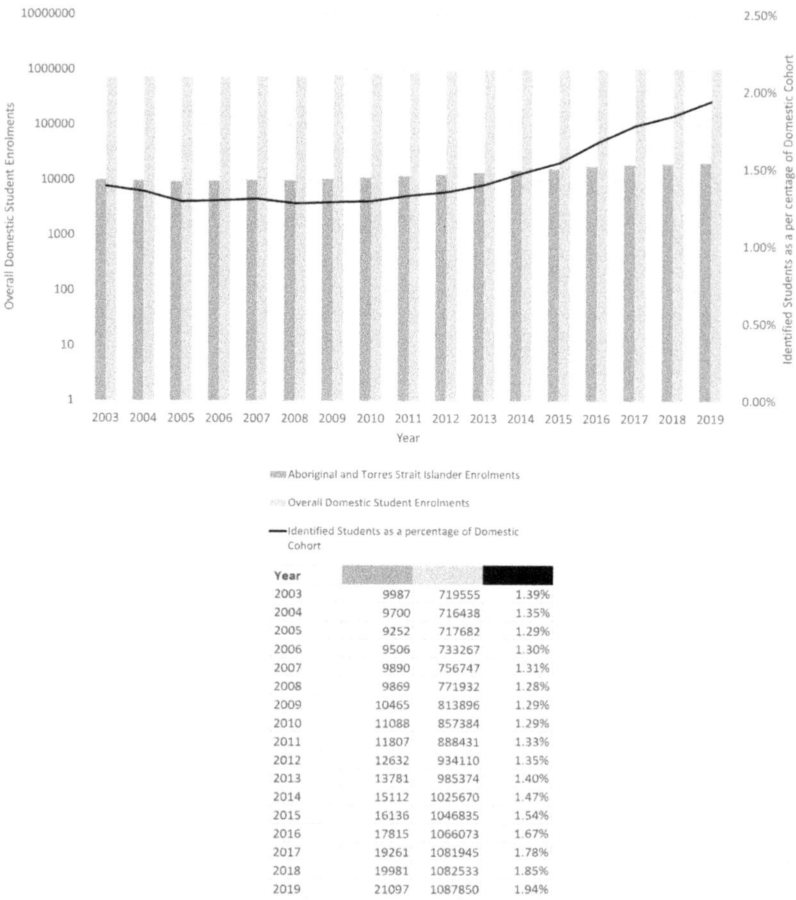

Year			
2003	9987	719555	1.39%
2004	9700	716438	1.35%
2005	9252	717682	1.29%
2006	9506	733267	1.30%
2007	9890	756747	1.31%
2008	9869	771932	1.28%
2009	10465	813896	1.29%
2010	11088	857384	1.29%
2011	11807	888431	1.33%
2012	12632	934110	1.35%
2013	13781	985374	1.40%
2014	15112	1025670	1.47%
2015	16136	1046835	1.54%
2016	17815	1066073	1.67%
2017	19261	1081945	1.78%
2018	19981	1082533	1.85%
2019	21097	1087850	1.94%

Figure 5.1 National domestic enrolments in higher education 2003–19. At time of publication, the figures for 2020 and 2021 were not available. Data prior to 2003 was not sourced for this chapter.

the development of the National Aboriginal and Torres Strait Islander Education Policy in 1989.[11]

The turn towards equity

The *National Aboriginal and Torres Strait Islander Education Policy* is a pivotal moment in the pursuit of equity in Australian higher education. The document marked a new era in collaboration between the federal government and the states and territories to support educational opportunities for Aboriginal and Torres Strait Islander students "in a manner that reinforces rather than suppresses their unique cultural identity".[12] The policy was driven not only by the "long expressed educational aspirations of Aboriginal people that have as yet not been realised" but also by the acknowledged "deficiencies in the provision and quality of educational services for Aboriginal people".[13] An Aboriginal Reference Group was formed to guide the reform and community consultation was embedded in the process. Some of the key recommendations of the work included: developing bilingual and bicultural programs; the need to adapt curriculum and teaching approaches; and the fundamental requirement to involve Aboriginal and Torres Strait Islander peoples in the decision-making process.[14] The ideas probably sound familiar because they continue to be central to discussions about higher education today.[15]

In 1990, the Department of Employment, Education and Training released the commissioned report A Fair Chance for All, which drew strongly on social justice principles.[16] The scope of the report was to identify disadvantaged groups, investigate equitable principles of access, and promote institutional change within universities. Goals were clear and ambitious. For Aboriginal and Torres Strait Islander students, success was to be defined by two measures to be achieved by 1995: a 50 per cent increase in Aboriginal enrolments in higher education; and improved graduation rates of Aboriginal students to a level comparable to the total student population. Self-determination was promoted and there was a push for higher representation of Aboriginal and Torres Strait Islander students in law, business, and medicine and health.[17] Like the National Aboriginal and Torres Strait Islander Education Policy, the report also recognised the need for Aboriginal and Torres Strait Islander peoples in educational decision making to progress the goals.[18]

There is a strong consistency in the position the Labor Party took during the 1990s. They recognised the need for meaningful change in the cultures of higher education providers and mandated that universities implement equity plans.[19] The goals of *A Fair Chance for All* were not met within the five-year timeframe; however, Labor strengthened the idea that listening to and working together with Aboriginal and Torres Strait Islander peoples was vital to long-term progress.

In 1996, the Liberal-National Coalition formed government and introduced a significant shift in attitude towards equity in higher education. This had a number of effects and stands as background to the *Learning for Life: Review of Higher Education, Financing and Policy* (the West Report) in 1998. The West Report noted that the policy initiatives of the late 1980s and early 1990s had done much to increase the opportunity for Indigenous students to enter into higher education but that their success rate was about 65 per cent compared to about 85 per cent for non-Indigenous students. A partial explanation: students reported that the complexities of navigating the requirements for ABSTUDY was a "major barrier and disincentive to study".[20] This is evidence of the layered complications students faced: it is not only the institutional culture and support offered by the university that matter, but also the structures and policies around access to higher education.

The West Report's recommendations included: incorporating Indigenous perspectives into the curriculum, supporting staff in higher education to better understand Indigenous experiences, and for universities to work in partnership with local Indigenous communities. The West Report offered several models for success including distinct centres for Indigenous learning, and incorporating "Indigenous languages, knowledge and ways of organising learning contexts" (also known as cultural competence) into Western tertiary systems. Perhaps the most telling comment of the report is that "nothing will change unless societal attitudes change towards Aboriginal Australians, both collectively and as individuals".[21] The report also emphasised the need for cultural change. How that might happen is important. Positive *representation* is crucial for student success. Incorporating knowledges adds *relevance* for students. To do this in a culturally appropriate way,

Aboriginal and Torres Strait Islander peoples need to be involved in the planning and delivery of the curriculum, which adds *recognition*.

When these ideas are combined with those expressed in the National Aboriginal and Torres Strait Islander Education Policy and A Fair Chance for All, the path forward is clear: genuine engagement with local communities, serious consideration of curriculum and pedagogy all contributing to a context that is culturally appropriate, as well as streamlined access to economic support for study.[22] The culture of a university is determined by its people. Both staff and students contribute to this. Government policies provide an overarching framework, but each university chooses its own policy path, implements its own strategies and is the arbiter of what is culturally appropriate and acceptable. This is an area where the higher education sector can direct its future.

Building a socially inclusive model

With a change of federal government from the Coalition to Labor in late 2007 came further considerations of higher education policy. The 2008 *Review of Australian Higher Education* (the Bradley Review) and the follow-up 2009 document from the federal government titled *Transforming Australia's Higher Education System* are contemporaneous with the advent of the Closing the Gap initiative (2009–present). The Bradley Review cites culture as a significant area for development: "Higher Education providers should ensure that the institutional culture, the cultural competence of staff and the nature of the curriculum recognises and supports the participation of Indigenous students."[23] The Bradley Review also echoes earlier reports in noting the need for changes to curriculum to ensure a deeper understanding of Indigenous culture for all students. Given the consistency of the message offered by the reports over decades, it is vitally clear what is needed, so the question becomes how can tertiary institutions do this well? Changing a culture may be a slow process, but each step towards this goal is important. And from a critical perspective, what opportunities have been missed to make positive and enduring change?

Closing the Gap set several targets that have been added to and in some cases altered over time. The suite of ideas has been part of the federal government's work since 2009 and continues to this day with varying degrees of success. *Closing the Gap* has a strong focus on completion of Year 12. The potential opportunities for further study mean that trends in success or failure in *Closing the Gap* have an impact on accessibility to higher education. While there are substantial areas where *Closing the Gap* has not met its targets, the area of Year 12 attainment has been one where steady gains have been made over time. From a 45 per cent attainment rate in 2008 to 66 per cent in 2018–19, more Aboriginal and Torres Strait Islander students are completing secondary education. One of the many complexities attendant with Closing the Gap is the ongoing need for cultural change not only within the education sector but also within the government (that is, a whole-of-government approach). The rhetoric of the various prime ministers who have delivered the annual report is evidence that the sustained cultural change needed by those in leadership is one of the greatest factors limiting the ambitions of the program. This is something that universities can learn from as well. Successful cultural change needs clearly visible support of the leadership. That is not to say that cultural change relies on leadership alone, or that leadership is only found at a senior management level of our institutions. In this context, leadership is also about speaking up, listening to advice about culturally appropriate ways to develop and deliver programs, including support to grow Aboriginal and Torres Strait Islander knowledges. So, we can look to identify leaders who promote culturally appropriate engagement within the university as the guide. What is in our strategies and what is upheld in our policies is all part of the culture of a university. When aspirational leadership is lacking elsewhere, the onus is on everyone to cultivate it, at every level of university practice.

A report that sought to provide guidance in this area was the *Review of Higher Education Access and Outcomes for Aboriginal and Torres Strait Islander People* (the Behrendt Review) in 2012. The Behrendt Review identified mechanisms of *support* as necessary for student success and, like the Bradley Review, advocated for *cultural change* enacted from the top. The Behrendt Review stressed that universities needed to take ownership of their practices and cultivate culturally safe environments for learning. The tenets of cultural safety emerged from the Māori nursing movement in the 1980s.[24] By 2011, the idea of cultural safety had evolved for the Australian context: "a culturally safe and secure environment is one where our people feel safe and draw strength in their identity, culture and community".[25] There was a growing interest in ensuring that people could bring their whole self to spaces and find a sense of belonging. The Behrendt Review drew upon this thinking and offered several suggestions for how cultural safety might be achieved: support Indigenous Education Units that provided culturally safe environments for Aboriginal and Torres Strait Islander students; audit pastoral care services, in particular "Elders in residence" counselling services; and develop methodologically sound protocols for Aboriginal and Torres Strait Islander research.[26] The Behrendt Review envisioned a transformation of practice embodied by a whole-of-university approach. So rather than there being culturally safe spaces on campus, the campus itself would evolve into a culturally safe space. Under this model, faculties would take a leadership role in providing student support within their discipline.[27] The extent to which universities implemented these recommendations underpins where the tertiary sector is today. Core to this has been the impact of the Higher Education Participation and Partnership Program (HEPPP) which arose from the Bradley Review, and which was showing great promise in terms of supporting universities to develop deeper connections and alternative admission pathways to higher education for disadvantaged schools, including rural and remote communities, by raising awareness about and aspirations for higher education. Over the past decade, funding for the partnership elements of this program has been progressively cut despite independent reviews showing considerable success, and potential for success longer term.

Cultural change in practice

Universities are very particular places. Even today with tertiary admissions at record levels, a university education is not something that everyone undertakes.[28] Across the Australian population (ages 20–64) about 35 per cent of people hold a degree.[29] University entry requirements, degree structures, and the administrative apparatus are challenging to navigate for many students including those from a low-SES background or those who are the first in their family to attend. The challenges can be magnified for Aboriginal and Torres Strait Islander students depending on the culture of the university they attend.

Location also matters. Degree holders are more likely to be found in urban areas. Physical access to tertiary institutions has a measurable impact on the ability of students to attend. A higher education can be rendered inaccessible in part by the nature of the education offered and in part because Australian universities tend to be clustered in urban areas. Beyond these factors, attending university does not automatically equate with completion of a degree, nor – for those completing their degree – a return to communities outside urban centres. Some degrees require specialisation training, internships, or other programs that are rarely available outside of the major centres.

During the decade that followed Dawkins' proposals and the resultant National Aboriginal and Torres Strait Islander Education Policy, there has been meaningful statistical change nationally in Australia. Aboriginal and Torres Strait Islander peoples with a higher education qualification jumped from around 0.82 per cent in 1991 to 2.93 per cent in 2001 when measured within the population (see Figure 5.2 for more details).[30] This is not the same as looking at parity with the Australian population, but it is indicative of greater rates of access to higher education and more completions. The upwards trend detailed in Figure 5.2 is a hopeful sign of what may be to come.

These shifts suggest that changing a culture is a process of gradual steps. Before changing the supports offered to students, there is a need for appropriate measures to encourage staff reflection on what defines the culture of a place. Listening to our local communities and working with the advice that was generously offered over 30 years ago is still what is needed. Involving Aboriginal and Torres Strait Islander peoples at the community and the student levels, and at the level of scholars and administrators, is not just a meaningful step to cultural change, but is essential for developing culture. Furthermore, the practice of being responsive to student needs in culturally appropriate ways is essential for student success.

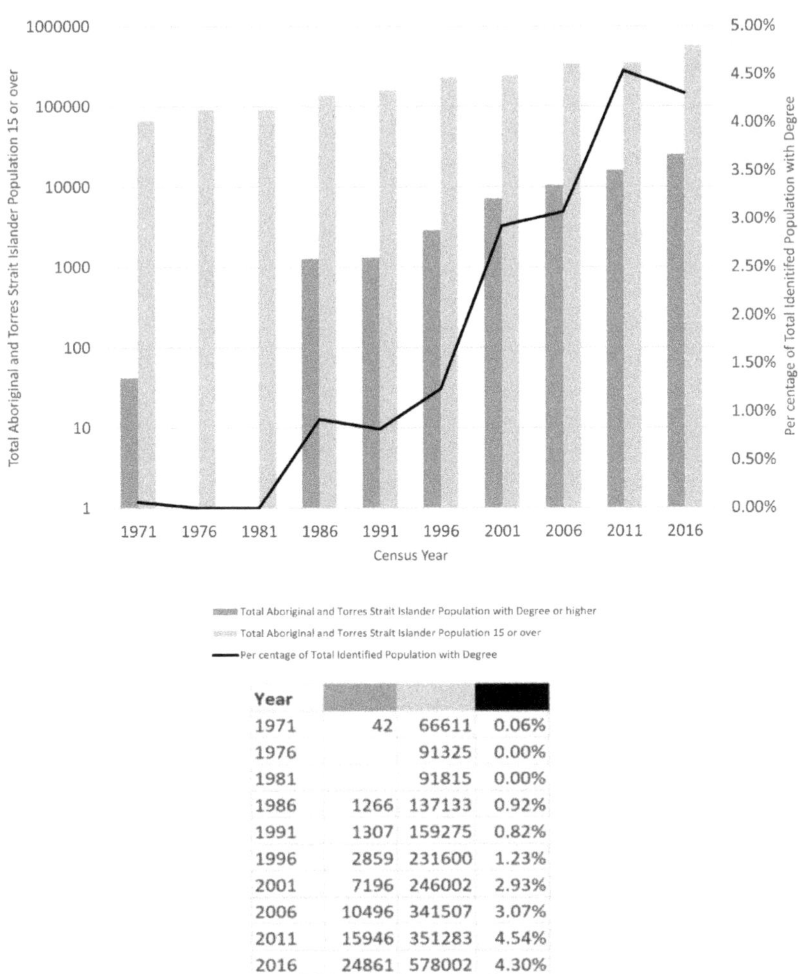

Year			
1971	42	66611	0.06%
1976		91325	0.00%
1981		91815	0.00%
1986	1266	137133	0.92%
1991	1307	159275	0.82%
1996	2859	231600	1.23%
2001	7196	246002	2.93%
2006	10496	341507	3.07%
2011	15946	351283	4.54%
2016	24861	578002	4.30%

Figure 5.2 National tertiary attainment – Aboriginal and Torres Strait Islander students. Please note that inconsistencies in accessible Census data means that figures for 1976 and 1981 are incomplete.

In this work, universities are supported by Universities Australia (UA), the peak national body. The UA's Indigenous Strategy 2017–20 acknowledged that "universities are cultural and intellectual hubs".[31] Recognising this is critical to building towards an inclusive future. The tertiary sector will further benefit by implementing their own strategies to engage with the experiences of their staff, students, and their local Aboriginal and Torres Strait Islander communities.

Conclusion

Universities have the power to create unique cultures of learning that allow students to thrive.[32] A deep appreciation of the history of Aboriginal and Torres Strait Islander peoples is part of the cultural development for higher education in Australia. This flows into understanding the significant journey of Aboriginal and Torres Strait Islander students today. They are building a legacy that will extend the opportunity of those who follow them. While lecturers and tutors are a consistent point of contact for students, we need to think carefully about policy as well. How do our systems, what we teach and how we teach, include or exclude students? For instance, in the contemporary university what are the consequences of having to verify your identity in multiple ways, multiple times a day? How can we ensure that the measures we put in place for cybersecurity touch lightly on the students and staff who must interact with them?

Each tertiary institution faces its own history and legacy. Each institution sits upon unceded lands. How imposing or welcoming does a university look to an Aboriginal and/or Torres Strait Islander student on their first day? How impenetrable does the place feel to someone who is the first in their family to attend university? How can universities build a culture of open and humble knowledge exchange that benefits every student and every member of staff? There are some tangible choices that help.

- Build strong relationships with local Aboriginal and Torres Strait Islander communities. Trust and respect are vital, and both are the product of time spent together, sharing, listening and collaborating. What initiatives are local communities working towards? How can the university help? The benefits that universities can offer are not always clear or obvious to people beyond their campuses – talking is the first step.

- Remember that there are many different organisations within communities that have a stake in higher education. Each will have their own way of conducting business and their own priorities. There will be competing viewpoints and contrasting perspectives. Building trust is created through mutual understanding and appreciating each other's strengths and limitations. Getting to know what drives and shapes the agendas of these organisations is important for developing shared practices.
- Appoint Aboriginal and Torres Strait Islander peoples to leadership roles. This brings with it many benefits – visible leadership shows what is possible. There is a developing sector-wide network of senior Aboriginal and Torres Strait Islander leaders (see Universities Australia for instance). These leaders can and will shape the strategies of tomorrow. Not all Aboriginal and/or Torres Strait Islander leaders need to be appointed into Aboriginal identified roles. Leadership opportunities for Aboriginal and Torres Strait Islander academics and professional staff to undertake non-identified roles need to exist across all areas of work in the sector.
- Engage meaningfully with cultural competence. This framework seeks to create a learning and working environment that is welcoming to all.[33] It is a way to ensure mutual respect as we meet on this land that has always been a place of knowledge exchange, healing, law and belonging. People need to feel comfortable in their own skin and, just as equally, they need to cultivate a respectful empathy for others. At its core, cultural competency seeks to facilitate people really connecting with this place we now call Australia and to which we belong.
- Show respect for Country. From learning how to offer a personal and meaningful Acknowledgement of Country to understanding the history of the lands on which the university sits, respect for Country changes how you do things. This might manifest in gardens that draw upon the local flora; it may involve embedding the important stories of the land, seas and skies into the building works; it will mean serious progress on sustainable practices.

Our chapter opened with the questions of how do you change a culture? What aspects should remain, and which should go? Who determines what change is needed? How do you manage the dynamic nature of change considering the need for the centrality of Aboriginal and Torres Strait Islander world views in Australian culture? Universities can take heart from the fact that we know how to change culture. It comes from listening and then meaningful action agreed to across the university or sector, and checking that actions have the intended effect. This is not a linear process, but a circular one. Actions need to be judged by how they are received, meaning we need to again engage in the process of listening. This circularity is vital for cultural change. Actions happen at every level but the decisions made by our leaders are significant as they shape what is acceptable and what is not. There are personal and collective responsibilities here.

And how do you know when you've succeeded in changing a culture? In the end each Australian university's success will be measured by how its Aboriginal and Torres Strait Islander students and staff *feel* when they are on campus. While we work to spread the word about our programs and supports for new students, there is always more that we as a community of scholars and professionals can do to bolster that sense of welcoming, that sense of belonging. The call for cultural change has been made for decades. We will grow as leaders and scholars by answering it deeply and committing to the long-term evolution that is needed to ensure we all thrive.

Notes

1 Pearson, Luke (2021). Appropriate terminology for Aboriginal and Torres Strait Islander people – it's complicated. IndigenousX, 15 June. https://bit.ly/3P5UTeT.

2 Early coverage emerged in 1957 in an article that names Margaret Williams (University of Queensland) and Irwin Lewis (University of Western Australia) as recipients of Aboriginal Scholarships: (1957) Aboriginal scholarship. *Honi Soit* 29(12): 3. By 1958, the local organisers for Abschol at the University of Sydney were clear about the deficiency of support amongst the student community when compared to Melbourne: Khan, Peter (1958). Aborigines and you. *Honi Soit* 30(13).

3 Clark, Jennifer (2001). Abschol: More than a Scholarship Scheme. *National Library of Australia News*, October: 13; Wilson, Eric (1973). Political Power in Aboriginal Affairs: Illusion or Reality? *Honi Soit* 46(30).

4 Department of Education, Training and Youth Affairs (2001). Higher Education Students Time Series Tables: Selected Higher Education Statistics. Commonwealth of Australia.

5 For detailed work on this subject see: Fletcher, J.J. (1989). *Clean, clad and courteous: a history of Aboriginal education in New South Wales.* Sydney: Southwood Press Pty Ltd.

6 Burridge, Nina and Andrew Chodkiewicz (2012). An Historical Overview of Aboriginal Education Policies in the Australian Context. In Nina Burridge, Frances Whalan, Karen Vaughan, eds. *Indigenous Education: A Learning Journey for Teachers, Schools and Communities*, 16–17. Rotterdam: SensePublishers.

7 Australian Institute of Aboriginal and Torres Strait Islander Studies (1973). Weilmoringle: a possible model. *New Dawn* 1 July 1973, 1. https://aiatsis.gov.au/collection/featured-collections/new-dawn.

8 These figures are derived from a number of sources including figures from the Department of Education, Employment and Workplace Relations (2008). Students: 2008 Summary of Higher Education Statistics. (Australian Government; Moodie, Gavin (n.d.). Australia: twenty years of higher education expansion. *Journal of Access Policy & Practice* 5(2): 1–21; West, Roderick (1988). *Learning for life: review of higher education financing and policy, final report.* Canberra: Commonwealth of Australia.

9 In the 1986 census, the population of Aboriginal and Torres Strait Islander peoples was counted at 227,645. This suggests that only about 0.87 per cent were enrolled in higher education. Castles, Ian (1986). Aboriginals and Torres Strait Islanders - Australia, States and Territories: Census of Population and Housing. Census 1986, Census 86, Commonwealth of Australia, 1. Please note that the Dawkins White Paper only refers to Aboriginal peoples and includes no mention of Torres Strait Islanders as a distinct group.

10 Dawkins, John Sydney (1988) *Higher education: a policy statement.* Canberra: Australian Government Publishing Service, 6, 57.

11 Department of Employment, Education and Training (1989), *National Aboriginal and Torres Strait Islander Education Policy.* This significant document recognised the distinction between Aboriginal peoples and Torres Strait Islander people. For analysis of the issue of equity in higher education consider: Macintyre, Stuart, André Brett and Gwilym Croucher (2017). *No End of a Lesson: Australia's Unified National System of Higher Education.* Melbourne: Melbourne University Publishing; Horne, Julia (2020) Mass Education and University Reform in Late Twentieth Century Australia. *British Journal of Educational Studies* 68(5): 671–90.

12 Department of Employment, Education and Training. *National Aboriginal and Torres Strait Islander Education Policy*, 7.

13 Department of Employment, Education and Training. *National Aboriginal and Torres Strait Islander Education Policy*, 6.
14 Department of Employment, Education and Training. *National Aboriginal and Torres Strait Islander Education Policy*, 8.
15 Education is not the only realm where reports on the concerns of Aboriginal and Torres Strait Islander peoples can appear current when they are decades old. Another example are the recommendations put forward in the 1989 *National Aboriginal Health Strategy* which are just as relevant today as when they were published.
16 Department of Employment, Education and Training (1990). *A Fair Chance for All: National and Institutional Planning for Equity in Higher Education: A Discussion Paper*, iii.
17 Department of Employment, Education and Training, *A Fair Chance for All*, 20. On the connection between degree types and self-determination, see: Macintyre, Stuart, André Brett, and Gwilym Croucher (2017). *No End of a Lesson: Australia's Unified National System of Higher Education*, 112–13. Melbourne: Melbourne University Publishing.
18 Department of Employment, Education and Training. *A Fair Chance for All*, 23.
19 On the friction this move created between universities and the government see: Macintyre, Brett, and Croucher, *No End of a Lesson*, 108.
20 West, Roderick (1998). *Learning for Life: Review of Higher Education Financing and Policy, Final Report*, 41. Canberra: Commonwealth of Australia.
21 West, *Learning for Life*, 140.
22 Siewert, Rachel (2020). *Adequacy of Newstart and related payments and alternative mechanisms to determine the level of income support payments in Australia*. Canberra: Commonwealth of Australia, 61–6.
23 Bradley, Denise, Peter Noonan, Helen Nugent and Bill Scales (2008). *Review of Australian higher education: final report*, xxvi. Canberra: Commonwealth of Australia.
24 Nursing Council of New Zealand (2011). *Guidelines for cultural safety, the Treaty of Waitangi and Maori health in nursing education and practice*. Wellington NZ: Nursing Council of New Zealand, 6.
25 Gooda, Mick (2011). *Social justice report 2011*. Canberra: Australian Human Rights Commission, 122.
26 Behrendt, Larissa, Steven Larkin, Robert Griew, Patricia Kelly (2012). *Review of Higher Education Access and Outcomes for Aboriginal and Torres Strait Islander People: Final Report*, 65, 85, 118. Canberra: Australian Government.
27 Behrendt et al., *Review of Higher Education Access and Outcomes for Aboriginal and Torres Strait Islander People: Final Report*, xii.
28 Universities Australia, "2020 Higher Education Facts and Figures", October 2020, 29, Figure 15. Overall university enrolment have been steadily increasing from 2001 (over 800,000) to 2018 (over 1.4 million).

29 Australian Bureau of Statistics (2020). "Education and Work, Australia, Attainment by level and field," Release, 11 November 2020, https://bit.ly/3z79O37.
30 Australian Bureau of Statistics, Census data 1991 and 2001.
31 Universities Australia (2016). *Indigenous Strategy 2017–2020*. Deakin: Universities Australia, 19.
32 Behrendt et al., *Review of Higher Education Access and Outcomes for Aboriginal and Torres Strait Islander People: Final Report*, xxiv.
33 See Frawley, Jack, Gabrielle Russell, Juanita Sherwood, eds (2020). *Cultural competence and the higher education sector: Australian perspectives, policies and practices*. Singapore: Springer Singapore.

6

Beyond "access" and "affordability"

Young people talk about university participation

Samantha McMahon and Valerie Harwood

We need to listen to young people who experience educational disadvantage. If we do not, the widening participation policy landscape will likely continue to fail to engage these young people with universities. A key reason for this policy failure is, we suggest, disturbingly elementary: young people who are the focus of these policies tend to understand the "problem" of university participation very differently to the policymakers trying to help them.

To make our case, we draw on findings from four research projects that, collectively, interviewed 553 young people who experience educational disadvantage across New South Wales, South Australia, Tasmania, Western Australia, Victoria and the Australian Capital Territory. The research participants were all young people ranging in age from 11–21 years, who can be identified as belonging to equity groups frequently the focus of widening participation policy. Whilst each project had its own research focus, all interviews with young people featured discussions of university participation. Given the timing of the Reinventing the Gap Year project[1], discussions about university participation in this study additionally focused on the impacts of natural disasters (fires and floods) and the COVID-19 pandemic on young people's university decisions.

We hope that in listening to young people's understandings of the "problem" of widening university participation, policymakers might find a new and more effective way for improving the university participation agenda.

Policy landscape

Policy analysts have long highlighted how various means of framing a policy problem result in varied policy solutions;[2] lack of agreement between policymakers and policy subjects will likely result in enduring social issues. The enduring problem of equitable participation in university is arguably made even sharper with the impact that the COVID-19 pandemic is having on education, particularly for those who experience educational disadvantage.[3]

Policy direction in widening participation policy landscapes can be characterised as "vague"[4] and there is a tendency for policy to attend to blunt fiscal mechanisms assumed to be levers for improving participation of underrepresented equity groups.[5] Given the troubled record of widening participation policy to date, we concur with Austin's concern about widening participation in the face of COVID-19 that will "continue to have, a profound impact on access to higher education".[6]

Widening participation policy can be broadly characterised as focusing on solving problems of university "access" and "affordability". The "access" policy problem is framed as the challenge of ensuring university populations are representative of the national population; seeking to ensure no groups identified as experiencing educational disadvantage are underrepresented in university enrolments and completion rates (for example, First Nations students, students from regional and remote areas and students who experience socio-economic disadvantage). The "solution" to the policy problem of "access" seems to be addressed through massification, and the creation of policies to increase university student places available in a given year. The logic of this solution seems to rest on the premise that if there are more university places available, there is more of a chance for young people who experience educational disadvantage to "get in". For example, the Australian federal government's demand-driven system (from 2012 to 2017) removed caps from degree enrolment and received a "mixed report card" in terms of its effectiveness for widening participation.[7] Driven by recommendations from the Bradley Report, policy responses – while flagging "social equity" – are, as Rizvi and Lingard argued, more complex, and infused with a "neoliberal imaginary".[8]

Policy problems of "affordability" tend to include policy approaches targeting redistribution of government funds to encourage universities to attract and retain educationally disadvantaged students. Examples include the Australian federal government's Higher Education Participation and Partnerships (HEPPP) funding programs and mechanisms aiming to reduce start-up costs and up-front fees for students experiencing educational and socio-economic disadvantage. Examples include the HECS-HELP loan schemes for deferring payment of public university fees, and the Job-ready Graduates Package efforts to offset costs of regional students moving to study at a university. Whilst these policies are promising, their effectiveness seems questionable given equity targets remain elusive, especially noting diversity of equity group representation in "elite" universities and degree programs.[9] We maintain policy effectiveness remains questionable because defining the widening participation issue as predominantly "access" and "affordability" elides the complexity of experiencing educational disadvantage and engaging with university. To demonstrate the profundity of this issue we explore what young people have to say about university "access" and related issues of cost and "affordability".

So, what about "affordability"?

Young people who experience educational disadvantage are concerned about the affordability of university, but not, necessarily, in the same ways that policymakers are when they respond to concerns of reducing the costs of university. In a large-scale project, Quin, Stone and Trinidad found that 56 per cent of regional NSW high school students state fear of debt as a barrier to university participation.[10] Considering this, Australia may have, arguably, the most successful university fee deferral policies in HECS-HELP, but if this still generates debt, most regional students are likely to feel dissuaded from university participation.[11]

Rethinking affordability: understanding how to respond to the affective fear of debt

Conversations with young people about affordability tend to focus on fear of debt and the day-to-day costs of studying at university. To illustrate this, we consider the case of young people from regional and rural NSW areas; and we have chosen this demographic because university participation of regional students has decreased over the last decade despite the policy targeting them as an equity group in the widening participation agenda.[12]

One young person interviewed in the Gap Year Study reminds us, "I think about the HECS debt … So I was kind of like, 'Oh, my god. How much money do I need?"[a] This statement is neither glib hyperbole nor melodrama; it is genuine exasperation and is representative of sentiment amongst young people we've interviewed. Whilst HECS-HELP repayments are inherently "affordable" because the payment amount is directly related to income tax scales, people located in these equity groups may experience the liability of HECS debt differently, especially when applying for a bank loan.

Rethinking affordability: day-to-day costs of university study

Young people are concerned about the affordability of university, especially day-to-day costs of studying, often identified as fuel expenses, food, textbooks, accommodation, as well as having reduced capacity for gainful employment due to the time demands of studying. "I was just thinking, 'Well, I'll just get a job and then I should be fine' but I wasn't really aware of how much it actually costs."[a] This key concern about experiencing poverty and food insecurity whilst at university seems strongly connected to the lack of review of Austudy and Youth Allowance to align with increasing costs of living,[13] and recent declines in hospitality and retail sectors during the pandemic. An extra $50 on the relocation costs grant offered in the Job-ready Graduates Package might assist with set-up costs but would, arguably, do little to incentivise regional students who are largely concerned with the *ongoing* living cost challenges associated with three- to five-year-long degree programs.

So, what about "access"?

Although the young people we interviewed valued non-ATAR pathways into university, they rarely comment about "access" difficulty, indicating a disconnect between lived experience and policy foci. Indeed, young people experiencing educational disadvantage often have incredibly strong and realistic aspirations in regard to university study.[14] Below are comments from two secondary school students in low socio-economic metropolitan schools:

> I always wanted to go to university. I know that I always wanted to pursue further education other than high school, so if anything it [a university outreach program] convinced me to go even more rather than changing my mind.[b]
>
> I've always wanted to go into tertiary education and I feel like it's just like motivated me rather than change my mind.[b]

As such statements were often made, we need to reappraise the assumption that concern about entry to university rests on whether or not these young people can or should access university. But if aspirations for the idea of a university education are strong, why are participation rates low? It seems that how young people imagine and understand university life and learning makes a big difference.[15] This finding, we argue, reframes the key policy problem as young people's restricted access to knowledge of what university life is like and how it might work for them.

Rethinking access: understandings of university being similar to school is a significant barrier to university access

Many perceived barriers to university seem to rest in misunderstandings of what university teaching, learning and place is like. A very common misunderstanding is that university is a "bigger" version of school.[16] For these young people, university is …

> A building, it looks like a school.[c]
>
> A really, really, really big high school.[c]
>
> Scary ... A giant school.[c]
>
> It's sort of like second base high school isn't it?[c]

These comments paint a picture of university as like a school, a way of imagining university that can be a barrier to wanting to attend.[17] Linked to this way of imagining universities as schools, is how university is depicted as though it is an intensified version of school. This intensity is spoken about by Jacinta, a young Aboriginal woman from regional Queensland. When asked what she'd think about if she was going to university tomorrow, Jacinta responded, "How busy and hard it would be."[c] Wendell, a young person from remote NSW explained he had never seen a university. When asked what happens at university Wendell replied, "Maths ... science."

The interviewer then asked Wendell the question, "If I asked you to describe a university – I know you've never been but what do you imagine a university to look like?" Wendell's response was, "Big building, lot of kids, lot of teachers. That's it."

And when asked, "What kind of people would go to the university?" Wendell responded, "Smart people."

Wendell's response to a question about whether he would consider going to university, and if he could get into anything he wanted, was, "Maybe" and what he would choose to do is "Football".[c] Choosing to do football speaks to the affective in Wendell's thoughts about what he would like to do at university.

There is, we suggest, an intensity in both Jacinta's and Wendell's responses; responses that might be thought of as a caricature of narrow stereotyped imaginings of what constitutes university subjects and what constitutes "smartness". The poignant question is just what exactly is meant by "smart"? To follow the flow of Jacinta's and Wendell's contributions to this discussion, it appears "smart" people are those who excel in maths and science. It is interesting that Jacinta decided to describe "how busy and hard it would be" and Wendell, an 11-year-old boy from a remote town in NSW with considerable disadvantage, decided he would like to go to university to study football. The key here is to connect with the feelings which, with colleague Anna Hickey-Moody, we have called "feeling futures".[18] Taken this way, we can productively engage with Wendell's comments to explore the diversity that can be available at Australian universities, and make connections with a young person's feelings and desires about their educational futures.

Thinking about university as meaning "*more school*", young people from Western Sydney, NSW, and from suburban South Australia made the following statements:

> I hate school. I've done 13 years of school and I don't need any more; I'm quite all right thank you.[c]
>
> Melody: [who'd] want another couple of years of schooling?
>
> Zac: I'd kill myself literally ... If I had to go to school for another few years.[c]

For many of the high school students, high school learning was not expressed as active, lifelong learning; instead, it was expressed as short term, for the purpose of passing exams and assessments and based on drill and memorisation.[19] This raises the question: "If learning feels like it does for the young people we spoke with, why would these young people want to do more learning in 'big school'/university?":

> Well, when I'm learning [at school] I'm like a hot air balloon. So, for example, when someone is like speaking, like the teachers, it's like the … hot air runs into the hot air balloon … It's like my brain because like it's getting filled with hot ideas and then when they're not letting the air in, I'm back onto the ground.[b]
>
> When I study, I think of myself like sticky tape, when you pull it out it's sticky, but if you leave it for a long time it doesn't get sticky as much.[b]

> So when I'm learning, I'm like a piggybank and I'm the inside of the piggybank and all the information and all the numbers and words and letters and topics and subjects go inside and then when it's exam time … you crack the piggybank open. It's full and then you empty onto the paper.[b]

For these students, university graduate attributes of lifelong learning are alien to their experiences of learning at school. If one is comparing choices of degrees to choices of HSC subjects, in school, there are limited elective subjects that you must commit to for up to two years at a stretch. In our interviews, the researchers highlighted university is not like school; explaining classes went for 12 weeks, there was flexibility afforded via mobility between majors, or capacity to transfer degree programs with course credits. However, we found the young people did not universally celebrate this more flexible aspect of university, or consider it helpful to deciding what to study:

> Oh, if I don't like it [the degree I choose] and I've got to change, that's a whole another year and like a whole another year of HECS debt. Like that is a real scary thing.[a]

This is not a one-off concern. Indecision about what to study was a barrier to university cited by 43 per cent of regional students in NSW.[20] Findings from the "Reinventing the Gap Year" (RIGY) project and common advice of higher education university outreach teams has been to overcome the barrier of indecision and to "make up your mind while you are at uni"; to select a generalist degree in your area of skill and interest (for example, arts, commerce, engineering, science), then discover your passions as you study a range of units. It follows, then, that the government's Job-ready Graduates Package policy that hiked fees for generalist degrees in arts and humanities means "indecision" is amplified, not squashed, as a barrier for regional students attending university, especially when coupled with the barrier of "fear of debt". Indeed, overcoming indecision via enrolment in generalist degrees, like this regional student did, is less plausible since the package:

> I'm studying an arts degree, which you look at it and it's just so broad but once you actually start and you get to choose your majors and – I don't think I even understood how that all worked until I started ... But once you're in it, you realise that it's fine and there's lots of choices.[a]

Rethinking access: lack of access to conversations about and experiences of university is a significant barrier for university access

Our research demonstrates educationally disadvantaged young people experience limited access to conversations about universities. Whilst we encountered occasional positive perceptions of university life, the ideas seemed overwhelming and anxiety provoking. When young people in the Imagining University Education (IUE) project[c] were asked to describe what they thought a university was like, they offered:

> *large-scale metaphors* such as learning in football stadiums, a giant Costco, a big warehouse, mansions, hotels, castles, movie theatres, and huge classrooms.
>
> *anxiety producing images* such as shiny floors, smelling like a hospital, a jail, government buildings and the oval office.
>
> *overwhelming images* such as heavy books, brick walls, getting lost, massive, buildings everywhere, so many offices.
>
> *isolating images* such as lecturers being physically far away from you and inaccessible, everyone in their own room at their own desk, sitting in a disconnected single desk or chair.[d]

The people at university are also often construed as inconceivable and so different to themselves that they would not fit in.

> Giants because they'd all be taller than me. Yes, because I'm so midget-like. I'd be scared; there'd be all these tall people running around and I'd be like ... tall people, intimidating people.[c]

In the interview excerpt below, Kyle, an Aboriginal young man in Year 9 at secondary school participating in the AIME program, describes how he learned about who can go to university:

> Yeah. It's just a reality check that anyone can go to university.

The interviewer then asks him about what he had previously thought, and Kyle's response is sobering:

> Interviewer: What did you think – who did you think went to uni?
>
> Kyle: *White* people, you know successful – people with money – you know what I mean?[e]

Based on these young people's understandings, not only is university a place indistinct from negative experiences of school, imagined in prevailingly negative ways, the people inhabiting these undesirable spaces would potentially make you feel alienated and ostracised. It took *access to conversations* with "real" university students, rather than imagined ones, to shift these misconceptions that would otherwise seem insurmountable knowledge barriers to university participation.

Conclusion

In summary, we will leave you with this question: *If you were one of these young people, would you consider university a desirable or plausible educational future?* Given this, government policy concerned with widening participation but which aims for massification would potentially only serve to amplify the undesirable in the eyes of possibly many young people who experience educational disadvantage. Policy that focuses on redistributions of government funds to incentivise universities to attract educationally disadvantaged students has extremely limited, if any, potential to address the problem of fear of debt and day-to-day costs of study. This dual strategy also has little impact on the persistent misunderstandings of university experienced by these young people, particularly those who do not have ready access

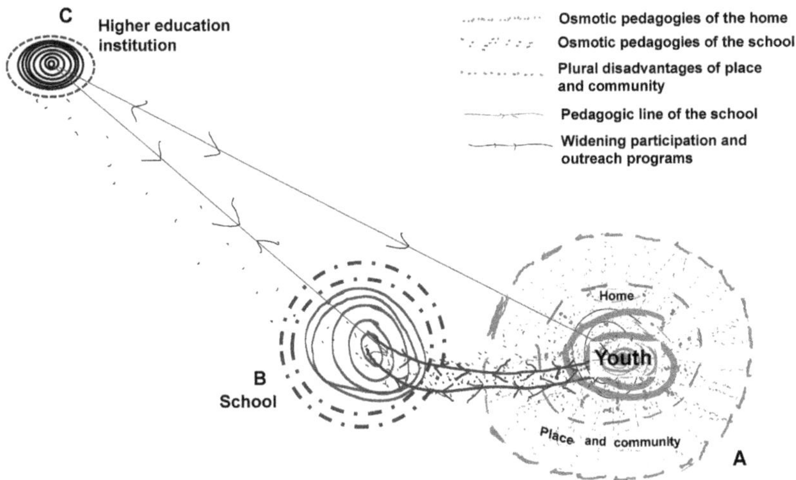

Figure 6.1 Diagrammatic pedagogies: mapping possibilities for outreach. (Reproduced from Harwood, Hickey-Moody, McMahon & O'Shea, 2017, p. 193)

to "real conversations" about university life. Whilst university outreach programs are designed to "bridge" this knowledge gap and offer such conversations of university life, that such misunderstandings persist is testimony to a need for a shift in focus for these programs, including a move away from marketing specific universities.[21]

Perhaps we could redefine the policy imperative? An important way to proceed is to acknowledge the current policy disconnect and to think differently about how understandings of young people might be improved and the policy disconnect decreased. A start could be to contemplate how the affective, or what we have termed "feeling educational futures", might be better supported, better planned for – and better embraced in policy. Our earlier work sought to create a way to "map possibilities for outreach" that offer improved ways of "conceptualizing the relationships young people with precarious relationships to education have to higher education institutions and the osmotic nature of their learning".[22]

One of the ideas this diagram helps to convey is the importance of an engaged practice of connection in considering what might need to happen in widening participation and, such as in this example, outreach programs. Policymakers are implicated in this process, and this means there is a key role to play in how subjectivities are constructed in widening participation (WP) policies. Southgate and Bennett persuasively target this failure in widening participation policymaking, stating "we want to make it more difficult for WP policy to restrain opportunities by narrowly defining subjectivities".[23] We certainly need to avoid policies that, even with attempts to ameliorate perceived access and affordability issues, continue to produce subjectivities that are alien to – and that can alienate – young people who experience educational disadvantage.

This puts the pressure on policy processes to create ways that connect with what the young people themselves know and experience. No doubt this is a considerable challenge when policymaking is arguably disconnected from the lives that are the object. To follow Ingold's argument, there is need to take a step towards the kind of education that occurs with what is held foremost in anthropology, the practice of participant observation.

> In participant observation ... anthropologists become correspondents. They take into themselves something of their hosts' ways of moving, feeling and thinking, their practical skills and modes of attention.[24]

This suggests that above all, policy needs to acknowledge its disconnect, and leaning into becoming "correspondents" may well be a step in a helpful direction for the many young people for whom university remains elusive.

As we have argued, we could sustain focus on the current policy imperatives of access and affordability, but we need to acknowledge these are not sufficient on their own to address the barriers to participation currently felt by young people who experience educational disadvantage. We also need to create policy sensitive to issues that matter to educationally disadvantaged groups including:

- fear of debt;
- indecision about studies;

- unsustainable living costs and limited employment during study; and
- understanding how schools and universities differ, especially in terms of teaching, learning and spaces.

And importantly, be able to *attend*, in the sense that Ingold conveys,[25] to the differences of the young people and learn with them.

Research projects referenced

[a] This data comes from the "Reinventing the Gap Year" (RIGY) project that established new forms of communications between universities, regional young people and parents to support accurate gap year and university decision making. This project (2019–21) was led by Samantha McMahon and equity practitioners and academics from the University of Sydney, University of Wollongong, and University of Canberra. Thirty-seven young people were interviewed.

[b] This data comes from the "Widening Participation and Outreach Longitudinal Evaluation". This project (2018–21) was led by Samantha McMahon and academics at Sydney, UNSW and Western Sydney University to evaluate a university outreach program for socio-economically disadvantaged high school students in the greater area of Western Sydney. One hundred and ten young people were interviewed.

[c] This data comes from the "Imagining University Education" project. This was an ARC funded Discovery project (DP110104704, 2011–14) led by Valerie Harwood. This study drew on interviews with over 250 young people across Australia who had been excluded from secondary school and their imaginings and narratives of university.

[d] For full analysis of these images of university, please refer to Chapter 8 of the book from the IUE study, *The politics of widening participation and university access for young people*, by Valerie Harwood, Anna Hickey-Moody, Samantha McMahon and Sarah O'Shea (2017).

[e] This data comes from a research partnership with the Australian Indigenous Mentoring Experience (AIME) (2012–ongoing). AIME is not a university outreach program, specifically, but this program is "an educational program proven to support Indigenous students through high school and into Uni or employment at the same rate as all Australians", so it is important to listen to the young people who attend. One hundred and forty-three First Nations high school students were interviewed. Funding for this research included the ARC Discovery Project (DP140103690, 2014–17).

Notes

1 For further details on this project, see McMahon, Samantha (2020). *New help for regional students thinking of taking a gap year*. https://www.aare.edu.au/blog/?tag=samantha-mcmahon; A-Star (2021). *Gap Year Guide*. https://astar.tv/page/gap-year-guide.
2 Bacchi, Carol, and Susan Goodwin (2016). *Poststructural policy analysis: a guide to practice*. New York: Palgrave Macmillan.
3 Austin, Kylie (2021). Facing the pandemic: considering partnerships for widening participation in higher education in Australia. *European Journal of Education* 56(1): 98–101.
4 Austin, Facing the pandemic, 99.
5 Reed, Richard, Anna King and Gail Whiteford (2015). Re-conceptualising sustainable widening participation: evaluation, collaboration and evolution. *Higher Education Research and Development* 34(2): 383–96.
6 Austin, Facing the pandemic, 98.
7 Productivity Commission (2022). The demand driven university system: a mixed report card. Accessed 17 December 2022. https://bit.ly/3JNqaBF.
8 Department of Education, Employment and Workplace Relations (2008). *Review of Australian higher education: final report*. Canberra, A.C.T: Department of Education, Employment and Workplace Relations; Rizvi, Fazal, and Bob Lingard (2011). Social equity and the assemblage of values in Australian higher education. *Cambridge Journal of Education* 41(1): 5–22.
9 Pitman, Tim, Daniel Edwards, Liang-Cheng Zhang, Paul Koshy and Julie McMillan (2020). Constructing a ranking of higher education institutions based on equity: is it possible or desirable? *Higher Education* 80: 605–24.
10 Quin, Robyn, Cathy Stone and Sue Trinidad (2017). Low rates of transition to university for high achieving students in regional NSW. NSW Department of Education. https://bit.ly/3ch4bpS.
11 Higgins, Timothy (2019). The Higher Education Contribution Scheme: keeping tertiary education affordable and accessible. In Joannah Luetjens,

Michael Mintrom, and Paul 't Hart, eds. *Successful public policy: lessons from Australia and New Zealand*, 59–86. Canberra: ANU Press.

12 Productivity Commission. The demand driven university system.

13 Temple, Jeromey, Sue Booth and Christina Pollard (2019). Social assistance payments and food insecurity in Australia: evidence from the household expenditure survey. *International Journal of Environmental Research and Public Health* 16: 455.

14 Harwood, Valerie, Samantha McMahon, Sarah O'Shea, Gawain Bodkin-Andrews and Amy Priestly (2015). Recognising aspiration: the AIME program's effectiveness in inspiring Indigenous young people's participation in schooling and opportunities for further education and employment. *Australian Educational Researcher* 42(2): 217–36.

15 Harwood, Valerie, Anna Hickey-Moody, Samantha McMahon and Sarah O'Shea (2017). *The politics of widening participation and university access for young people: making educational futures*. Abingdon: Routledge.

16 McMahon, Samantha, Valerie Harwood and Anna Hickey-Moody (2016). 'Students that just hate school wouldn't go': educationally disengaged and disadvantaged young people's talk about university education. *British Journal of Sociology of Education* 37(8): 1109–28.

17 McMahon et al., Students that just hate school wouldn't go.

18 Harwood, Hickey-Moody, McMahon & O'Shea, *The politics of widening participation*.

19 McMahon, Samantha, Meghan Stacey, Valerie Harwood, Nada Labib, Alexandra Wong and Sheelagh Daniels-Mayes (2021). Exploring students' metaphors for learning in Western Sydney schools. *Critical Studies in Education*, DOI: 10.1080/17508487.2021.1943476.

20 Quin, Stone and Trinidad, Low rates of transition, 3.

21 Austin, Facing the pandemic, 99.

22 Harwood, Hickey-Moody, McMahon & O'Shea, *The politics of widening participation*, 192.

23 Southgate, Erica, and Anna Bennett (2014). Excavating widening participation policy in Australian higher education: subject positions, representational effects, emotion. *Creative Approaches to Research* 7(1): 40.

24 Ingold, Tim (2018). *Anthropology and/as education*. Abingdon: Routledge: 70.

25 Ingold, *Anthropology and/as education*.

7
International students in Australia since the early 1900s

Julia Horne

Australia's history of international students is significantly longer than many realise. In this chapter, I provide an historical perspective to offer alternative viewpoints on the present which are worth exploring in regard to the "public good". I argue that we should be devising ways in which we broaden our relationships with international students, specifically by engaging philosophically with the idea of "welcome" as an ethical practice. The philosopher and cultural theorist Kwame Anthony Appiah expresses it this way: we should consider what we might "owe strangers by virtue of our shared humanity". In other words, at the heart of "welcome" is our "shared humanity" and the offer to "strangers" – such as international students – to belong.[1]

As my brief history shows, the Commonwealth government has, since 1901, been the sole arbiter of policy that governs the lives of international students in Australia. At various points it has imposed harsh entry restrictions, stern often unforgiving requirements about a student's length of stay, and placed such constraints on students as to affect their quality of life. At other times, especially in the 1960s and 1970s, there was a lighter and more conciliatory attitude to having international students study in Australia on much the same basis as Australians, viewing them as long-term residents and even potential citizens. But what for the 21st century? While the past is by no means perfect, it reveals not only what we shouldn't do – such as restrict students on the basis of race – but also what we might do.

Origins

In February 1923, a Japanese ocean liner docked in Sydney. On board was N.Y. Shah, a young Chinese man who had voyaged from Wuhan, China, to study at the University of Sydney. Shah – whose name may have been anglicised from Xia – had recently graduated from Wesley College in Wuchang, a post-secondary educational establishment founded by British Methodists. According to a local news report, he expected to study for a year, after which he planned to return to Wuhan to "enter upon the teaching profession at the Union Normal School", an independent educational establishment partially funded by missionary organisations.[2]

Beyond friendly mentions of his arrival in the local press, there is no other explicit record that tells us about his study program, where he stayed, or how and why he came to be at the University of Sydney. Perhaps Shah was supported by missionary organisations, though also possible was contact with British academic networks in this period, and the intriguing lines of communications between British academics across the British Empire. One such line of communication may have been Arthur Sadler, who in 1922 was appointed Professor of Oriental Studies at Sydney University. It's a tenuous connection, but his more than ten years of teaching in Japan and close ties to British diplomatic missions in the region (including China) make it possible. Sadler was open to the idea of educational and cultural exchange between Australia and Asia, especially Japan.

The choice of Sydney University is interesting, not so much for possible missionary connections, but because of its successful experiment in teacher-training involving university study, a first in Australia, with the emphasis on teacher education, not just skills acquisition. Shah's goal to become a teacher made the University of Sydney an obvious choice. Alexander Mackie, appointed the first Professor of Education in Australia in 1910 and principal of the Sydney Teachers College, was undertaking widely known innovative and exciting work on pedagogy and the professional training of teachers, and this reputation itself may have been reason enough for Shah to travel across the seas with the purpose of study.[3]

Shah's enthusiasm for educational transformation to prepare him for his chosen professional life is part of a broader story of educational movement in the early 1900s. At that time, there was a small but growing movement of students internationally who travelled to study in the English-speaking world. In the US, for example, estimated numbers of foreign students rose from 600 in 1905, to 1,800 in 1912, and almost 10,000 in 1930. Most came from China, Japan and the Philippines, followed closely by students from Europe, and then Canada. As Paul Kramer explains in his study of the US situation prior to the First World War, globally mobile educational endeavours were largely orchestrated by missionary groups who assisted talented students from China and Japan to enter denominational colleges in the US, to both attain a degree and sharpen their Christian faith. After the war, an additional interest group emerged, the new breed of internationalists who aimed to build peace through fostering cultural understanding, primarily through education in other lands, and their efforts ignited the expansion of numbers in the 1920s.[4]

As Kramer shows, these educational endeavours were often complicated, with potential students mostly bemused and muddled by US Congressional immigration restrictions and the often suspicious attitudes of Port authorities. Similarly in Britain, the reception of students from China and Japan could be troubled, especially when the local press relished reports of uncorroborated crime allegedly committed by "foreign" student scoundrels. Nonetheless, the global movement of university-aged students shows that many were prepared, even encouraged, to leave their countries and travel vast distances to study at higher education institutions in foreign lands.

There was from this early time specific interest from potential students from neighbouring countries such as China, Japan and India to study at Australian higher education institutions. Universities were also open to, even cautiously enthusiastic about, such educational and scholarly exchange that clearly crossed the Commonwealth's "colour line". David Walker explores the Asia-Pacific interest of a few Australian intellectuals in this period including University of Sydney academics who believed in Australia's Asian future despite increased national anxiety about the proximity of Asia.[5]

However, as Amit Sarwal and David Lowe argue, the Australian government barely tolerated the presence of such students, even when they had the required authority and documentation to travel to Australia and be admitted as students into Australian higher education institutions. While government attitudes were to change later, in the first part of the 20th century they were shaped by racial arrogance and the desire to create and maintain Australia as a white nation. Students from China, Japan, India and elsewhere were not part of this vision, even though their admission to Australia was a consequence of agitation by locals who recognised a universal good in such relationships.[6]

One of the founding acts of the first Australian parliament in 1901 was to introduce immigration restrictions. Colloquially known as the White Australia Policy, the legislation encoded racism and made it almost impossible for people of colour to enter Australia, except under strict exemptions. From the early 1900s, such exempted categories included students, along with merchants and tourists, but exemptions were not automatic. One customs official responded to a reporter's query about a case of declined entry in 1912, claiming that "all a coloured student from India need do was to get a passport from the Indian Government and he would be admitted to the Commonwealth for 12 months". And if 12 months was inadequate to undertake a university degree? The official explained: "An extension of the term would be considered when it had expired."[7] It sounds relatively simple, but as political scientist Tony Palfreeman argued, the whole process, including a dictation test in a European language that was administered to people of colour, was at the minister's discretion. Only the minister himself could grant a "certificate of exemption" from the dictation test, which he could as easily cancel, a not uncommon occurrence.[8]

The Commonwealth responded case by case, it seems, to allow exemptions for students accepted by an Australian university to enter Australia for one year, which realistically only enabled a taste of Australian university study and life for a very small number of determined students. We know that the exemption system often failed, and there are reports of people who were stopped at their port of origin from boarding ships to Australia, despite having the necessary paperwork. We also know local authorities occasionally attempted deportations, not understanding how exemptions for Chinese, Japanese and Indian students, or other people of colour, functioned within the context of the government-imposed colour bar. While over the next four decades students from Asia trickled in under Commonwealth exemptions to live in Australia and attend university for a year, both entry and departure could be fraught. The "law", it seems, hovered over students like Shah for the entirety of their stay in Australia and cast deep shadows over whether they were really welcomed at all, even with all the goodwill of professors and friendly community members who championed their stay.

Postwar "goodwill" and "neighbourliness"

During the two decades that followed the end of the Second World War, various forces at play nudged the Commonwealth government to consider small changes to its immigration restriction policies. Foremost was the awareness that war had forever changed Australia's relationship to the Asia-Pacific region, especially with the emerging reality of the collapse of the British Empire and the subsequent rise of new nation-states. Outside government circles there was a progressive shift towards Asia.[9] And slowly, changes were made to Australian government policy from a nation that once defined itself largely in terms of the British Empire, to one that articulated a new role for Australia in the region, transforming the government's appetite for Asian students.

Gwenda Tavan's evocative phrase, "The *long*, slow death of White Australia", captures the spirit of these decades: the continuation of policies designed to protect cultural and racial homogeneity that began to be adjusted to accommodate the changing geo-political reality and increasing humanitarian concerns. This gradual shift eventually led to the repeal of the White Australia Policy by the Whitlam government.[10]

While the original immigration restriction legislation was significant in reducing the number of Asian students who came to study in Australia in the early 20th century, its dismantling in the postwar decades resulted in an exponential increase. In 1947, 300 non-European students studied in Australia.[11] By 1955 there were 1,800 foreign students in higher education, rising to 7,300 in 1966. Of the higher education students who came mostly from Asian countries, 16 per cent enrolled to study at colleges of higher education and 80 per cent at universities.[12]

As Sarwal and Lowe explain, the increase was partially due to Australia's efforts to promote Australia as a "good neighbour" in the Asia-Pacific region and trade on education as a form of humanitarian aid. In 1958, Alick Downer, the Minister for Immigration, expressed the government's mood for change and acceptance of overseas students as demonstrating Australia's "goodwill" towards "our Asian neighbours", a sentiment that was a far cry from the previous relentless defence of Australia's racist immigration policies. Education as a form of " soft diplomacy" to spread influence became a favoured government approach.[13]

Yet the "goodwill" which these schemes were intended to support was not especially altruistic. As Anna Kent and Genevieve Dashwood caution, Australia's government scholarship schemes were ultimately designed to serve the " national interest". They sought to create a new image of Australia as welcoming and hospitable to students from the Asia-Pacific region, regardless of race, and despite the fact that half-a-century of a vigorously enforced colour bar was still on the books, if no longer fully enforced. Good will and neighbourliness often had strict boundaries, especially when it came to the social and economic wellbeing of the sponsored students who came to live and study in Australia.[14]

The best-known government-sponsored overseas student scheme was the Colombo Plan, which Daniel Oakman reminds us was an "international creation" of the British Commonwealth rather than being "exclusively Australian". It was initiated with great fanfare in 1951 and, according to Tavan, became the "cornerstone of Australia's 'good neighbour' policy". It succeeded in bringing in new cohorts of scholarship-assisted students from Asia, including from Thailand, Indonesia and Malaysia, and became the model for other educational assistance schemes such as those mobilised by Australia in the Pacific.[15] But so prominent was the Colombo Plan in the Australian imagination, it is still incorrectly believed to have been the first major source of overseas students.

Australia's "private overseas students" policies

Most Asian students who arrived in Australia in this period were not part of the government's scholarship and assistance programs. Rather, they were classified as "private overseas students" to distinguish them from "sponsored students" under government aid programs such as the Colombo Plan. They were part of the same student lineage as N.Y. Shah in the early 20th century, but were now able to enter Australia more easily under new immigration regulations designed to encourage students from the Asia-Pacific region. Lyndon Megarrity, whose work on changing government policy towards private overseas students in the 1950s and 1960s remains a landmark study, estimates that the Colombo Plan brought less than a fifth of overseas students to Australia in the 1950s and 1960s.[16]

From the 1940s, some universities began a more sustained call for changes to Australian immigration restrictions to allow students from Asia to be educated at Australian universities. This policy change was almost certainly a consequence of the increased communications between universities and the Commonwealth government via the Australian Universities Commission, established by the government in 1943 as part of postwar national reconstruction and made a permanent government body in 1945.[17] But the call also highlighted the belief that our public universities had a role and responsibility to not only educate Australians, but to extend that opportunity to the citizens of our neighbours as they emerged from their respective colonised pasts. And this meant creating a more formalised means of entry to Australia that allowed students freedom of movement to stay here for the duration of their study and beyond. Within government circles, this scheme was informally called the Private Overseas Student Programme.

The result was that by the 1950s many, but not all, universities admitted private overseas students to their degree programs under the same matriculation requirements and conditions as were accorded to

Australians. There was not yet a different category of fees specifically for these students; this did not emerge until the 1980s.

From the 1950s, the children of Chinese diaspora parents from South-East Asia began to arrive in Australia, go to school and matriculate to university. Increased student numbers led to more interactions with Australian university students and staff creating a discernible trend of "Australian-Asian sociability", according to Kate Darian-Smith and James Waghorne, that helped raise awareness of the irrelevance of the White Australia Policy to modern Australia. One practical outcome of this campus sociability was the publication of Control or Colour Bar? *A Proposal for Change in the Australian Immigration System* (1960), an influential treatise that helped shape public and, eventually, government opinion over the following decade.[18]

By 1966, 8.9 per cent of students in Australian universities were classified as "private overseas students" who had come to Australia for the purpose of university study.[19] From 1966 to 1979, while the number of overseas students at universities increased, the proportion remained under 9 per cent as a consequence of exponential growth in domestic enrolments.[20] Nonetheless, there was obviously something about Australian education and society that appealed to our Asian neighbours, and attracted them to Australia, where they lived for five years and more.

Overseas student experience

In the late 1990s, I began a three-year archival project that surveyed and interviewed about 80 private overseas students mostly from Malaysia, Singapore, Hong Kong and Thailand, who studied at UNSW in the 1950s to 1970s. The students' "voices" were in response to mostly open-ended questions I posed where respondents were encouraged to provide a memoir about their student experience. The questions included educational and social background, reasons for coming to study in Australia and student experience including what many termed the "Australian way of life". While caution is needed in generalising from the responses, the project has informed the following observations of how the simple change to Australia's immigration laws that allowed students from Asia to study and work here, helped amplify the welcome that many experienced.[21]

It was apparent that most came from modest families, attracted by the cheaper fees of Australian universities, and the possibility of gaining Australian Commonwealth scholarships, which some did. They went to Australian schools – many to public high schools – sat for university matriculation and, upon matriculation, proceeded to university, either funded by the Commonwealth Scholarship scheme, or by paying subsidised university fees on the same basis as the Australian students they studied alongside.[22] Education costs of both school and university were largely borne by the state and federal governments. Even when overseas students enrolled at independent schools or paid university fees because they had not secured a Commonwealth scholarship, these were nonetheless subsidised by governments, just as they were for Australians. The notion of private overseas students being distinguished as "full-fee paying" and creating an "income stream" for universities was still decades away.

Some universities introduced admission quotas on the number of private overseas students, with the result that overseas students began to ignore them and instead place other universities as their first preference, such as UNSW and Monash, which were more accommodating to these private students.

The high cost of international travel meant that no one I interviewed returned to their country of origin over the four or more years they were in Australia. Most worked during the long summer vacation – in department stores, as bus conductors and even as seasonal fruit pickers, often alongside their Australian university student cohort – to raise money for their academic year. Many accepted invitations to dine with the families of school or university friends, or travel to country areas to stay on farms, sometimes organised through community organisations like Rotary. And in the 1960s, new regulations meant that after graduation they could remain in Australia to work in their chosen profession for several years.

I don't want to suggest that their Australian experience was always easy. My cohort of students was reflecting on their Australian experiences of 30 or more years ago in a way that could smooth over racial conflict or loneliness in order to emphasise the adventurous nature of the experience. But some memories stuck. Amongst my 1950s cohort there were complaints about over-zealous immigration officials. There were also stories of older Australians telling them to go back to where they came from. Many mentioned the various cultural adjustments they made, such as their bewilderment in the face of certain Australian social customs and manners, the intellectual independence expected of university students and, not the least, adjusting to Australian food. There was no appetite for "cold" sandwiches prepared by kindly landladies, and alternatives were sought such as the meat pie, all that gravy and hot chunky meat which made a culturally more appealing lunchtime substitute for them. The first time I heard the story of the delicious Australian pie, I thought there was a mistake until I heard it again and again from different students from different countries.

They also benefited from the gradual loosening of immigration restrictions which gave private overseas students who had lived in Australia for at least five years – which most had by the end of their degree – access to Australian citizenship. On the other hand, overseas students under schemes like the Colombo Plan were in Australia for shorter periods and were generally required to depart upon completion of their study.

From 1966 there were significant policy changes for private overseas students, which included a stronger Commonwealth government welfare commitment which was previously virtually non-existent. And amongst some government officials, there was an increasing awareness that the substantial experience of these students of the many facets of Australian life, including living, studying and working with other Australians, would make them good Australian citizens.[23]

A new approach for the 21st century

Which brings us back to Kwame Anthony Appiah's idea of the power of "shared humanity". International students have been an essential part of the development of Australian universities since the mid-20th century up until now, not an addition, nor easily excised. Yet we have reached an awkward impasse between desiring the economic benefit they bring to Australia, but overlooking the cultural and social benefits. Historically, there have been significant periods dating from federation when the federal government has not welcomed international students, even though it legislated mechanisms for their entry to Australia. And there have been times from the 1960s to the 1980s when a sympathetic dialogue within government began to contemplate international students as potential and worthy immigrants – because of their Australian education – who should be encouraged to stay with the option of Australian citizenship. The "welcome" derived from community programs, university life and the lessening of government restraints around their presence in Australia especially once they had graduated.

We know that international students are important to the 21st century Australian economy. Their economic participation includes the hefty fees they pay to study at universities, as well as more diffuse contributions from payments they make for accommodation, food, travel, and other goods and services. It also includes their labour in the often lowly paid jobs many undertake in service industries to support their study. And let's not forget the government taxes they pay as consumers and workers.

Despite these significant contributions, the current political and community environment is not as warm and welcoming to the tens of thousands of international university students who come to Australia, live in our university cities and towns, and contribute to our wellbeing as many of us might hope.[24] Politicians are selectively aware of the economic consequences of their absence, yet seem unwilling to make a virtue of the social benefits of their presence. As a significant proportion of international students are young people prepared to invest a few years of their youth to study, live and work in Australia to gain an Australian degree, theirs is an investment that should be acclaimed and welcomed, not shunned and unnoticed.

Our current approach assumes that Australian universities are only for Australians, which was not exactly the case in the 1960s, when almost 10 per cent of the student population were overseas students admitted to university on the same basis as Australians. Furthermore, there tends to be an assumption that international students are generous interlopers – not genuine residents – either with deep pockets or willing to fill the hard and unglamorous low-paying casual and part-time jobs Australian employers struggle to fill. Their contribution to the " national interest" is economic. Furthermore, the public investment in the higher education of Australian citizens and residents is regarded as contributing to Australia's long-term public good. But why no place for international students in this vision?

The "public benefit" of international students is framed as an "export industry" to earn valuable foreign currency for Australia through the payment of tuition fees to study at Australian universities, a logic that generally insists on their imminent departure at or soon after completion of study (with the possibility of extending visas for a limited time). The logic is sometimes softened with promises of short-term post-study work rights, dreams of " soft diplomacy" and the greater good served by Australian-educated international students returning to their countries of origin and spreading goodwill. But there is precious little government policy to indicate how we invest in this goodwill, nor much to show for the effort. Nor is there any serious consideration as to whether our "soft diplomacy" dream would be served better if we genuinely encouraged these graduates to remain part of our workforce and become permanent Australian residents, even citizens.

The political rhetoric either ignores the reality of their presence, or confounds it by reducing international students to a simple logic of cashed-up consumers in a marketplace, to help address current workforce shortages caused by the pandemic, or to help "bridge gaps" in the Australian workforce.[25] We mostly ignore what it means to have amongst us a group of intellectually-able young adults from a diverse range of cultural and educational backgrounds, who are optimistic about the future, eager for adventure in a new land where they hope to meet a variety of different people, expand their horizons and experience interesting and diverse ways of living. They have chosen Australia for an opportunity of a lifetime which they are unlikely to ever forget, hopefully for good reasons. Yet there's little appetite to devise serious strategies to encourage and nurture these relationships, present Australia as another "home" beyond study, recognise the students' potential to enrich our diverse society, and invite those who wish to stay to become Australian citizens.

The current system encourages a short-term view of international students, one which sees education as simply an export commodity with visa extensions available upon graduation to enable a short period of valuable work experience. We expect most to depart, rather than invite them to stay so that Australia might reap the benefits of their Australian education.

If Australian graduates depart Australia, we lament the "brain drain" and the loss of young workers with great potential. In contrast, we don't talk of "brain drain" in relation to departing international students. Once their fees are paid, work experience is finished, and visas have expired, they mostly depart Australia for places that reap the benefits of young graduates with an Australian education and knowledge of Australia. Some universities develop relations with these alumni, but there's little in government policy which relishes the possibility of keeping them here.

Treating them as additions to the national balance sheet, rather than welcoming them "by virtue of our shared humanity", undermines Australia in the long term, its foreign policy aspirations, and its social fabric as a culturally diverse society. We need to see our international students in new ways to safeguard Australia's future cultural and economic security and prosperity. We need concepts like "shared humanity" to redefine how we welcome them during their Australian stay. And if they choose to depart, they need to know they will be welcome to return to the place where they educationally came of age.

Notes

1 Appiah, Kwame Anthony (2006). *Cosmopolitanism: ethics in a world of strangers*. New York: W. W. Norton and Company, xxiv–xxi; Horne, Julia (2010). The cosmopolitan life of Alice Erh-Soon Tay. *Journal of World History* 21(3): 419–45.
2 *Northern Star* (1923). "Chinese Student", Tuesday 6 February 1923, 4.
3 Sherington, Geoffrey (2019). *Alexander Mackie: an academic life*. Sydney: University of Sydney, 58–60, 63, 68–69, 74–94.

4 Kramer, Paul A. (2009). Is the world our campus? International students and the US global power in the long twentieth century. *Diplomatic History* 33(5): 775–806. See 791.

5 Walker, David (2012). *Anxious nation: Australia and the rise of Asia 1850–1939.* Crawley: UWA Publishing, 211–216.

6 Sarwal, A. and D. Lowe (2021). 'Behind the white curtain': Indian students and researchers in Australia, 1901–1950. *History of Education Review* 50(2): 212–25. See 214–15.

7 *Newcastle Morning Herald and Miners' Advocate*, Tuesday 16 July 1912, 7.

8 Palfreeman, A.C. (1974). Non-white immigration to Australia. *Pacific Affairs* 47(3): 344–57. See 345.

9 Walker, David (2019). *Stranded nation: White Australia in an Asian region.* Crawley: UWA Publishing.

10 Tavan, Gwenda (2013). Creating multicultural Australia: local, global and trans-national contexts for the creation of a Universal Admissions Scheme 1945-1983. In Triadafilos Triadafilopoulos ed. *Wanted and welcome? Policies for highly skilled immigrants in comparative perspective*, 41, 39–59. New York: Springer; Tavan, Gwenda (2005). *The long, slow death of white Australia.* Carlton North, Vic: Scribe, 71–167.

11 Megarrity, Lyndon (2005). Under the shadow of the White Australia Policy: Commonwealth policies on private students 1945-1972. *Change: Transformations in Education* 8(2): 31–51. See 32.

12 Commonwealth Bureau of Census and Statistics (1967). *Official Year Book of the Commonwealth of Australia*, 627. Canberra: Commonwealth Bureau of Census and Statistics. The percentages are based on figures in the 1970 *Official Year Book*, p.659.

13 Sarwal and Lowe, Behind the white curtain, 220–22.

14 Kent, Anna (2018). Australian scholarships for PNG and the South Pacific: mandates and mis-steps, 1948-2018. PhD thesis (unpub.), Deakin University; Dashwood, Genevieve (2021). "Mutual understanding and goodwill": international students, publicity, and policy in mid-twentieth century Australia. PhD Thesis (unpub.), UNSW.

15 Oakman, Daniel (2004). *Facing Asia: a history of the Colombo Plan.* Research School of Pacific and Asian Studies, The Australian National University: Pandanus Books, 2–3, 126–54; Anna Kent, Australian Scholarships, 6–31.

16 Megarrity, Lyndon (2010). Regional goodwill, sensibly priced: Commonwealth policies towards Colombo plan scholars and private overseas students, 1945–72. *Australian Historical Studies* 38(129): 88–105. See 97. Megarrity, Lyndon (2007). A highly-regulated "free market": Commonwealth policies on private overseas students from 1974 to 2005. *The Australian Journal of Education* 51(1): 39–53. Also, Megarrity, Under the shadow, 31–51.

17 Macintyre, Stuart (2015). *Australia's boldest experiment: war and reconstruction in the 1940s.* Sydney: NewSouth, 2015, 214–16; Croucher, Gwilym and James Waghorne (2020). *Australian universities: a history of common cause.* Sydney: UNSW Press 61–62.

18 Darian-Smith, Kate and James Waghorne (2016). Australian-Asian sociability, student activism, and the university challenge to White Australia in the 1950s. *Australian Journal of Politics and History* 62(2): 203–18.
19 Megarrity, Regional goodwill, 103.
20 *Official Yearbook of the Commonwealth of Australia*, Commonwealth Bureau of Census and Statistics, 1967 to 1981. The yearbooks cover student enrolment numbers for 1966 to 1979. Note that the information on overseas student numbers is variable across the years and means the proportional figures I provide are a well-judged estimate rather than being exact.
21 The "overseas students collection" I created is dispersed across several collections, held in the UNSW Archives and comprises 37 oral history interviews and about 40 in-depth questionnaires. The questionnaires are part of a larger survey I conducted on student life from the 1950s to 1970s. The questionnaires completed by "overseas students" are in the following collections: 1950s Student Experience at the New South Wales University of Technology/University of New South Wales, 96A96, UNSW Archives; 1960s Student Experience at the University of New South Wales, 97A86, UNSW Archives; 1970s Student Experience at the University of New South Wales, 02A55, UNSW Archives.
22 See Susan Goodwin and Ariadne Vromen's chapter in this volume which gives a brief account of the Commonwealth Scholarship system introduced in Australia in 1951.
23 Megarrity, Regional goodwill, 100–102.
24 See Gaby Ramia's chapter in this volume which explores this issue in depth.
25 Hawke, Alex and Frydenberg, Josh (2022), "Joint media release with the Hon. Josh Frydenberg MP – Student and Working Holiday Maker visa holders," ministerial media release, 19 January 2022, https://bit.ly/3z76Ag1; Hawke, Alex (2021). "Visa changes to support the reopening of Australia and our economic recovery", ministerial media release, 25 November 2021, https://bit.ly/3RvWIUl. The recently announced migration program for international students is intended to "bridge gaps ... in the Australian workforce" which significantly limits the immigration potential of many international students who would, regardless, make suitable Australian residents and citizens: *Australian Strategy for International Education 2021–2030*, Australian Government, 2021.

8

International students

During, before and after

Gaby Ramia

During: or, a pandemic hits

It was 3 April 2020. The nation was in lockdown. Days before, the federal government had announced the introduction of a raft of policy measures designed to provide financial compensation to Australians for the effects of the pandemic on those who could not work. There was a new JobSeeker payment for those who were unemployed. There was a JobKeeper payment, channelled through employers, for employees who had lost their job or were not able to keep working because of ongoing restrictions. A Coronavirus Supplement was also offered to the unemployed and others in receipt of social security benefits. There was a range of other initiatives, including new and more effective measures to counter homelessness, and new protections for people renting.[1]

For the first time in three quarters of a century, the welfare state in Australia was growing in a meaningful way, albeit only temporarily. From government, the temporality was as unequivocal as it was unapologetic. Yet it had come as a major surprise to many observers that the most conservative-leaning government in living memory would introduce a social protection regime more akin to those in social democratic Scandinavia. It is what social policy experts call a "universalist" welfare state; nobody is left behind, with a social solidarism built in that suggests "we are all in it together". And it seemed that the Australian public – who were usually and by tradition anti-universalist and anti-welfare – were in favour.

But on that 3rd of April, Prime Minister Scott Morrison made an additional announcement, which went against the generosity of mood. As much as we were "all in it together", those who were in Australia on temporary visas – many of whom were unable to leave the country – were somehow not in it with us. Morrison made it clear that international students would not be eligible to receive financial compensation. They apparently had options the rest of us did not have. "International students", he said, "have to give a warranty that they are able to support themselves for the first twelve months of their study." They are "not held here compulsorily", and "there is the alternative for them to return to their home countries".[2]

Yet the vast majority of international students who had been employed part time to pay the bills – as had always been allowed under their visa conditions – could not keep working. For various reasons, including the unaffordability and unavailability of flights, many could not go back to their home countries. Like everyone else, they were in lockdown and subject to the effects of social isolation. Therein lies the point. International students were living in Australia, as part of the resident population. Like many others who could not work, they were unable to earn an income in wages. Unlike others, however, they were unable to receive financial compensation. Many were plunged into poverty, given that their families back home were also dealing with the social and economic effects of the pandemic, and that many of those countries did not have the near-universalist welfare packages that the Australian government had introduced.

Based on a survey of over 7,000 international students before the pandemic, and a bit over 700 during the main national 2020 lockdown, Alan Morris and his colleagues found that, mainly because of the lockdown, 45 per cent had to borrow money from friends or family in Australia or overseas.[3] Almost 30 per cent had gone without meals. Twenty-five per cent pawned or sold something to pay for life's expenses. Loneliness among international students doubled, from 30 per cent to just over 60 per cent. Thirty-five per cent could not heat their dwelling or room. Almost 30 per cent were at least somewhat worried about losing their accommodation. Forty-six per cent said that the pandemic was having an impact on their studies. Only 26 per cent said that their landlord or real estate agent was "sympathetic" to their situation. This was all despite generous if ad hoc assistance from local non-government organisations and state governments in the form of food vouchers and parcels, and free legal and other services.

Before: or how "new" was the pandemic for international students?

Given the crisis in international student welfare that arrived with the pandemic, it might be tempting to think that government policy was substantively different before the 2020 lockdown. The truth of the matter, however, is that the government's policy response to the pandemic in 2020 represented a continuation of pre-pandemic policy. On that fateful day in April, Morrison introduced nothing new, and he repealed nothing in relation to international students.

Yet, a crisis like COVID-19 was always going to be significantly worse for international students than for domestic students. Why? First, international students are more likely to suffer social exclusion. Most of Australia's international students come from countries where English is not the first language. Then there are the cultural differences between the home and the host countries. International students are more likely than domestic students to be lonely and socially isolated. Despite the multicultural structure of Australian society, and the fact that a significant proportion of domestic students are from migrant backgrounds, international students are more likely to suffer discrimination and racism.[4] At times, the reality of this comes to the fore and is demonstrated in tangible ways; as in 2009 and 2010 when Indian students were subject to a wave of racially charged violence against them, in Melbourne and to a lesser extent Sydney.[5] The prompt for government to act, however, was not the actual phenomenon of racism. It was the fact that the racism would cause – as it turned out, *did* cause – a downturn in international student numbers. The downturn lasted four years, interrupting a longer-term pattern of major growth.

If the first reason that international students would be hit worse by the pandemic than domestic students relates to social exclusion, the second relates to social "citizenship". British postwar sociologist Thomas Marshall defined the latter in terms of the rights that accrue from eligibility for the benefits and services of the welfare state. More precisely, he emphasised a range, from "the right to a modicum of economic welfare and security to the right to share to the full in the social heritage and to live the life of a civilised being according to the standards prevailing in the society".[6]

It must be acknowledged, of course, that even for domestic students and the wider permanent-resident population of Australia, generous is not a word that describes the nation's welfare state, either before the pandemic or since the winding back of the 2020 reforms nine months after they were introduced. Equally, there is a range of factors which bring into sharp relief the different position that international students are in, and have always been in. International students must pay full fees up-front for all courses, whereas domestic students pay subsidised (undergraduate) or lower (postgraduate coursework) rates and can defer fees until their income reaches a mandated minimum. Independent of the pandemic, international students have no rights in the realm of income compensation, whereas their domestic counterparts can qualify for rent assistance and/or limited, admittedly low-level social security assistance if formally independent of their parents. Domestic students also qualify without cost for access to the Medicare health system, whereas international students must pay to be able to access similar health rights. International students must also pay taxes on any earned income in Australia, like their domestic counterparts. In short, domestic and international students contribute equally in economic terms, but the latter receive far fewer social and economic benefits in return.

If that is the state of play, let us not be in doubt about the benefits to Australia of international students. Independently of the necessary comparison between their rights vis-à-vis the rights of domestic students, we should not forget the cultural enrichment the former offer Australia and Australians, and the contributions of international students to life on campus.[7] Politically, the presence of international students increases the soft power of host countries through enhanced incentives for positive diplomacy and productive trade. Educationally, international students contribute to diversity and choice in course offerings. Some courses would simply not be available if it were not for the boosting of enrolments through internationalisation. In addition, domestic students are better able to realistically aspire to the now-common graduate attribute of "global citizenship" because of their everyday dealings and team-based discussions and assessments alongside international students. International students bring with them different and diverse skills, rooted in a diversity of cultural home-country contexts, which also provide greater choice in labour supply for employers.

If these factors do not convince nationalists, conservatives and other sceptics, consider that economically, education represents 8 per cent of total Australian exports, and education is the fourth top source of export revenue, after coal, iron ore and natural gas respectively.[8] In his 2010 Boyer Lectures, Glyn Davis pointed out that for every dollar an international student spent on their tuition another two dollars were spent on services, food, housing and entertainment.[9] Let us also not doubt Australia's importance as a host to international students, because before the pandemic, 8 per cent of the world's mobile students chose to study here, and we had the same share in percentage terms as the UK. The two countries were equal second, after the United States.[10] And let us not forget the human capital that international students inject into the economy, which has flow-on positive effects on national productivity and living standards.[11]

International students are themselves diverse as a population category, and they constitute nearly one quarter of all students in Australia. In 2018, and hence before the pandemic, 48 per cent of them were female.[12] Of the 756,000 of them studying in Australia as at 2019, the year before the pandemic hit, the top source countries respectively were: China (211,000), India (115,000), Nepal (53,000), Brazil (27,000) and Vietnam (26,000). And it is often not realised that the vocational education and training (VET), English language and schools sectors together enrol about as many of them as universities do.[13]

Given our economic reliance on international students – and the fact that until the pandemic they just kept coming, no matter how expensive an investment it was for them – we might be tempted to believe that we can and should charge full and up-front fees to international students. They have been coming to Australia to benefit from "our" higher and vocational education systems for decades, and as the chapter by Julia Horne makes clear, they have been studying in Australia on a commercial basis for longer than was recognised until recently. But only since the early 1990s have they been coming in economically significant numbers. Up until the pandemic, their welfare was not prominent in the minds of many Australians. It was generally thought that if they have the means to come to Australia and to pay the fees, they must be living financially within their means. In other words, it was generally believed that the self-regulatory market approach is good enough for them.

That view, however, does not hold up for some or many international students, as demonstrated in longstanding and recent research which has highlighted a range of welfare deficits, including in relation to: housing; social isolation, loneliness, civic engagement and domestic-international student interaction; personal safety risks due to crime; racism; personal finances; and exploitation and underpayment in employment.[14]

Despite formal recognition from time to time by government agencies, such as the Council of Australian Governments (COAG) International Round Table, successive Australian governments have done little in policy and law to address the situation. The *Education Services for Overseas Students* (ESOS) *Framework*, which combines the *ESOS Act* and the accompanying *National Code of Practice for Registration Authorities and Training to Overseas Students* for education providers, does not compel either the government or providers to provide meaningful welfare support or services.[15] Instead, they mandate *information provision* on services. Student rights are mentioned in Standard 6 of the Code, under "support services", stating that institutions "must support the overseas student in adjusting to study and life in Australia by giving the overseas student information on or access to an age and culturally appropriate orientation program that provides information about" a range of services. Specifically, the Code mentions: "English language and study assistance programs"; "legal services"; "the registered provider's facilities and resources"; "student complaints and appeals processes"; "requirements for course attendance and progress"; any factors "adversely affecting" individual students' education; and "employment rights and conditions" for students who are casually or part-time employed. In addition, institutions must have “critical incident policies” in place for all students. However, with the exception of students under 18 years of age, where there are more specific terms, at no point is there detail on substantive responsibilities for the material living conditions of international students.

This market-based approach to policy and law is not common to all major international education provider countries. To be sure, the other Anglo-majority countries do largely conform, though Europe is different. All European Economic Area (EEA) countries offer the same fee regime to students whose home country is within the EEA. This applies also to social security system coverage. In addition, France and Germany offer students from around the world – and thus not only from the EEA – a free or low-fee education, and France provides equal access to health and social security rights.[16]

After: or thinking beyond the pandemic

What about the post-pandemic context, if and to the extent that we are able at this time to contemplate it meaningfully. It is important to say that if this chapter only discussed the pre-pandemic or the during-pandemic contexts, and not both, the central recommendations would remain the same. That itself speaks again to the point made earlier – that not much in policy terms changed during the pandemic. To be sure, yes, as the extensive report by Morris and his colleagues demonstrates, a significant proportion of international students were thrown into poverty in 2020.[17] And there are many other serious consequences for wellbeing that accompany the poverty. However, the tragic phenomenon of increased poverty was not the result of any diminution in government assistance. The assistance from the federal government provided to international students was the same before and after the 2020 lockdown. That is, the ESOS Framework provided the central legal and policy basis for assistance before and after. In 2020, the major innovations in social policy for the benefit of permanent residents were denied to international students, though it must be acknowledged that the 2021 lockdown measures included international student qualification for the Disaster Payments program.[18] Students were considered eligible to receive up to $500 per week if they were working 20 hours or more before the lockdown, and lost all of those hours, and $325 per week if they lost under 20 hours of paid employment.

The options presented to the new Labor Government, elected in May 2022, are wide-ranging. The approach of a country such as France, which provides highly similar benefits in social protection to domestic and international students, is an option, but it is very unlikely to be consistent with the approach to be taken in Australia. A second and more politically possible option would be to overhaul the ESOS Framework, to mandate the actual provision of the kinds of services mentioned in ESOS, as opposed to the mere provision of *information* on them. That is, the services specified in ESOS could be made compulsory to provide by either education providers or the government, or preferably both together in some form of collaborative governance arrangement. Unfortunately, given that neither of the two main sides of politics has had that on its policy radar, it is unlikely to materialise. There may be some middle ground between the first and second options.

The most realistic avenues for action are more austere. The then minister for education, Alan Tudge, laid out some possibilities in his speech at the 2021 Australian International Education Conference.[19] The possibilities included the opening of borders at the end of 2021, and unless unravelled by new waves in the pandemic and new border closures, the return of international students in 2022. But they went further. The minister also wanted to see students coming from a greater diversity of source countries, thus reducing reliance on China and India in particular. The government also signalled that it would support more offshore provision, without providing detail on whether that might mean more physical presence in the form of Australian university campuses placed in other countries, or if that meant more students studying online from their home country. And if education providers do not enact changes, the minister hinted that the government may step in to force their hand. He did not provide detail on what that would mean in policy or strategic terms.

Setting aside the understandable critiques of that government's broader higher education policy approach, as detailed in other chapters of this book, there is not a great deal in the minister's suggestions on international students that is materially different to erstwhile policy. Some universities themselves have been strategising on how to diversify their international student base, and some have been exploring more offshore provision through overseas campuses. The strategy behind campuses offshore is that they may make up for revenue shortfalls from international student fees if the numbers of international students onshore in Australia are set to decrease on an ongoing basis. Monash University in Melbourne, for example, has opened its Indonesia campus during the course of the pandemic. But international students are at the centre of additional priorities for Australia's universities. Their fees have been funding an increasing proportion of the research that universities undertake, as well as the significant growth that has characterised the sector. This has happened at the same time as – and because of – the decreasing proportions of total university funding that have come from government. The previous government did not seriously address the funding shortfall, and it worked to deflect political attention from it.

In general, unless the new government is planning a policy overhaul, universities are left with compelling constraints on their strategic planning. If universities wish to better cater for international student welfare, they face two quandaries in relation to their approach to international student recruitment. First, they can seek to ensure welfare in an autonomous fashion, independently of government incentives or mandates. That is, they may unilaterally introduce services that are not required by the ESOS Framework. In so doing, they can go beyond the information-only approach to services. After all, successive governments have shown no signs of changing the predominant policy approach, so why not "go it alone"? And, or second, universities can look to fund their research using formulae that do not depend on ever-increasing numbers of international students. The central question is, from which sources? In the coming years and decades, the public reputation of universities may rest partly on their decisions in these realms.

Notes

1 Ramia, Gaby and Lisa Perrone (2021). Crisis management, policy reform and institutions: the social policy response. *Social Policy and Society*, online early, 2021. doi:10.1017/S1474746421000427.
2 Gibson, Jane and Alexis Moran (2020). As Coronavirus spreads, "'It's time to go home' Scott Morrison tells visitors and international students." *ABC News*, 3 April 2020. https://ab.co/3o4sw4Z.
3 Morris, Alan, Catherine Hastings, Shaun Wilson, Emma Mitchell, Gaby Ramia and Charlotte Overgaard (2020). *The experience of international students before and during COVID-19: housing, work, study and wellbeing*. Sydney: University of Technology Sydney.
4 Marginson, Simon, Chris Nyland, Erlenawati Sawir and Helen Forbes-Mewett (2010). *International student security*. Cambridge, Melbourne: Cambridge University Press.
5 Ramia, Gaby (2021). Crises in international education, and government responses: a comparative analysis of racial discrimination and violence towards international students. *Higher Education* 82: 599–613.
6 Marshall, Thomas H. (1950) [1963]. *Sociology at the crossroads, and other essays*. London: Heinemann.
7 Hughes, Joanna. (2019). Why international students are so important to their host countries. Keystone Academic Courses. https://bit.ly/3uOKlZK.
8 Department of Foreign Affairs and Trade (2021). Australia's Top 10 Goods and Services Exports and Imports. https://www.dfat.gov.au/trade/resources/trade-at-a-glance/Documents/top-goods-services.html.
9 Davis, Glyn (2010). *The republic of learning*. Sydney: Harper Collins.
10 OECD (2021). *Education at a Glance*. Paris: OECD Publishing.
11 Deloitte Access Economics (2016). *The value of international education to Australia*. https://internationaleducation.gov.au/research/research-papers/Documents/ValueInternationalEd.pdf.
12 Larkins, Frank P. (2018). Male students remain underrepresented in Australian universities. Should Australia be concerned? *Melbourne Centre for the Study of Higher Education Paper*. https://melbourne-cshe.unimelb.edu.au/__data/assets/pdf_file/0012/2894718/Gender-Enrolment-Trends-F-Larkins-Sep-2018.pdf.
13 Department of Education, Skills and Employment. (2021). International Student Data. https://internationaleducation.gov.au/research/international-student-data/pages/default.aspx.
14 These problems are identified in individual publications, with a range of authors in relation to individual life-domains. The best summative but comprehensive accounts are: Marginson et al. (2010), for the longstanding research; and Morris et al. (2020) for the pandemic context.
15 Department of Education, Skills and Employment. (2018). *National Code of Practice for Providers of Education and Training to Overseas Students*

2018. https://internationaleducation.gov.au/regulatory-information/Pages/National-Code-2018-Factsheets-.aspx.

16 CampusFrance. (2018). Health, Social Security and Insurance. https://bit.ly/3ceTbJI.

17 Morris et al., *The experience of international students before and during COVID-19.*

18 Australian Government (2021). Temporary Australian Government Assistance for Workers. Prime Minister of Australia. Accessed 26 December 2021. https://www.campusfrance.org/en/healthcare-student-social-security.

19 Tudge, Alan (2021). International Education: The Road Back. *Keynote address delivered to the Australian International Education Conference Online*, 8 October 2021. Accessed 26 December 2021. https://ministers.dese.gov.au/tudge/international-education-road-back.

Part 3

Rethinking structures

9

Who should pay for university?

Eight logics of higher education funding in Australia

Gareth Bryant

This chapter maps out the workings of Australia's system of funding domestic students at public universities.[1] I take a political economy approach that places university funding within changing economic, budgetary and policy contexts. The main contribution of the chapter is to identify eight distinct logics that are bundled together in the architecture of fees, loans and grants that finance the education of Australian university students. I show how the eight logics have been activated to facilitate the expansion of universities over the last 30 years, but with socially uneven outcomes. I argue that, as ever, the problem of paying for expansion remains the primary challenge facing Australian universities – a challenge that has been made more acute and visible by the COVID-19 crisis.

Public debate following the onset of the COVID-19 pandemic has primarily focused not on managing expansion, but arresting decline. Writing in *The Monthly*, Emeritus Professor Judith Brett commented that "COVID-19 has now turned an incremental decline into an existential crisis".[2] For Brett, the pandemic had exposed and exacerbated pre-existing symptoms of decline, such as the reliance on casualised teaching, and cuts to arts and humanities programs. Brett traced the beginning of the decline to the Dawkins reforms implemented by the federal Labor government in the late 1980s that required students to again make contributions to the cost of their education. This move, according to Brett, ended the "golden age in Australian universities" ushered in by the Whitlam government's introduction of free education in the mid-1970s.

Yet, the period of decline described by Brett was, on another measure, a period of mass expansion of access to universities. Pressures within universities have emerged in the context of a great opening up of tertiary education across Australian society. What was still a relatively elite university system in the 1980s is now a truly mass system of higher education, particularly for young Australian women. In 1989, 13 per cent of men and 10 per cent of women aged 25–34 had a bachelors level degree. In 2021, that number had reached 37 per cent of men and 50 per cent of women in that age group.[3] Compared globally, the funding system has produced rates of educational attainment in Australia that are above OECD and EU averages, and a comparatively large number of world-class public universities, with far lower levels of institutional inequality than exist in the USA.[4] At the same time, the expansion of universities has been far from socially even. Expansion has opened university to more people from Aboriginal and Torres Strait Islander, low socio-economic status, rural and regional, and disability backgrounds, but has been less successful in lifting the relative share of these students in university enrolments.[5]

The COVID-19 pandemic nonetheless revealed the limits of the current mode of expansion. Since the Dawkins reforms, governments have steadily shifted the domestic funding mix from grant funding to student fees while holding real per-student income for universities relatively stagnant.[6] Universities responded by turning to international student fees to fund their expansion, especially in research. This has left Australia with comparatively low levels of "public" spending on universities by global standards, at around 0.7 per cent of GDP, and comparatively high levels of "private" spending.[7] It has also made the education of Australian students increasingly marginal to the financial position of major universities. At the University of Sydney, for example, less than one quarter of 2019 total revenue came from domestic student fees and teaching funding.[8] The sudden closure of borders in 2020 and the impact this had on the international student market exposed the risks of insufficient public investment in Australian universities.

The COVID-19 crisis should foster renewed attention on how to reconfigure the funding landscape to properly support the integral role of universities in a 21st century economy and society. The eight logics identified in this chapter are intended to serve as a map, both for understanding the political economy of the funding system that has led to this point, and for navigating what might be changed to facilitate future rounds of expansion on a more equitable and sustainable basis. Taken together, the eight logics are, at different times, and in different combinations, complementary, contradictory, incoherent or eclectic. After outlining the eight logics, I demonstrate how they have configured successive funding regimes between 1989 and 2021, identifying turning points in how particular logics have been emphasised, bundled and applied, before reflecting on how the dominant logic of fiscal austerity might give way to that of the public good.

Eight logics of university funding

One – fiscal austerity

The logic of fiscal austerity, which demands a trifecta of low taxes, low debt and low spending from governments, is the starting point of the post-1989 university funding system. While governments have usually not lived up to their austerity rhetoric in practice, the bipartisan pursuit of budget surpluses has held a tight grip over Australian politics. The logic of fiscal austerity is a near permanent feature of university funding precisely because universities are an expanding part of the modern economy. Without regular efforts to rein in costs, public spending on universities would outpace political goals of "budget discipline", even though these costs could be readily financed via the Australian government's fiscal and monetary powers. Fiscal austerity logics sit behind the long-term trend towards increasing student fees and reducing the share of government contributions. As will be demonstrated, the other seven logics of higher education financing have tended to be subsumed within this overarching goal.

Two – human capital

Understanding higher education as human capital emphasises higher education as a "private good". In standard economics, a private good is a product purchased in a competitive market by an individual who enjoys its benefits to the exclusion of others. This economic thinking was applied to higher education by Chicago School economists such as Gary Becker, who pioneered "human capital" theory in the 1960s. Higher education was reconceived as an individual investment in the human capital of students, which delivered private benefits in the form of higher lifetime earnings for graduates. Human capital theory reframed higher education in distinctly economic terms, encouraging students to engage with their education as a process of appreciating their own "capital". Human capital logics were evident in the introduction of student fees, and have been used to justify differential fee levels between courses with different earnings potentials. From the perspective of human capital theory, university fees should be set to reflect this private benefit that accrues to university graduates.

Three – cost recovery

Cost recovery logics have been implemented as part of the pursuit of "efficiency" in public services. Whereas human capital logics focus on returns on investment for individuals, cost recovery logics are concerned with charging fees to recoup the costs of service delivery. Cost recovery logics are part of the suite of New Public Management reforms that sought to neutralise the competitive advantages of governments compared with markets, implemented in Australia as "competition policy". In higher education, this has been translated into efforts to match funding and fees to the efficient "unit cost" of delivering education - something that differs wildly between courses with different staffing and infrastructure needs, and between institutions.

Four – workforce planning

Workforce planning logics refer to the use of university funding arrangements in ways that respond to and seek to influence Australia's labour market requirements. Workforce planning logics have driven the expansion of Australia's university system over the last three decades. They are also applied when differential fee levels and the allocation of places between courses are used to shape the skills profile of graduates. Governments may attempt to increase enrolments in areas deemed to be workforce priorities or linked to skills shortages, or reduce enrolments in other areas not deemed to meet these criteria. University funding therefore sits alongside other skill-oriented programs such as migration and apprenticeships. Workforce planning logics often push against human capital and cost recovery logics in practice. It has been common for governments to selectively decrease fees in areas of study that align with certain professional pathways, irrespective of their teaching costs or earnings potential. For this reason, fee levels have never perfectly tracked private benefits, nor the cost of delivering courses.

Five – status maximisation

Universities primarily compete for students based on institutional status, rather than the price or quality of education. They seek to maximise their positions within status hierarchies, measured by things like international rankings. Status maximisation logics encourage a model of cross-subsidisation where income from higher fee, lower cost courses are used to subsidise high status research which, in turn, attracts student enrolments (and research income). The status maximising logic of universities further alters the operation of fees as the "price" of education. In contrast with conventional economic understandings of how markets work, reduced prices do not signal value-for-money but rather lower status. Former UNSW Vice-Chancellor John Niland described this in terms of a "Veblen effect", after institutionalist political economist Thorstein Veblen, who explained how demand follows higher prices for the "conspicuous consumption" of certain status goods.[9] Status maximising logics are strongest where universities have autonomy over student enrolment patterns and fee levels.

Six – income-contingency

The design of the Higher Education Contribution Scheme (HECS), the public loan system introduced in 1989 to cover the up-front cost of domestic student fees, is underpinned by a logic of income-contingency.[10] While HECS is presented as a debt, the repayment structure reflects many aspects of the income taxation system. Ben Spies-Butcher and I have attempted to capture this through our description of HECS as a tax-loan "hybrid".[11] First, income-contingency means no repayments are made until a person reaches a certain level of income. This operates in practice like the tax-free threshold that exempts low-income earners from paying income tax, and delinks debt levels from regular repayment amounts, unlike a conventional term loan. Once workers are earning above the income threshold, repayment rates are progressively increased, and collected by the Taxation Office. Second, the indexation of debts to inflation means there is no market interest rate. Indexation is a tool used throughout the tax and transfer system to ensure that tax thresholds and payment rates maintain real values over time. When applied to HECS, indexation attempts to ensure that graduates are not advantaged or disadvantaged if they repay their debts either quickly or slowly because of their income level. Together, these features blunt the impact of fees on decisions to attend university and between courses with different fees. The logic of income-contingency can be applied with different levels of progressivity, depending on the level at which the income threshold is set, and the extent to which the repayment rates reflect ability to pay.

Seven – financial asset

The loan-like properties of HECS, which is advanced by the government as a loan, with a student liability attached, infuses financial asset logics into the management of HECS by governments. HECS is accounted for as a financial asset on the federal government's balance sheet. This is highly significant in fiscal terms because, unlike direct grants, the cost of issuing HECS loans is not counted as government expenditure, unlocking a source of income for universities that does not put direct pressure on federal budget surpluses and deficits. Governments with fiscal austerity goals therefore have strong incentives to shift the balance of university financing from Commonwealth contributions, funded through grants, to student contributions, funded by loans. However, this financial asset logic creates other pressures for governments to manage, and maintain, the "fair value" of accumulated HECS debts, as assets, on the government's balance sheet. These pressures have materialised in various attempts to reduce the concessional, income-contingent elements of HECS, such as by lowering the income threshold for repayments and increasing the interest rate on debt.

Eight – public good

There is a strong level of support in the community for a broader understanding of universities as a public good. The logic of universities as a public good can be seen in the way these wider economic and more-than-economic benefits are reflected in the funding system. More narrowly, the public good features of university degrees are the "spill over" economic benefits of a more educated workforce, such as higher taxes paid by graduates, as well as increasing productivity and economic growth. This is what is behind economic calculations of the public share of benefits of university education (such as Deloitte's 2017 estimate of a 55–45 public-private split in benefits from undergraduate degrees).[12] However, a broader understanding of universities as a public good focuses on their role in pursuing public missions and addressing inequalities, by promoting social progress, civic participation, and individual opportunity. As will become clear across the post-1989 history of funding, it is perceived attacks on the broader public good logics of universities, linked to concerns about equity, that drive the democratic politics of higher education funding.

Funding regimes and turning points: 1989–2021

Introduction of fees

The introduction of university fees in 1989 was heavily influenced by a combination of fiscal austerity, human capital and workforce planning logics. In the context of a political commitment to fiscal constraint, fees provided a way to finance an expanded university system without increasing public funding to the same extent. Global economic pressures and the transition to an increasingly feminised service economy created demand for more university places as a pathway to the skills needed for workforce participation, especially for women.

Understanding higher education through the logic of human capital provided a political rationale for moving from free to fee-based university education. The idea that higher education created private benefits that should attract a private cost fitted within the Hawke-Keating government's framework of fiscal constraint and "economic reform". However, the decision to introduce fees, initially set at $1,800 per year, via an income-contingent loan system reflected ongoing public good logics embedding universities. HECS, underpinned by the architecture of the income taxation system, was used by the government to argue that fees would not hinder access to universities, and that costs would reflect ability to pay.

Fee increases and fee bands

The Howard government made two major changes to fee levels and repayment arrangements in 1997 and 2005, reflecting a curious combination of various higher education funding logics. The first set of changes, which commenced in 1997, increased fees and lowered repayment thresholds. Fees were increased from $2,442 per year for all courses to a new fee structure comprising three bands of courses, set between $3,300 and $5,500. At the same time the repayment threshold was reduced from $28,494 to $20,700 per year. The 2005 changes had elements of both continuity and change. Fees were again increased across the three existing bands, to a maximum of $8,018. A fourth, lower cost, "national priority band" was also introduced, at $3,847, creating a much wider range of fee levels. However, this time, repayment thresholds were raised to $35,000.[13]

The steady increase in fees primarily reflected the fiscal austerity logic of HECS and its articulation with accounting for HECS as a financial asset. With the introduction of the accrual accounting-based "underlying balance" in the 1996/97 budget, the cost of HECS advances were removed from the budget bottom line. Accounting helps construct reality, and this changed the fiscal reality of HECS. The accounting change created a budgetary incentive to shift higher education funding from block grants to student fees, which neatly aligned with the Howard government's politics of budget surpluses.

The financial asset logic of HECS also helps explain the change in policy direction in the application of income-contingency via the repayment threshold, which accompanied the fee hikes. Just as the costs of issuing HECS are not counted as government expenditure, nor are HECS repayments counted as government income. As underlying budget measures came to dominate over cash measures, imperatives to increase repayments as a means of boosting budget surpluses dissipated. The Howard government took advantage of this in 2005 by using the increased repayment threshold to offset the political costs of fee increases.

The introduction of differential fee bands was driven by a combination of human capital and workforce planning, rather than cost recovery logics. Human capital logics were evident in the highest fee band courses. Lower teaching cost courses such as law, and from 2008 business and economics, were combined with higher teaching cost courses including medicine, dentistry and veterinary science, reflecting higher income earnings potential in these areas. Lower fee band courses included both lower teaching cost (for example, arts and humanities) and higher teaching cost (for example, nursing and education) courses. While there remains a strong wage premium for all university education, compared to not attending university, many of these areas of study have lower average earnings than those that were placed in higher bands.[14] Lower fees in these areas in part reflected the relatively lower human capital (measured in market terms) associated with these courses, a calculus that, as will be explained below, was reversed by the 2020 "Job-ready" reforms.

Some courses were placed in lower fee brackets due to workforce planning logics as a way of addressing projected skills shortages. This was made explicit with the creation of a national priority band in 2005, which was in place until 2012 and included, at different times, nursing, education, maths and science. While there is little evidence that differential fee bands changed course preferences, they play useful political roles for governments wanting to be able to point to areas of fee decreases, in the context of overall increases in fees.

Demand-driven funding

The introduction of demand-driven funding by the Rudd-Gillard Labor government, completed by 2012, showed a different use of the financial asset logic of HECS. Demand-driven funding reforms uncapped the number of HECS places that would be available, allowing universities to enrol as many students as they could attract. Prior to this, governments had set the number and distribution of places between universities, and to some extent between courses, in part reflecting workforce planning logics.

As with fee increases, demand-driven funding used the financial asset logic of HECS to provide income to universities that sits off the government's yearly budget. Whereas fee increases did so by increasing student debt, demand-driven funding used this logic to increase access, boosting places from 444,000 in 2009 to 541,000 in 2013.[15] However, this mechanism also encouraged universities to act in a more competitive manner, intensifying the role of status maximising logics in the sector. This may have undermined the capacity of governments to directly exert planning logics, but demand-driven funding nonetheless provided an automatic mechanism to adjust places to population dynamics, and generated enrolment growth in priority and skill shortage areas. While more people of all social backgrounds, including those from disadvantaged backgrounds, were attending university, the share of students from the latter only marginally improved. In addition, both full-time graduate employment rates and graduate income premiums – measures of return on human capital investment – continued their longer-term decline.[16]

Demand-driven funding was partially ended in 2018 as the expansion of university places triggered the reassertion of fiscal austerity logics. As places expanded, so too did fiscal pressures from the Commonwealth's contribution to supported places, which increased from $3.6 billion in 2007–08 to $6.9 billion in 2016–17.[17] The Turnbull Coalition government responded by partially severing the link between Commonwealth contributions and HECS. Commonwealth contributions were capped, but universities were able to "over-enrol" above this cap and receive HECS-funded student contributions only, which remained uncapped, and uncounted as government spending.

Deregulation debate

Prior to the changes to demand-driven funding, the Abbott Coalition government's failed attempt to deregulate student fees in 2014 was the most publicly debated university funding issue since the introduction of HECS. At its core, the proposal would cut direct government funding of places by 20 per cent, and allow universities to set their own, much higher, HECS-financed fees without limit. Deregulation was therefore somewhat paradoxical in being the only recent government attempt to expand per-student income available to universities, while cutting direct public funding. Deregulation aimed to satisfy fiscal austerity logics for a government wanting to put a lid on the escalating costs of demand-driven funding, while appealing to the status maximisation logics of universities.

Deregulation was a heated political issue that revealed the strength of public good logics in public opinion about university funding. University managements, wanting autonomy in income-generation to cross-subsidise research needed to enhance their status, largely supported the proposal, while also committing to use extra revenue to fund equity programs. However, staff unions, student representatives, and public opinion was overwhelmingly opposed to the policy.[18] The National Tertiary Education Union, National Union of Students, and the Greens and Labor parties ran highly effective "$100,000 degree" campaigns that convinced the Senate to ultimately vote down the legislation.

The efficacy of this campaign was rooted in public good logics about fairness and equality that asserted limits to the framing of university as a private good. In doing so, the campaign implicitly recognised how status maximisation logics would translate to fee setting behaviour by universities, which were more likely to engage in upwards, rather than downwards, price competition, to signal higher status. There was some pre-existing evidence for this, such as when fees were set as maximum not mandated levels in 2005, universities quickly moved to charge the maximum.

Spectre of doubtful debt

Increasing reliance on HECS-financing has seen outstanding HECS debts steadily increase in value, to $66 billion in 2020 (a tripling in ten years).[19] This has shifted fiscal austerity logics to the problem of "doubtful debt". In 2015, the Department of Education estimated that about 23 per cent of outstanding debts, which are eventually written off from deceased estates, were unlikely to ever be repaid (although some of these debts were from VET sector loans).[20] Doubtful debt has been identified as a problem by bodies such as the Parliamentary Budget Office because it erodes the "fair value" – an estimate of realisable market value – of HECS assets on the government's balance sheet. This part of government finances does not directly concern the surplus or deficit, but rather the government's net wealth position. The introduction of fair value accounting was part of the same set of corporate-sector-inspired accounting reforms that removed the cost of issuing HECS debts from the budget, which relieved fiscal pressures on one hand, while creating new fiscal pressures on the other.

The spectre of doubtful debt drove successive moves by the Abbott-Turnbull-Morrison Coalition government to charge real rates of interest, and reduce the income thresholds, for repayments of HECS debts. Doubtful debt is baked into the income-contingent logic of HECS. These moves target this logic by tightening the concessional, or tax-like, features that implement it. The failed deregulation package included a proposal to change the indexation of HECS debts from inflation to government bond yields. Ostensibly, this would cover the interest costs incurred from government borrowing used to issue HECS debt. It would also make HECS debt more attractive to investors in any future move to sell off, or "securitise", the government's loan book, as has occurred in the UK.

The Turnbull and Morrison Coalition governments did successfully reduce income thresholds for repayments. From 2019, the threshold was reduced to $45,880 – about half of average full-time weekly earnings. This represented an erosion in the human capital logic of HECS, because graduates earning this income are unlikely to be experiencing significant returns from their university education. In line with concerns about doubtful debt, the change did not result in higher total repayments (which are not counted as revenue anyway), but rather increased the share of people with a HECS debt making repayments.[21]

The lowering of the repayment threshold showed how, just as with the income tax system, the logic of income-contingency can be implemented in a more and less progressive way, mimicking policy decisions about the design of income tax systems. The impact of this change on the progressivity of HECS was mixed. The change made some lower income-earning graduates make repayments for the first time (itself a regressive change). This effect was countered, however, by a somewhat progressive smoothing out of repayment rates, by introducing lower repayment rates at the bottom (down from 4 per cent to 1 per cent of income) and higher repayment rates at the top (up from 8 per cent to 10 per cent of income).

Job-readiness

Finally, the Job-ready Graduates reforms of 2020–21 instituted a highly confused combination of cost recovery and workforce planning logics to ultimately achieve fiscal austerity goals. In spruiking the package, the education minister declared that fees in STEM, teaching, nursing, English, other languages, and agriculture would be reduced to as low as $3,950 per year because they were linked to the "jobs of the future". In contrast, law, business, economics and other humanities and social sciences (HASS) courses would be charged $14,500 per year – up to a doubling of the previous cost.

The Morrison government therefore primarily mobilised workforce planning logics to justify the change. Critics were quick to point out the lack of evidence base behind this, noting that it did not match data on future employment growth, graduate outcomes by course, and student price sensitivity.[22] Indeed, the justification given by the government completely reversed the human capital logic of HECS. Whereas high fee courses were previously justified based on higher incomes by graduates, now they were being used – at least politically – as a price disincentive for areas of study deemed less "job-ready".

When the overall package was brought into view, it became clear that the main goal of the package was to further shift the funding mix in favour of private contributions, up from 42 to 48 per cent of the funding ratio. The Morrison government justified its reduction of grant funding using a cost recovery logic. It claimed that the overall level of income received by universities for teaching domestic undergraduate students would match the costs of teaching that had been calculated by Deloitte. This aims to prevent cross-subsidisation of research by domestic teaching, which presents a structural challenge to the teaching and research nexus for academic staff.

The confused combination of logics in the Job-ready Graduates package sent contradictory signals to students and universities. Job-ready Graduates created incentives for universities to reduce enrolments in lower fee STEM courses because it cut their per-student income. In contrast, with the cost of student fees blunted by the income-contingency of HECS, Job-ready Graduates created incentives for universities to increase enrolments in higher fee areas. Paradoxically, Job-ready Graduates softened caps on places in law, business and HASS by making Commonwealth contributions financially immaterial for universities, while placing much harder caps on so-called priority areas.

Concluding thoughts

Across each funding regime, the other seven logics of higher education funding have been activated in service of a dominant logic of fiscal austerity, which has held back the public investment needed to expand universities fairly and sustainably. Successive funding regimes for Australian universities have been products of a constant search by governments for a "fix" that can finance expansion without increasing budget pressures. It is students, both domestic and international, who have increasingly provided the answer to the question of "who should pay for the costs of university?"

With government contributions towards the costs of educating Australian students inching perilously close to a minority share, the fix may be reaching its political limits. Recent attempts at funding reform, both successful and unsuccessful, have demonstrated strong public opposition to proposals that are viewed as privatising universities. Further, the fragility of the current funding situation was exposed at a time, during the COVID-19 crisis, when many of the fiscal rules that had been constraining governments were being rewritten. Indeed, reaching the levels of base public funding that review after review has recommended would come in at a small fraction of the fiscal outlays incurred in the COVID-19 response.[23]

For supporters of public universities, the central challenge is creating a political constituency that can be mobilised, not only to oppose bad reforms, but to support a better funding system. The makeup and strategy of this constituency – across young people and their parents, unions, business, and civil society, working with universities – is the topic for another essay, and political organising. What this chapter has shown is the level of political malleability in how the eight logics can be emphasised, bundled and applied in funding regimes. However, it will take a strong political constituency in support of public universities to force governments to activate higher education funding logics in ways that serve, and are dominated by, the public good.

Notes

1 Many thanks to Ben Spies-Butcher, Mike Beggs, Annamarie Jagose, Julia Horne, Matthew A.M. Thomas and a reviewer for their very helpful feedback and guidance.

2 Brett, Judith (2021). The bin fire of the humanities. *The Monthly*, 1 March.

3 Australian Bureau of Statistics (2021). Highest non-school qualification: bachelor degree level or above by age by sex, Table 35. *Education and work, Australia*, May 2021. Canberra: Australian Bureau of Statistics.

4 OECD (2021). Education at a Glance: OECD Indicators. Paris: OECD Publishing.

5 Department of Education, Skills and Employment (2020). Selected Higher Education Statistics – 2019 Student Data. Canberra: Department of Education, Skills and Employment. https://bit.ly/3P20Sl0.

6 Norton, Andrew (2020). Why did universities become reliant on international students? Part 1: Government funding cuts. *Andrew Norton* (blog), 1 June. https://bit.ly/3z1Griu.

7 OECD. Education at a Glance.

8 The University of Sydney (2020). Annual Report 2019. Camperdown: The University of Sydney.

9 Hare, Julie and Andrew Trounson (2014). Price and quality 'will be confused' by deregulation of university fees. *The Australian*, 16 September.

10 Now formally known as the Higher Education Loan Program (HELP).

11 Bryant, Gareth and Ben Spies-Butcher (2020). Bringing finance inside the state: how income-contingent loans blur the boundaries between debt and tax. *Environment and Planning A: Economy and Space* 52(1): 111–29; Spies-Butcher, Ben and Gareth Bryant (2018). Accounting for income-contingent loans as a policy hybrid: politics of discretion and discipline in financialising welfare states. *New Political Economy* 23(6): 768–85; Spies-Butcher, Ben and Gareth Bryant (2018). Universities: a paradox of privatisation. In Damien Cahill and Philip Toner eds. *Wrong way: how privatisation and economic reform backfired*, 239–53. Carlton: La Trobe University Press / Black Inc.

12 Deloitte Access Economics (2016). Estimating the public and private benefits of higher education. Australian Government Department of Education and Training.

13 Ey, Carol (2021). The Higher Education Loan Program (HELP) and related loans: a chronology. Canberra: Parliament of Australia. https://bit.ly/3yHCH4r. All further references to fee levels, and repayment thresholds and rates, are from this source unless otherwise noted.

14 Aungles, Phil, Gabrielle Hodgson and Simon Parbery (2021). Graduate incomes: insights from administrative data. Canberra: Department of Education, Skills and Employment.

15 Kemp, David and Andrew Norton (2014). *Review of the demand driven funding system*. Canberra: Australian Government.

16 Productivity Commission (2019). *The demand driven university system: a mixed report card*. Canberra: Commission Research Paper.

17 Department of Education and Training (2017). *Portfolio Budget Statements 2017–18: Education and Training Portfolio 2017*. Canberra: Commonwealth of Australia; Department of Education, Employment and Workplace Relations (2008). *DEEWR Budget Statements – Outcomes & Performance – Outcome 3*. Canberra: Commonwealth of Australia.

18 Massola, James and Heath Aston (2014). University fee deregulation opposed by most Australians, says Fairfax Ipsos Poll. *Sydney Morning Herald*, 2 November.

19 Ferguson, Hazel (2020). HELP Statistics 2019–20. Canberra: Parliamentary Library. https://bit.ly/3z47jP5.

20 Australian National Audit Office (2016). Administration of Higher Education Loan Program Debt and Repayments. Text. Canberra: Australian National Audit Office.

21 Mackey, Will (2019). Most people will pay less under the new HELP thresholds. *Grattan Institute* (blog), 5 September. https://grattan.edu.au/news/most-people-will-pay-less-under-the-new-help-thresholds/.

22 The University of Sydney (2020). Job-ready Graduates Package – draft legislation submission. Camperdown: The University of Sydney. https://bit.ly/3azpJh1.

23 Department of Education and Training (2015). *Higher education in Australia: a review of reviews from Dawkins to today*. Canberra: Department of Education and Training.

10
Fees and HECS and the politics of access to university

Gwilym Croucher

Introduction

The Higher Education Contribution Scheme (HECS) is a significant Australian innovation. HECS, and its successor the Higher Education Loans Program (HELP), has come to dominate the politics around university education in Australia. Built on ideas advanced a generation earlier by economist Milton Friedman and others, it has become a policy copied around the world. Its success lies in the fact that it delivers what it claims – expanding the availability of higher education with a direct student financial contribution that is varied according to assessed capacity to pay. Despite its success as a public policy, it has created discrete challenges and brought unintended consequences. By solving logistical and ethical problems of access to university, it has amplified the unresolved issue of what is an equitable amount for students to contribute to the cost of their education and what loan settings are needed to ensure the scheme supports equity.

Who should pay?

HECS has been an influential development in Australian higher education because student tuition costs and how they are levied has influenced who attends university. At different points during the development of the Australian higher education system fees had the effect of excluding many people in the community who would otherwise have chosen to enrol, even if the cost of tuition was not the only factor preventing their participation.

From the time of the establishment of Australia's first universities, scholarship schemes have ensured some without the means to pay fees have been able to attend; however, these were far from universal. While those provided by state governments, and later through the Commonwealth Reconstruction Training Scheme (CRTS) and then Commonwealth scholarships provided wide support, these schemes favoured some students, often those already with means, and were not designed to widen access in the way that it is often thought about now.

It was not until the introduction of highly subsidised tuition brought in by the Whitlam government that fee-free tuition became central to the question of equity and access. The policy was introduced by the Whitlam government in March 1973 but had been long foreshadowed and was part of his 1969 election platform. Whitlam had criticised the social constituency of Australian universities as being still largely for those in the middle class. The policy was to address the proposition that "we are all diminished when any of us are denied proper education".[1] In this way, Whitlam's policy explicitly joined access to university to the question of fees. Rather than increasing the number of Commonwealth student scholarships, the Whitlam government argued that no student should be excluded by financial barriers, and so removed annual tuition fees, and replaced previous forms of Commonwealth assistance with the Tertiary Education Allowance Scheme (TEAS), a means-tested benefit to support the cost of living of those "in need". To make higher education "free" to students, the government abolished the system of Commonwealth scholarships and agreed to support those students that a university was willing to enrol, within the funding provided. This meant that there was opportunity for some students who would not have been eligible for the

Commonwealth scholarship, while removing the incentive for other students to take "bonded" scholarships that required service after graduation, such as those for many teachers.

From before the time of Whitlam's policy of "free to student" education, there had been strong public arguments about the regressive nature of providing fully subsidised higher education. This was because it would largely benefit students who were already highly privileged. Many of these critiques had been anticipated prior to the abolition of fees, summarised in a 1971 report by H.G. Brennan, an economist at the University of Adelaide, who was commissioned by the Australian Vice-Chancellors' Committee to investigate such issues. Brennan concluded that "the argument against fee abolition … is not that it fails to remove certain of the disadvantages under which [students of lesser means] operate but that it does not go far enough in doing so".[2]

The period of "free to student" education served to change only marginally the demographics of those who attended university, and while it was the reason that many people without the capacity to pay for fees were able to attend, it did not address one of the central challenges of growing access to university: how to expand the number of university places while at the same time ensuring that wealthy students were not subsidised by the taxes of those who did not wish to attend.

The justifications for government providing student financial support rested on the assumption that universities fulfilled a public function in educating students, and this was rightly something the Australian community should support. The first Australian universities were public institutions, with obligations to educate professionals, but also to provide other public services where academic expertise was called upon.[3] At the same time it was also recognised that university education provided considerable private benefits to their students, through their advantage in the labour market and significant capacity to earn higher wages.

The question of who should pay went further. There has long been ambiguity in justifications advanced for how and why students are financially supported to attend higher education, including recognition that not only were graduates needed for the economy, but also to support perceived national need, such as during wartime.[4] For other countries, the provision of "free to student" education, such as in many

European states, had been tied to student academic achievement without an explicit equity dimension.

It was in the context of these habitual debates about how and why education was provided that the HECS scheme was developed. As more and more Australians wished to undertake bachelor or postgraduate education, the public came to broadly support their aspiration, and so a case emerged to increase the number of available places and widen the opportunity for admission. This meant a problem for government: providing more places would be very costly if they continued to be fully subsidised. However, given the private financial advantage higher education provided, it was unclear if this cost could be palatable for those Australians not aspiring to university education.

How did HECS come about?

The reintroduction of a student contribution was floated in 1983 when Prime Minister Bob Hawke asked John Dawkins, who was at that time minister for finance, to consult universities on how to expand the number of places in the system. The proposal was greeted with little enthusiasm due to a variety of concerns.[5] There were obvious political difficulties for Labor to overturn "free education" introduced by a former Labor government. However, the argument that higher education conferred private as well as public benefit had come to be accepted across the political spectrum, and there was some public sympathy for a form of direct student contribution to cover part of the cost of an education.

The Hawke government was quick to show that university student demographics remained stubbornly unchanged despite increase in enrolments following the Whitlam government's abolition of student fees.[6] Although women achieved parity with men in terms of their overall representation in the student body in 1987, they remained strikingly underrepresented in many disciplines.[7] Other groups were underrepresented too, including the children of post Second World War migrants, especially those from non-English speaking backgrounds, Aboriginal and Torres Strait Islander peoples, as well as people with a disability.[8] This was cited as prima facie evidence for establishing a fairer system including both more places and a student contribution.

There were proposals floated at the time to expand the number of places through a student contribution in the form of a "graduate tax" that would be deferred until after graduation. Yet some commentators saw this as flawed because students provided no collateral and could simply not graduate to avoid repayment. Overseas experience, such as in some states of the United States, had shown high rates of default on student loans.[9]

Other arguments made were that upon joining the professional workforce, students would pay higher taxes and so should not have to pay the levy. While graduates continued to earn higher wages and therefore pay higher taxes, this was seen by many as a weak argument. Why should those who do not attend university nonetheless pay the same amount of tax without the benefit of a university degree?

Dawkins appointed a panel – chaired by the former premier of New South Wales, Neville Wran, the Chair of the CSIRO – to review the options and come up with a scheme for the government to implement. Dawkins asked the committee to design a deferred payment scheme that would be efficient, equitable and administratively feasible. Bruce Chapman, an academic at the Australian National University and later an adviser to the treasurer, was appointed consulting economist to the committee and would be instrumental in the final design of the HECS.

The terms of reference were explicit: how to achieve "far greater access to higher education by people from financially and other disadvantaged backgrounds" so that it did "not continue to be the preserve of the relatively privileged". The terms of reference also stated that "the advantaged who use and benefit directly from higher education ought to contribute more directly to the cost of the system", and that "employers and industry also benefit financially and should contribute directly to the cost".[10] The committee considered the role of support from industry, arguing that businesses benefited from trained graduates and should therefore make a direct contribution towards the cost of provision of higher education teaching. However, the committee stopped short of proposing a levy for industry, saying "the issues are complex and the question of industry contribution to higher education must be considered in the broader context of the entire education and training system".[11]

The committee ultimately recommended that students contribute up to 20 per cent of the cost of their education, only when their personal taxable income exceeded the average earnings of all working Australians. They would pay in increments of 2 per cent of taxable income each year until their maximum contribution amount was met. To address the issue of how to seek direct contributions but ensure that it was administratively feasible, the committee proposed that the student contribution be recovered from graduates through the tax system.[12] This was in many ways a notable departure, and although in later years would come to seem unremarkable, when such a collection mechanism was initially proposed it was opposed by the Australian Taxation Office (ATO). The intervention of the treasurer, Paul Keating, ensured this new role for the ATO.

University staff and student organisations vehemently rejected the Wran Committee's recommendations, prompting the government to write to all currently enrolled students explaining the changes and how they would affect them. The universities' administrators were more agnostic, and in light of the government's determination to increase the student contribution, their response was measured. In public statements the universities stressed the need to establish the actuarial details of the scheme and model its likely effects on student demand. The Australian Vice-Chancellors' Committee, the national body representing the interests of Australian universities, questioned the revenue calculations provided by Wran saying they fell short of the amount needed to meet the enrolment targets. It urged the Commonwealth to commit to an industry levy to broaden the funding base and, as a condition of the new arrangements, called on the government to restore its spending on higher education, which had fallen to 0.83 per cent of GDP in 1988. Dawkins dismissed the call as an "unrealistic and fanciful hope". The proposal faced significant opposition within the government although after some negotiation it was supported. The Australian Labor Party could maintain its stance that higher education would not directly cost the student at the point of entry.

While the Commonwealth implemented HECS without modelling to show whether it would create a significant barrier to university entry, there was a strong rationale supporting predictions it would not. When the Hawke Labor government finally introduced HECS it revived an earlier emphasis on the economic value of university graduates. This benefit derived from the dramatic expansion of the university system, aimed at propelling Australia's emergence as a "clever country".[13] John Dawkins argued that "the larger and more diverse is the pool from which we draw our skilled workforce, the greater is our capacity to take advantage of opportunities as they emerge".[14] In only a few years the number of enrolments had grown from 380,000 students in 1987 to over 560,000 in 1992.[15]

Deferred and income contingent

The government had settled on what was in effect a "graduate tax" in the form of an income-contingent loan collected through the tax system. The alternative was to pay fees up-front. Almost all Australian undergraduate students choose to defer their financial contribution rather than pay up-front fees. The key for access to education is the element of deferral and income-contingent repayment.

As its designers intended, direct contribution makes expansion of the system more politically manageable as government has fewer public policy trade-offs to make. Deferral also means an equal zero price for all students at the point of entry. But *how* HECS/HELP defers is also important. By collecting the contribution through the tax system, increasing the value of the loan only by inflation and making the repayments income contingent, it changes the actual contribution each student makes, and hence is more equitable. This goes some way to removing the structural financial barrier to access, especially for those who expect to take time out of the workforce for caring duties. In doing so it changes the incentives students and governments face.

As Bruce Chapman points out, because graduates pay back over a number of years based on their unique income patterns, so too is there a unique true tuition price for each student.[16] An extreme example illustrates this. If you earn nothing over a lifetime you pay nothing for your education. If you expect to earn nothing, you expect that your education will be fully subsidised. The contribution for each student thus in effect changes depending on their expectations.

This has had some notable implications for the effect of the policy and the politics around it. First, the settings for the loan, the repayment schedule and the characteristics of the student all interact to affect the equitableness and fairness of the scheme. Second, the advertised or "sticker price" of domestic higher education does not matter as much as it does for most goods and services. The signal it sends changes between individuals and over the passage of time. This is a problem for the former Morrison Government's Job-ready Graduates Package of policies implemented in 2020, which were aimed at incentivising different areas of study by changing their price. For the small proportion of students that pay their contribution at the time of enrolment, the change in the advertised price is a change for them. For most, however, it means much, much less, as the price they face will be a discounted present value of the expected HELP repayments, and this will be different for each student. Third, depending on the settings, the cost to the public of providing the loans changes dramatically, as the real value of the loan diminishes unless a real interest rate is applied. Yet, because the loans have historically been treated as an asset in the Commonwealth budget, there was incentive for government to want to increase HELP instead of a more predictable and potentially cost-neutral direct subsidy, especially if it expects loans never to be repaid.

Has it worked as intended?

Access to higher education in Australia has grown significantly in recent decades. This has come through a suite of measures and efforts, following the Commonwealth government's 1990 *A Fair Chance for All* policy statement that sought targeted support for designated underrepresented groups to redress imbalances of power and access.[17] Mandated changes ranged from detailed policies to basic requirements that university buildings have disabled access. Six disadvantaged population groups were identified in *A Fair Chance for All*: people from low socio-economic backgrounds, Aboriginal and Torres Strait Islander peoples, women in non-traditional fields, non-English speaking migrants, people with disabilities, and rural and regional Australians.[18]

Despite the successes of *A Fair Chance for All*, greater access to higher education in Australia has come through the expansion in available places more than from any targeted scheme. This expansion was not dependent directly on the introduction of HECS; the government, after all, could have subsidised many more places if it had so chosen. However, the politics of expanding the number of higher education places, aside from the substantive equity issues that the policy of "free" education was unable to address, meant that it was the de facto enabler. The fact that many people do not know even broadly what the contribution amount is for their chosen course, the "cluster" rate, is a testament to its effectiveness. On the face of it, HECS has largely worked as originally proposed – to make university study financially feasible for students. This is particularly the case in so far as student choice is concerned. By and large, students do not select courses based on price and there is little compelling evidence that the variations in HECS (now HELP) charges cause students to select different courses of study, with most analyses reporting no statistically significant relationships being discovered.

Furthermore, HECS seems to have removed the barrier to entry for an advertised contribution amount which is relatively high. Because potential students are aware that HECS defers this payment and makes it contingent on their income, their decision whether or not to study appears less affected by the price, which they discount into the future. Aggregate enrolments appear to be insensitive to price changes when the contribution a student is asked to make is increased, as it has been several times since the introduction of HECS. Any reduced demand that follows a price change appears to diminish after a few years, and the announcement of a price change seems to only have a fleeting influence. There have been stable trend levels of growth of domestic enrolments through a 30-year period of quite variable HECS settings. The Australian experience is mirrored in the UK, which has much higher relative fees for all courses. For example, the trebling of prices in 2011, from £3,000 to £9,000 per full-time student year, was followed by an increase in enrolments within a year of the change.[19]

Yet HECS has not come without unintended consequences and implications going forward: the devil, as always, is in the detail. The loan settings matter for equity. Small changes can punish some students and undermine the central reason for having an income-contingent scheme. Not thinking of price, a disingenuous government could burden the most vulnerable with huge debts. At the end of the day, there is a limit to what higher education is worth, compared to other options such as Vocational and Educational Training (VET). Moreover, if the loan is treated as an asset in the future, it can skew government decision making in weighing the costs and benefits of different policy options. If it is counted as an asset it is tempting for government to put any new system expansion through the loan scheme, knowing it will not dissuade students. This is the case even when, as Andrew Norton and others have shown, the net present value of the loan book is significantly lower.[20] Removing the price signal takes the sting out of the politics for both better and worse.

It also raises the question of what "widening access" to higher education means. This in part depends on the goal. If we are looking towards ensuring that those who have traditionally been underrepresented at university are enabled to come in greater numbers, such as Aboriginal and Torres Strait Islander students, then the expansion of places that HECS brought is likely a necessary but not sufficient condition. It must work in concert with other targeted measures. For example, many of the universities that were established during the creation of the Unified National System, such as the University of South Australia and Charles Sturt University, have been proactive in recruiting Aboriginal and Torres Strait Islander students and have enrolments that exceed population parity, in contrast to the older universities of Sydney and Melbourne where the proportion of Aboriginal and Torres Strait Islander students remains lower than their relevant proportion in the general population.

Conclusion

The end of "free" higher education for students in Australia reflected debates about the public and private benefits of university education, and whether it had been the best policy to widen access and support equity. The introduction of HECS allowed this expansion, while concurrently reducing the need to allocate university places as a reward for merit. HECS meant that universities had entered the era of "user pays" in the public imagination, even if not in practice on university balance sheets. Yet having a functioning loan system only sharpens the question of "access to what?" It does not relieve us from asking what policy measures can achieve and improve access. It is important to consider whether in policy terms there are wins we should focus on in the *context* of HECS. These are not easy questions and prescriptions. We need a system that is driven by student needs, and this has implications for where and how resources are delivered.

Notes

1 Gough Whitlam, Speech, delivered at Sydney, NSW, 1 October 1969. https://electionspeeches.moadoph.gov.au/speeches/1969-gough-whitlam
2 Brennan, H.G. (1971). Fee abolition, an appraisal. *The Australian University* 9(2).
3 Horne, Julia and Geoffrey Sherington (2012). *Sydney: the making of a public university*. Carlton, Vic: Melbourne University Publishing, 4–5.
4 Croucher, Gwilym, and James Waghorne (2020). *Australian universities: a history of common cause*. Sydney: UNSW Press.
5 Croucher and Waghorne, *Australian universities*.
6 Anderson, Don (1990). Access to university education in Australia 1852–1990: changes in the undergraduate social mix. *Australian Universities' Review* 33(1–2): 37–50.
7 CTEC. *Selected University Statistics*, various years.
8 Department of Employment, Education and Training (1990). *A Fair Chance for All: National and Institutional Planning for Equity in Higher Education: A Discussion Paper.* Canberra: Australian Government Publishing Service.
9 Hansen, W. Lee and Marilyn S. Rhodes (1985). *Student debt crisis: are students incurring excessive debt.* Wisconsin Center for Education Research, School of Education, University of Wisconsin-Madison; Edwards, F.M. (1988). Piecemeal solutions won't reduce the default rate on guaranteed loans. *The Chronicle of Higher Education* 17(44); Wilson, R. (1988). Student-aid analysts blast loan program, urge big overhaul; observers doubt that Congress will approve sweeping changes. *The Chronicle of Higher Education* 27(1).

10 Wran, Neville (1988). *Report of the committee on higher education funding.* Canberra: Australian Government Publishing Service, xv.
11 Wran, *Report of the committee on higher education funding*, xv.
12 Milner, Glenn (1988). Minister warns on leaks. *Sydney Morning Herald*, 8 March; Edwards, Meredith (2001). *Social policy, public policy: from problem to practice.* Crows Nest, NSW: Allen & Unwin, 116, 127–32; Chapman, Bruce (1998). Economics and policy-making: the case of the Higher Education Contribution Scheme. *Canberra Bulletin of Public Administration* 90: 120–4.
13 Hawke, Bob (1990). Speech delivered at Brisbane, Queensland, 8 March 1990. https://electionspeeches.moadoph.gov.au/speeches/1990-bob-hawke, accessed 24 July 2020.
14 Dawkins, John Sydney (1988). *Higher education: a policy statement.* Canberra: Australian Government Publishing Service, 7.
15 Australian Government, Selected Student Statistics, various years.
16 Chapman, Bruce (2008). *The Australian university student financing system: the rationale for, and experience with, income contingent loans.* EABER Working Paper Series, East Asian Bureau of Economic Research.
17 Department of Employment, Education and Training, *A Fair Chance for All.*
18 Martin, Lin (1994). *Equity and general performance indicators in higher education.* Canberra: Australian Government Public Service.
19 Murphy, Richard, Judith Scott-Clayton and Gill Wyness (2019). The end of free college in England: implications for enrolments, equity, and quality. *Economics of Education Review* 71: 7–22.
20 Norton, Andrew (2016). Equity and markets. In Andrew Harvey, Catherine Burnheim, and Matthew Brett, eds. *Student equity in Australian higher education,* 183–206. Singapore: Springer.

11

The 2020 Job-ready Graduates Package and what it means for students

Tim Payne[1]

Introduction

In October 2020, the Australian parliament passed legislation that arguably made the most significant changes in a decade to the way the federal government funds places for domestic students seeking a university education. The Morrison government's *Job-ready Graduates Higher Education Reform Package* (JRG Package) commenced on 1 January 2021, heralding a new era for Australian students and higher education providers. Today, 35 per cent of Australians aged 20–64 have at least a bachelor degree. More than 400,000 domestic students commence higher education each year and nearly two thirds of young Australians do so by age 22. Our economy and labour market have transformed over the last 30 years, with by far the strongest jobs growth occurring in fields that require higher order skills and post-school qualifications.[2] Participation in higher education by young Australians has become ubiquitous, increasingly important to the economy, and to individuals in terms of their work and life outcomes. With the Australian Labor Party's win in the May 2022 federal election and a looming boom in school leavers requiring tertiary education, it is timely to take stock of the JRG Package's key elements and to consider their implications for students from different backgrounds.

Responding to and capitalising on a crisis

In June 2020, in the middle of the COVID-19 pandemic and recession, then federal education minister, Dan Tehan, released the Morrison government's proposals for major change to Australia's system of higher education funding. The JRG Package demonstrated the Coalition's recognition that continuing to freeze core public funding for universities at 2017 levels would not be in the national interest. The key factors behind this realisation were the recession's expected counter-cyclical increase in demand for higher education as people looked to upskill and retrain, the anticipated strong increase in numbers of 18-year-olds seeking places due to the so-called "Costello baby boom" of the 2000s, and labour market forecasts completed before the pandemic predicting that the economy would require even more highly skilled workers over the next decade. The Morrison government realised that without a circuit breaker, demand for Commonwealth-supported places could start to far exceed availability from as early as 2021.

The JRG Package was presented publicly with a sense of urgency around the need for it to be adopted in time for the start of the 2021 academic year. Less than a week was provided for consultations on the draft legislation, which was introduced to parliament in late August 2020. On 8 October 2020, after the briefest of inquiries, the Senate passed the package's enabling legislation by just one vote, and with a few amendments negotiated with Pauline Hanson's One Nation Party and South Australian independent senator, Stirling Griff, in return for their votes. As a result, key elements of the JRG Package commenced on 1 January 2021, beginning a new era for Australian higher education students and providers.[3]

A driving purpose of the JRG Package was to provide more Commonwealth-supported places for Australian students, without incurring any substantial additional costs for taxpayers. When introducing the package to parliament, Minister Tehan advised that it would deliver 39,000 extra places by 2023 and 100,000 by 2030. Since 2021, funding for these places has been allocated through a formula weighted to favour regionally based universities, followed by those serving metropolitan areas experiencing higher rates of population growth. In its pandemic-delayed emergency budget of October 2020, the Morrison government also committed $550 million for a further 12,000 full places for students commencing studies in national priority areas in 2021, as well as 50,000 places for short-course places targeted to support people seeking to upskill or retrain due to disruption caused by the pandemic.[4]

Price signals to influence students' study choices

With its JRG Package the Morrison government sought to send strong price signals to students to select courses in fields it viewed as national priorities and areas of predicted jobs growth such as building, teaching and healthcare. It did this by making it cheaper, in some cases much cheaper, for students to study in areas where the government expects there to be strong jobs demand in the future. As Ministers Tehan and Cash stated when releasing the package in June 2020:

> To power our post-COVID economic recovery, Australia will need more educators, more health professionals and more engineers, and that is why we are sending a price signal to encourage people to study in areas of expected employment growth.[5]

From 2021, new students studying units exclusively in agriculture, science, engineering, teaching or nursing pay $3,950 each year, compared to those starting courses in the humanities, communications, law or social sciences, who pay $14,500 annually.

A new approach to setting funding levels

The JRG Package sought to align total funding for each domestic student (the Commonwealth plus student contributions) more closely to the government's understanding of universities' average cost of teaching each student in different fields. Critically for universities, this calculation disregarded the costs they incur sustaining the base level of research that is required for registration as a university in Australia, and which prior to the JRG Package was an accepted part of university "base funding" – provided to support universities' core education and research activities.[6] Recognising the implications of this change when combined with the disruption caused by the pandemic, in July 2020 the federal education minister established a working group of vice-chancellors to advise the government about sustainable approaches to research funding for universities. The October 2020 federal budget contained a $1 billion commitment of emergency funding for university research. However, this measure was not extended in the subsequent budget, leaving major questions still to be answered about how Australia's sovereign university research capacity will be sustained during COVID-19 and beyond.[7]

Students pay more, on average, while providers receive less per student place

The JRG Package's funding changes mean that the overall split of funding for higher education in Australia linked to domestic student enrolments continues to shift further towards students and away from taxpayers; from 58 per cent paid by the government and 42 per cent by students pre-2021, to 52 per cent by the government and 48 per cent by students from 2021. Moreover, the average net funding providers receive for each Commonwealth-supported student was reduced by around 6 per cent. To put this in perspective, for the University of Sydney, if not for transition arrangements that will apply until 2024, the JRG Package's student fee changes would have resulted in a $27 million funding cut in 2021, compared to 2020.[8] By shifting more of the overall cost to students, reducing the average value of funding per place that providers receive, and by ignoring the costs they incur sustaining core research capabilities that were previously an accepted part of funding linked to domestic student places, the JRG Package delivered Minister Tehan's promised additional Commonwealth-supported places at a marginal, if any, additional cost to the government.

The JRG Package's transfer of financial responsibility for higher education back from the state to students and families was the latest step in what appears to be an inexorable 30-year trend, since the Higher

Education Contribution Scheme (HECS) was introduced in 1989. Direct comparisons between countries' rates of public and private support for local students accessing higher education must be treated with caution because of structural, financial and data collection differences. Nevertheless, according to the OECD data, in 2018 Australia's rate of private expenditure on *tertiary* education was already roughly twice the OECD average and reported as among the highest of all member countries.[9]

Winners and losers

The package intentionally creates new groups of students who are winners and losers. Continuing (pre-2021) Commonwealth-supported students who were enrolled in courses (or units of study) where their fees drop, benefit from paying the lower rates for these subjects. They will graduate with smaller HECS debts and pay them off more quickly once employed. The package's grandfathering arrangements mean that current students in courses where fees have increased continue to pay the old rates for the duration of their studies in these courses. These students may also benefit from the lower fees in some fields – if they complete such units for credit towards their substantive degrees.

New students benefit if they enrol in courses where the fees decrease, whereas those studying in areas where fees rise will incur higher fees, and larger HECS debts if they defer payment. At the extremes, the cost gap of different fields of study is substantial. For example, new students in agriculture or mathematics courses in 2022 have fees of $3,985 indexed per year – 58 per cent less than previously. Meanwhile, students choosing to study units exclusively in the humanities, communication and social sciences must pay $14,650 each year, or 113 per cent more than before. For a standard three-year degree, future students graduating from the highest-cost courses will have HECS debts of more than $40,000, or almost four times more than students enrolling in the new lowest-cost fields. A post-2021 student studying a five-year combined Arts/Law degree will graduate with a HECS debt of more than $70,000, compared to around $50,000 pre-2021.

In March 2021 the then new federal education minister, Alan Tudge, released early data suggesting new domestic student enrolments rose by 11,000, or 7 per cent, compared to the same time in 2020. While the minister highlighted that the strongest increases were in courses made cheaper by the JRG Package, the data also showed strong growth in society and culture courses, where annual fees increased the most. In June 2022 it was reported that the latest Universities Admissions Centre (UAC) data showed the proportion of year 12 students applying for society and culture courses in NSW increased 9 per cent between 2020 and 2022.[10] Many factors influence students' course choices. Most students commencing courses in 2021 and 2022 would have started making their study preference well before the JRG Package became law, while history shows university enrolments increase when the economy experiences downturns. It is still too early to determine if the package's changes to fees will have the effect desired by the Morrison government of altering students' study choices to favour certain fields at the expense of others. What we do know is that while women cluster in the health, teaching and some other disciplines that have modest fee decreases under the JRG Package, they also account for two thirds of students in society and culture courses, which have the largest fee hikes under the JRG Package.

We also know that prior to the JRG changes, over 50 per cent of Aboriginal and Torres Strait Islander students were enrolled in fields like management/commerce, society and culture and the creative arts, which now attract the highest course fees. If women and Aboriginal and Torres Strait Islander students continue to prefer generalist fields of study, it is likely that they will be disproportionately affected by the JRG Package's fee increases. There is considerable research suggesting that previous changes to the fees Australian students pay through HECS have not led to major long-term changes in the study choices of students. However, recent research for the NSW Department of Education has found that fear of debt, concerns about living costs while studying and indecision about course selection pose significant barriers to university-level study for school leavers from regional areas who are uncertain about pursuing higher education, including students from low SES and Aboriginal and Torres Strait Islander backgrounds.[11]

Application of the 50 per cent Pass-Rate Rule to Commonwealth-supported students

The JRG Package introduced requirements to make all higher education providers, including public universities, more accountable for the academic preparedness of the domestic students they enrol, and for supporting their students to succeed, especially in the first year of study. This includes extending the so-called "50 per cent Pass-Rate Rule" to Commonwealth-supported and postgraduate fee-paying domestic students who commence studies after 2022, where previously it applied only to students with FEE-HELP assistance enrolled with non-university higher education providers. Under this change, students who fail more than 50 per cent of their first-year subjects will no longer be able to access a Commonwealth-supported place with a HECS-HELP loan to continue in their chosen courses. Students affected by this policy will only be able to continue in their preferred courses of study if their institutions determine that special circumstances (beyond a student's control) apply, or by paying the full course costs up-front until their pass rates reach 50 per cent again.[12]

This measure has the worthy intention of improving student success rates and reducing their HECS-HELP debts incurred for failed subjects. It seeks to do this by providing a financial incentive for higher education providers to focus on the academic and pastoral support services they provide to their students. However, it is a very blunt instrument, which risks needlessly increasing anxiety and stress levels for all new domestic students from 2022, negatively affecting their learning and personal growth during this crucial and formative time of transition. Here, it is important to note that many Australian school leavers who commenced university studies in 2022 have experienced two years of disrupted schooling and development, as well as heightened levels of anxiety, stress and depression because of the prolonged school closures caused by the COVID-19 pandemic.[13] Recent research concludes that the pandemic has added new psychological challenges for young women in particular – during their developmentally critical years.[14] Additionally, a survey of 2021 NSW school leavers conducted by the Universities Admissions Centre (UAC) found that 50 per cent of respondents rated "mental health" as a "key" worry overall, up from 44 per cent for the class of

2020.[15] Australian higher education providers are currently coping with significantly increased requests for special consideration and are trialling how to assist students equitably in ways that will help keep them in their studies.[16]

Providers will, in cases where they determine that special circumstances exist, retain discretion to allow failing students to continue in their chosen courses with Commonwealth support. However, some providers (especially those experiencing financial stress) may be reluctant to exercise this discretion, because in each instance the provider must repay the fees and funding linked to the student's Commonwealth-supported place. Students from affluent backgrounds who fail courses and cannot prove special circumstances may still be able to continue in their preferred courses of study by paying up-front. This option is unlikely to be available for students from disadvantaged backgrounds unless commercial lenders, education providers or other organisations step in to provide fee relief or loan options to cover tuition fees. Students who lose access to Commonwealth-supported places in their preferred courses of study may still be eligible for supported places at the same institution in another course, or with another provider. A wide range of personal and institutional factors can influence students' academic success and progress in the first year of post-school education. However, inevitably, the students most likely to be impacted by the extension of the 50 per cent Pass-Rate Rule are those who are less academically prepared, Aboriginal and Torres Strait Islander students, mature-age students, those who study remotely or part-time, and those who experience family, financial and mental health pressures.[17]

The JRG Package's approach to access and equity

The package included a raft of measures in response to the National Regional, Rural and Remote Education Strategy (Napthine Review) released in 2019, which confirmed that higher education participation and attainment rates remained significantly lower in rural, regional and remote (RRR) Australian areas compared to metropolitan areas. According to the JRG Package discussion paper:

> Individuals in RRR areas are less than half as likely to obtain a bachelor degree or above qualification by the time they are 35, compared to those from metropolitan areas. People living in regional areas account for 27.3 per cent of people aged 15–64 years, but only 21.5 per cent of domestic undergraduate enrolments.[18]

The Morrison government's response set a target of halving these gaps in regional educational participation and attainment by 2030. This, according to its modelling, would increase Australia's GDP by around $25 billion annually by 2050 and deliver significant benefits for individuals, regional communities and the nation.[19]

The JRG Package included a commitment of $6 million over four years to appoint and support an independent Rural Education Commissioner to oversee the implementation of the strategy, through working with all levels of government to halve the disparity of educational outcomes between regional and metropolitan students by 2030. From 2021, campuses directly serving regional communities receive an annual 3.5 per cent funding increase for non-medical domestic bachelor growth places, compared to 2.5 per cent growth for those located in high-growth metropolitan areas, and 1 per cent for other campuses.

To encourage and assist Year 12 school leavers from outer regional and remote areas to commence tertiary education immediately following school, the JRG Package established a one-off Tertiary Access Payment (TAP) of $5,000 for eligible students who need to relocate to undertake full-time, higher level (Certificate IV or above) studies. The study must be full-time in a course that runs for at least a year, and the student's home must be 90 minutes or more by public transport from the campus at which they are enrolled. A combined parental income test of $250,000 is applied. The Morrison government estimated that some 8,100 students could receive this payment in 2021.

Measures like the $5,000 TAP for students from regional and remote areas may sound good and helpful on the surface. But it is important to note that the TAP will benefit a relatively small number of students each year (around 8,000 in 2021), many of whom are likely to be from more affluent backgrounds and would have pursued tertiary education regardless. Moreover, the TAP is one-off, provided in two instalments during a student's first year of study. After that, students from low SES backgrounds will still need to meet their living expenses through Youth Allowance, ABSTUDY and paid employment. The JRG Package included no meaningful improvements to the ongoing levels of income support available to students from the most disadvantaged backgrounds, especially those who must move away from home to study.

In recognition of the very low higher education participation rates of Aboriginal and Torres Strait Islander students from regional and remote communities, since 2021 any First Nations student from these areas who is offered a place in a bachelor degree program by a public university has been guaranteed a Commonwealth-supported place. The Morrison government estimated in 2020 that this targeted demand-driven funding measure would see an additional 160 Aboriginal and Torres Strait Islander students access higher education in 2021, rising to 1,700 students by 2024. While some First Nations students from regional and remote communities may benefit from this measure, the more than 50 per cent of Aboriginal and Torres Strait Islander peoples who live in or around major cities are not eligible.[20]

Before the implementation of the JRG Package, public universities received funding under the Higher Education Participation and Partnership Program (HEPPP) based on their shares of domestic undergraduate students from low SES backgrounds only. In line with the JRG Package's strong regional focus, since 2021 HEPPP funding has rewarded providers for their respective shares of students from regional and remote areas (45 per cent) and Aboriginal and Torres Strait Islander students (10 per cent). Moreover, from 2024 the HEPPP, Regional Loading and other relevant funding schemes will be combined into a single Indigenous, Regional and Low SES Attainment Fund (IRLSAF).[21] These changes provide financial incentives for providers to enrol students from regional and remote communities, including First Nations students from those areas.

Conclusion

Through the JRG Package of 2020, the Morrison Coalition government capitalised on the COVID-19 crisis to further expand domestic students' access to higher education to 2030, without substantially increasing the cost for taxpayers. It did this by following the long-term trend, pursued by successive Labor and Coalition governments, of progressively shifting more of the total costs from the state to students, and by redirecting funding Australia's universities have traditionally relied upon to support their core research activities. With the JRG Package, the Coalition unashamedly sought to send price signals to students, encouraging them to select courses with clear employment pathways as well as STEM, English and foreign languages subjects, rather than generalist courses in the arts and social sciences. It was also unapologetically focused on lifting access to higher education by students from regional and remote Australia, and especially Aboriginal and Torres Strait Islander students from these areas.

Most of the JRG Package's student fee and funding changes commenced on 1 January 2021. Higher education providers in receipt of Commonwealth-supported places have until 2024 to adjust to the full impact of these very significant changes to the way they are funded. While the package's changes to student and Commonwealth contribution amounts provide strong financial incentives for students to choose courses favoured by the government, they also have the perverse effect of rewarding providers financially for enrolling more students in arts, humanities, social science, law, economics, business and commerce subjects. Decoupling funding for teaching and research linked to domestic students has finally realised the Coalition's long-held goal of being free to allocate Commonwealth-supported places to teaching-only private and other non-university higher education providers. This started to happen in 2021 with the distribution of places for COVID-19 emergency online short courses. It may become an increasing feature of Australia's higher education funding system, with the objectives of increasing student choice, provider diversity and efficiency through competition.

Only time will tell what impact measures such as student fee changes, the 50 per cent Pass-Rate Rule and the many other elements of the JRG Package will have on Australian students' access to higher education, their study choices, levels of stress and anxiety, and the quality of the education and associated experiences they receive. The impacts of the JRG Package's changes on students from different backgrounds need to be considered carefully by the incoming Albanese Labor government. Any early signs of adverse outcomes for COVID-19 school leavers, women, mature-age, low SES and Aboriginal and Torres Strait Islander students will need to be identified and swiftly addressed.

Notes

1 Any views expressed in this chapter are those of the author alone and are not made on behalf of or represent the views of the University of Sydney.
2 Australian Bureau of Statistics (2020). Education and Work, Australia, Table 10, Release, 11 November 2020, https://bit.ly/3z79O37; Department of Education, Skills and Employment. Selected Higher Education Statistics – 2019 Student data, Table (i). https://bit.ly/3z7MO43; Productivity Commission (2019). *The demand driven university system: a mixed report card*, Commission Research Paper, 2; Philip Lowe (2014). *Address to the Australian Business Economists (ABE) Annual Dinner*, Reserve Bank of Australia, 25 November 2014, Graphs 6 and 7. https://bit.ly/3cgDJwO.
3 Australian Government (2020). *Job-ready Graduates, Higher Education Reform Package 2020, Discussion Paper.* Canberra: Commonwealth of Australia; *Higher Education Support Amendment (Job-Ready Graduates and Supporting Regional and Remote Students) Bill 2020.* https://bit.ly/3yENGvn.
4 Australian Government (2020). *Budget 2020–21, Budget Measures, Budget Paper No.2.* Canberra: Commonwealth of Australia, 78.
5 Cash, Michaelia and Dan Tehan (2022). "Job ready graduates to power economic recovery," Media release, 19 June 2020, https://ministers.dese.gov.au/tehan/job-ready-graduates-power-economic-recovery.
6 Lomax-Smith, Jane, Louise Watson and Beth Webster (2011). Higher Education Base Funding Review, Final Report. Canberra: Commonwealth of Australia, 81.
7 Tehan, Dan (2020). "Research sustainability work group," Media release, 1 July 2020, https://ministers.dese.gov.au/tehan/research-sustainability-working-group; Australian Government, Budget 2020–21, Budget Measures, Budget Paper No.2, 79.
8 Figures from unpublished analysis of the JRG Package undertaken by Universities Australia and the University of Sydney.

9 OECD (2021). Education at a glance 2021, OECD Indicators. Paris: OECD, Publishing, 259.
10 White, Daniella (2022). Students flock to humanities degrees despite huge fee increases. *Sydney Morning Herald*, 6 June. https://bit.ly/3yAKhxS.
11 Tudge, Alan (2021). "Job-ready Graduates package sees more Aussies enrolling in key courses," Media release, 25 March 2021, https://bit.ly/3QGese2; Chapman, Bruce. (2020). The Government's planned changes to HECS-HELP Charges: A submission to the Job-Ready Graduates Package draft legislation consultation, August; The University of Sydney (2020). Submission to the Senate Education and Employment Legislation Committee's Inquiry into the Higher Education Support Amendment (Job-Ready Graduates and Supporting Regional and Remote Students) Bill 2020. Sydney: The University of Sydney, 4.
12 Australian Government (2020). *Job-ready Graduates Discussion Paper.* Australian Government, *Overview – draft legislation to implement the Australian Government's Job-ready Graduates Package*. Canberra: Commonwealth of Australia, 5.
13 Teeson, Maree and Mark Stears, ed. (2021). *COVID-19 and Australia's mental health: An overview of academic literature, policy documents, lived experience accounts, media and community reports*. Sydney: Australia's Mental Health Think Tank.
14 Grant, Sara, Jianyun Wu, John Uesi, Nancy Jong, Ian Perkes, Katherine Knight, Fenton O'Leary, Carla Trudgett and Michael Bowden (2022). Growth in emergency department self-harm or suicidal ideation presentations in young people: Comparing trends before and since the COVID-19 first wave in New South Wales, Australia. *Australian & New Zealand Journal of Psychiatry.* Published online March 3, 2022. https://journals.sagepub.com/doi/full/10.1177/00048674221082518.
15 Universities Admission Centre (2022). *Student Lifestyle Report 2022.* Sydney, 28. https://www.uac.edu.au/assets/documents/submissions/student-lifestyle-report-2022.pdf.
16 Tran, Khanh and Fabian Robertson, "Will five-day extensions remedy Special Consideration's inhumanity?" *Honi Soit*, 23 August 2022. https://bit.ly/3BDXmJc.
17 Tertiary Education Quality and Standards Agency (TEQSA) (2017). *Characteristics of Australian higher education providers and their relation to first-year student attrition*. Melbourne: Commonwealth of Australia, 24; Higher Education Standard Panel (HESP) (2017). *Final Report – Improving retention, completion and success in higher education*. Canberra: Commonwealth of Australia.
18 Australian Government, *Job-ready Graduates Discussion Paper*, 28.
19 Australian Government, *Job-ready Graduates Discussion Paper*, 28.
20 Department of Education, Skills and Employment (n.d) "More opportunities for regional Australia," https://bit.ly/3o1DWXq. On 10 December 2021, the Australian government announced that eligibility for the TAP would be

extended to include students from *inner regional* areas as defined by the Australia Bureau of Statistics. https://bit.ly/3AO8TWG.

21 Napthine, Denis et.al. (2019). *National Rural and Remote Tertiary Education Strategy Final Report.* Canberra: Department of Education, Skills and Employment; Australian Government, *Job-ready Graduates Discussion Paper*, 32–38.

12

Twenty years of research in Australia's universities and implications for the future

Alan Pettigrew

Introduction

We often hear how universities are Australia's research powerhouses, advancing knowledge in ways that contribute to the greater public good. But with the gap between government funding and the real cost of research growing, it is timely to consider the long-term trends in the scale and scope of research across the university sector and the implications that arise for the future.

There is a large amount of data compiled by the Australian government on research activity in each of Australia's 42 universities that operate within the single, unified national system that has been in place since the Dawkins reforms of the early 1990s. These annual data, which include levels of income and expenditure on research, numbers of staff, and numbers of students who have completed their research degrees, reveal a high degree of diversity in the scale of research activity across the sector. Indeed, half of Australia's universities now account for 88 per cent of research conducted in the sector. Data from the Excellence in Research for Australia program, which rates the quality of research in different disciplines at each university, reveal a similar diversity in the scope and quality of research undertaken across the sector. The financial data also reveal the extent to which Australia's university research effort and competitiveness has been reliant on other revenue sources in university budgets, principally student fees.

A critical issue emerging from the following analysis concerns how government policies should recognise and address the diversity in scale and scope of research across Australia's universities. Foremost within this issue is the strategy for funding of research such that our universities can realise their full potential and capacity to benefit the widespread Australian population and our economy, especially in the face of immediate and emerging challenges.

The scale of research in Australian universities

Total external funding for research in Australia's universities has grown from $1.16 billion in 2001 to $5.11 billion in 2020. These funds are sourced from a complex array of government agencies and grants as well as industry and philanthropic sources, but they do not flow evenly across the sector. To understand the broad policy implications of this complexity it is necessary to find a suitable, consistent measure by which we can assess the relative scale of research across all universities.

In addition to external competitive funding awarded to researchers through granting agencies and other systems, the Australian government annually provides a Research Block Grant (RBG) to each university to partially support the indirect costs of research that are not covered through research grants and to support training research students enrolled in masters and doctoral degrees. The RBG for each university is determined on the same basis using data on all externally sourced income for research as well as completions of higher degree by research (HDR) candidates.[1] Thus, the RBG provides a convenient measure of each university's overall scale of research activity.

The distribution of RBG allocations across all eligible universities in 2001 and 2020 is shown in ranked order in panels A and B in Figure 12.1.[2] Over this period, the total RBG quantum has increased from $0.9 billion to $1.9 billion but this has not kept pace with the growth in total external funding for research. The data reveal the consistent, significant diversity in the scale of research across Australia's universities. Changes over time in the ranked order reveal changes in relative scale of research between universities.

The principal feature of these distributions is that the RBGs to the top ranked "Group of Eight" (Go8) universities have always been the largest, with the order amongst this group varying only slightly over the period. On the other hand, some universities in the mid-range of the ranked order have significantly increased their percentage share of total RBG funds while others have declined. Universities in the lower part of the distribution have varied little in their relative position across the period.

Categories of research funding and performance

The government's determination of each university's RBG is largely based on its success relative to all others in acquiring external income for research. The relevant income data are aggregated in four major categories: Commonwealth Competitive Grants schemes (Category 1), priority-directed Commonwealth, state and local government funding (Category 2), funding from local and international industry, not-for-profit organisations and philanthropy (Category 3), and Cooperative Research Centre funding that combines government, industry and university resources (CRC, Category 4).[3] These four categories of research income have different purposes, criteria and processes for the award of funding. However, in general, the decisions taken by governments, funding agencies and other organisations to award funding in any of these categories are usually made on an assessment of the capacity and previous research performance of researchers as well as the scope and feasibility of the research that has been proposed. Hence, income for research secured by universities through each of these four RBG categories reflects the scale, capacity and record of achievement in research at that institution. Similarly, the number of HDR completions at each university reflects outcomes in research training.[4]

To gain a picture of relative research performance across the sector over time, it is instructive to compare groups of universities with similar levels of overall performance, as summarised through the RBG allocation methodology.[5] The 42 universities eligible for RBG funding

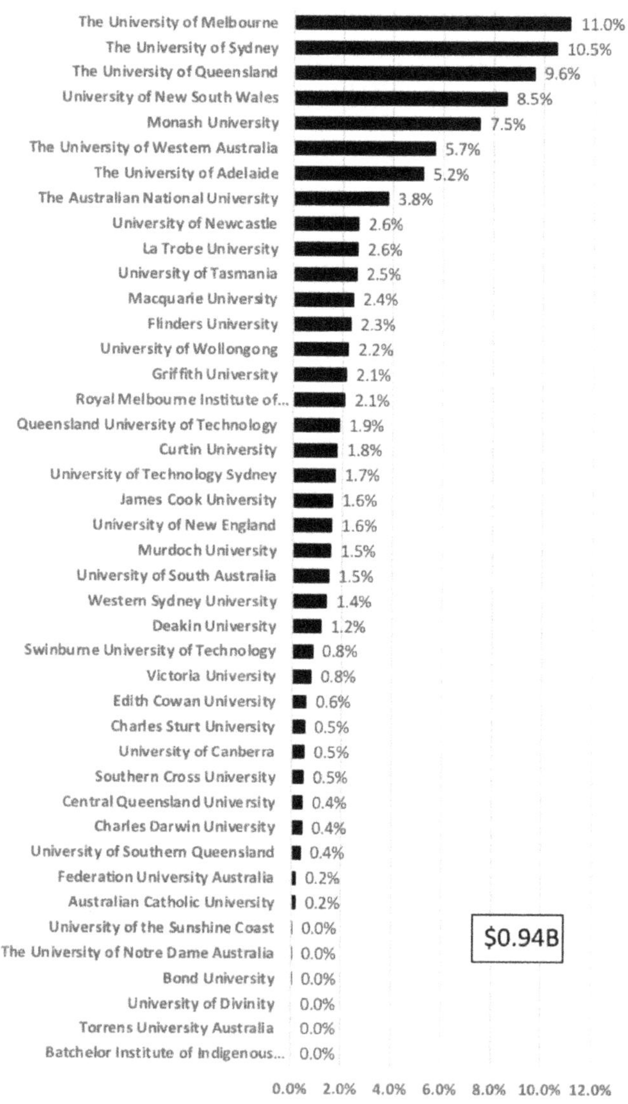

Figure 12.1a Distribution of RBG allocations in 2001.

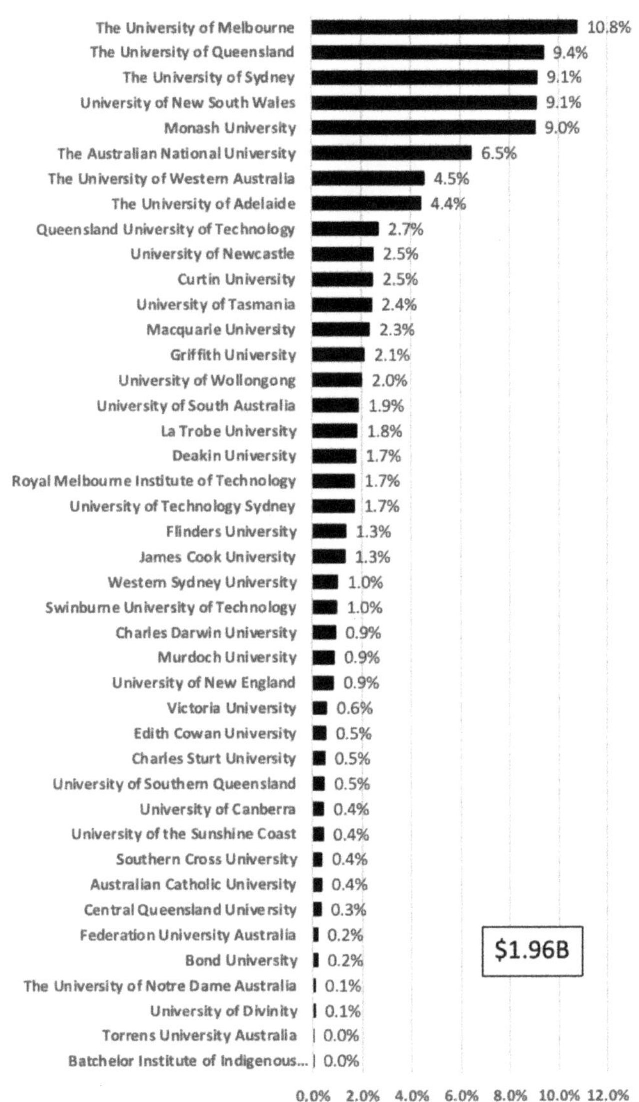

Figure 12.1b Distribution of RBG allocations in 2020.

have been divided in this analysis into three groups, based on their ranked RBG allocation in 2020. These groups are labelled in Table 12.1 as Go8, G9–20 and G21–42. These data show the percentage shares for each group of the total RBG in 2001 and 2020 and the total funding awarded in each of the four categories of research funding in 2000 and 2019.[6] Also shown are the percentage shares of total HDR completions across the sector.

There are several points to note. First, as is well known, the Go8 group has dominated research funding and HDR completions by a significant margin over these 20 years. Second, there are three changes to this pattern, namely, the shift of 3 per cent share of Category 1 income, 23 per cent share of Category 4 income and 5 per cent share of HDR completions away from the Go8 universities to the G9–20 group. These changes show the slow but important growth in the scale of research activity in the G9–20 group of universities over the last 20 years.

Whilst the levels of Category 4 (CRC) funding in 2019 across the Go8 and G9–20 universities are variable, the range of funding levels across both groups is now very similar (approximately $1 million–$7 million). The data reveal that the share of CRC funding over the period 2000–19 has fallen in five of the Go8 universities, remained stable in two universities (Universities of Adelaide and Western Australia) and has grown in only one (Monash University). The data suggest that many of the Go8 "research-intensive" universities have taken strategic decisions to reduce their involvement in the CRC program. In contrast, all but two of the G9–20 universities have achieved increases in their CRC funding over the period, presumably because they see a strategic opportunity for funding that will benefit their ambitions in research and development. For those universities though, the overall level of funding for the CRC program, compared to the funding in the other three categories, has been low and has barely increased over these 20 years ($81 million in 2000 and $89 million in 2019).

Third, across the 20-year period, the G21–42 group of universities have lost shares in all the funding categories to the other two groups of universities ranked higher on the RBG scale. Whilst these percentage changes are small, the changes in funding are nevertheless significant for each of these universities of smaller scale. The change reflects an

Table 12.1 Changes in Research Block Grant categories.

Research Block Grants	**Go8**		
	2000/2001	**2019/2020**	**Change**
Total Group Research Block Grant	61.8%	62.8%	1.0%
Category 1 – Commonwealth Competitive Grants	71.2%	68.1%	-3.1%
Category 2 – Commonwealth-State-Local Government Funding	58.3%	62.8%	4.5%
Category 3 – Industry Funding	66.7%	69.9%	3.2%
Category 4 – Cooperative Research Centre Funding	57.4%	34.2%	-23.2%
Higher Degree Completions	55.1%	49.6%	-5.5%
Research Block Grants	**Go8**		
	2000/2001	**2019/2020**	**Change**
Total Group Research Block Grant	24.5%	25.3%	0.8%
Category 1 – Commonwealth Competitive Grants	18.0%	21.4%	3.5%
Category 2 – Commonwealth-State-Local Government Funding	25.2%	25.7%	0.5%
Category 3 – Industry Funding	23.0%	20.8%	-2.2%
Category 4 – Cooperative Research Centre Funding	25.1%	48.4%	23.3%
Higher Degree Completions	28.8%	34.2%	5.4%

Research Block Grants	G21–42		
	2000/2001	2019/2020	Change
Total Group Research Block Grant	13.7%	11.9%	-1.8%
Category 1 - Commonwealth Competitive Grants	10.8%	10.5%	-0.3%
Category 2 - Commonwealth-State-Local Government Funding	16.4%	11.4%	-5.0%
Category 3 - Industry Funding	10.3%	9.4%	-0.9%
Category 4 - Cooperative Research Centre Funding	17.5%	17.4%	-0.1%
Higher Degree Completions	16.0%	16.3%	0.3%

increasing domination in research activity amongst the higher 50 per cent of RBG-ranked universities in the sector.

Numbers and roles of academic staff

The scale and productivity in research of all universities is critically, but not solely, dependent on the academic staff who lead and undertake the research. The total number of academic staff (full-time equivalent, FTE) across the sector has increased by 60 per cent over the period 2000–19, along with increased numbers of students. However, amongst this growth there has been a doubling of university staff FTE classified as "Research-Only". Most of this gain occurred in the period 2000–13, when research funding was growing, but has remained relatively steady since then, reflecting the stable level of competitive grant funding over the latter period.[7]

Not surprisingly, there is a general correlation between the total number of academic staff FTE and a university's success in acquiring a larger share of the total RBG. However, there are some important differences in the comparative scale in academic staff numbers and relative performance in research across the sector. In 2019, the larger Go8 universities together employed 41.5 per cent of the total academic FTE whose research outcomes are reflected in winning 62.8 per cent of the total RBG distributed across the sector in 2020. In contrast, the G9–20 universities employed 34.1 per cent of total academic FTE who won 25.3 per cent of the total RBG. The G21–42 smaller universities together employed 24.2 per cent of the total FTE who won just 11.9 per cent of the total RBG. This suggests the importance of scale in research but also the relative research productivity of staff in the Go8 and the G9–20 in comparison to the G21–42 group.

A further observation relevant to consideration of research scale and productivity concerns the ratio of "Research-Only" staff to "Teaching and Research" staff. In 2019, the Go8 group had an average ratio of 0.90 (range: 0.52, Australian National University to 1.62, University of Queensland) whilst average ratios in the G9–20 and G21–42 groups were 0.51 and 0.27 respectively.[8] Four universities in the G9–20 group that have shown significant uplift in research activity as judged by their proportion of total RBG over the last 20 years have ratios that are similar to those across the Go8 group. It would appear, in general terms, that the research performance of universities is correlated at least in part with the proportion of their academic staff who are regarded as "Research-Only".

One of the positive developments in staff numbers across the sector over the period 2000–19 has been the increased proportion of female staff at senior academic levels. Whereas the percentage of female academic staff at lower academic levels (A and B) has declined very slightly (-0.8 per cent and -2.2 per cent to 51.0 per cent and 51.8 per cent respectively), the percentage of female staff at levels C (Senior lecturer) and D and E (Associate Professor and Professor) has increased by 16.8 per cent and 19.0 per cent to reach 46.5 per cent and 35.2 per cent respectively.

These data can be further broken down by academic role to understand how women contribute to research performance. Table 12.2 shows the percentage of female Research-Only and Teaching and Research staff at different academic levels across the three groups of universities in 2001 and 2019. Also shown are the changes in these percentages over that period. Any variations in percentage sums in Table 12.2 are the result of rounding.

As Table 12.2 shows, between 2001 and 2019 the percentage of female Research-Only staff at professorial levels (D and E) increased in the Go8 and G9–20 groups of universities from just 13.6 per cent and 18.9 per cent respectively to reach 37 per cent in 2019. Similar increases can be observed in the percentage of female Teaching and Research staff at levels D and E. There have also been smaller increases in female staff representation at lecturer levels B and C in both the Research-Only and Teaching and Research classifications in the Go8 and G9–20 universities, reaching levels of 42 per cent to 55 per cent. It is still the case, however, that after these 18 years, the proportions of female staff at the higher academic levels (C, D and E) of both classifications across the two groups of universities with higher levels of research activity are still less than 50 per cent (average 43 per cent, range 30 per cent to 46 per cent).

Internal funding for research

Universities use internal funds to cover research costs such as land, buildings, other capital costs, labour costs, scholarships and other current expenditure that are not met from their RBG allocation, competitive grants and other external sources. These are labelled in the public Commonwealth data as "General University Funds" (income) for research.[9] The sources of these funds include Australian and overseas business partnerships, donations, investment income, asset management, bequests and foundations, as well as student fees from domestic and international fee-paying students.

Total General University Funds expended on research across the sector have increased from $2.62 billion in 2004 to $6.82 billion in 2018 (+161 per cent).[10] The percentage of total expenditure on research in 2018 that is represented by General University Funds for each university, ranked in the order of their RBG allocation in 2020, is shown in Figure 12.2.

For the sector as a whole, universities have provided on average 56 per cent of total university expenditure on research from their own

Table 12.2 Percentage of female Research-only and Teaching and Research staff by academic level.

% Female Staff (FTE)		Go8		
		2001	2019	Change
Research Only staff	Lecturer Level A	52.7%	45.8%	-6.9%
	Lecturer Level B	38.2%	46.6%	8.3%
	Senior Lecturer Level C	25.6%	44.8%	19.3%
	Associate Professor (D) + Professor (E)	13.6%	36.7%	23.1%
Teaching and Research staff	Lecturer Level A	50.7%	53.9%	3.2%
	Lecturer Level B	46.5%	52.1%	5.7%
	Senior Lecturer Level C	28.6%	43.7%	15.1%
	Associate Professor (D) + Professor (E)	14.7%	30.2%	15.6%

% Female Staff (FTE)		G9–20		
		2001	2019	Change
Research Only staff	Lecturer Level A	49.7%	47.9%	-1.8%
	Lecturer Level B	35.1%	46.8%	11.7%
	Senior Lecturer Level C	33.1%	41.8%	8.7%
	Associate Professor (D) + Professor (E)	18.9%	36.6%	17.7%
Teaching and Research staff	Lecturer Level A	54.0%	56.8%	2.8%
	Lecturer Level B	45.8%	55.4%	9.6%
	Senior Lecturer Level C	32.7%	46.0%	13.2%
	Associate Professor (D) + Professor (E)	20.1%	37.1%	17.1%

% Female Staff (FTE)		G21–42		
		2001	**2019**	**Change**
Research Only staff	Lecturer Level A	44.7%	49.8%	5.1%
	Lecturer Level B	27.7%	52.1%	24.4%
	Senior Lecturer Level C	39.6%	49.7%	10.1%
	Associate Professor (D) + Professor (E)	30.5%	34.2%	3.7%
Teaching and Research staff	Lecturer Level A	57.1%	51.5%	-5.6%
	Lecturer Level B	47.4%	56.3%	8.9%
	Senior Lecturer Level C	31.9%	47.5%	15.7%
	Associate Professor (D) + Professor (E)	20.2%	38.9%	18.7%

resources (although there is considerable variation across universities). This is little changed from the situation in 2004 when the percentage was 61 per cent. Thus, universities in Australia have for at least two decades maintained a diverse funding strategy to support the sector's contribution to research and development.

More importantly, however, the percentages of the sector's total internal expenditure on research represented by the Go8, G9–20 and G21–42 groups of universities in 2018 were 56 per cent, 31 per cent and 13 per cent respectively. Thus, the top 50 per cent of universities ranked on RBG in 2020 provided 87 per cent of total internal financial resources to support research in 2018. In the next section, we will examine the relationship between student fee income and expenditure on research.

Student fees and research

One of the more substantial sources of funds to universities over the last 20 years has been the fees paid by students for their degree programs, be they domestic or international undergraduate or postgraduate

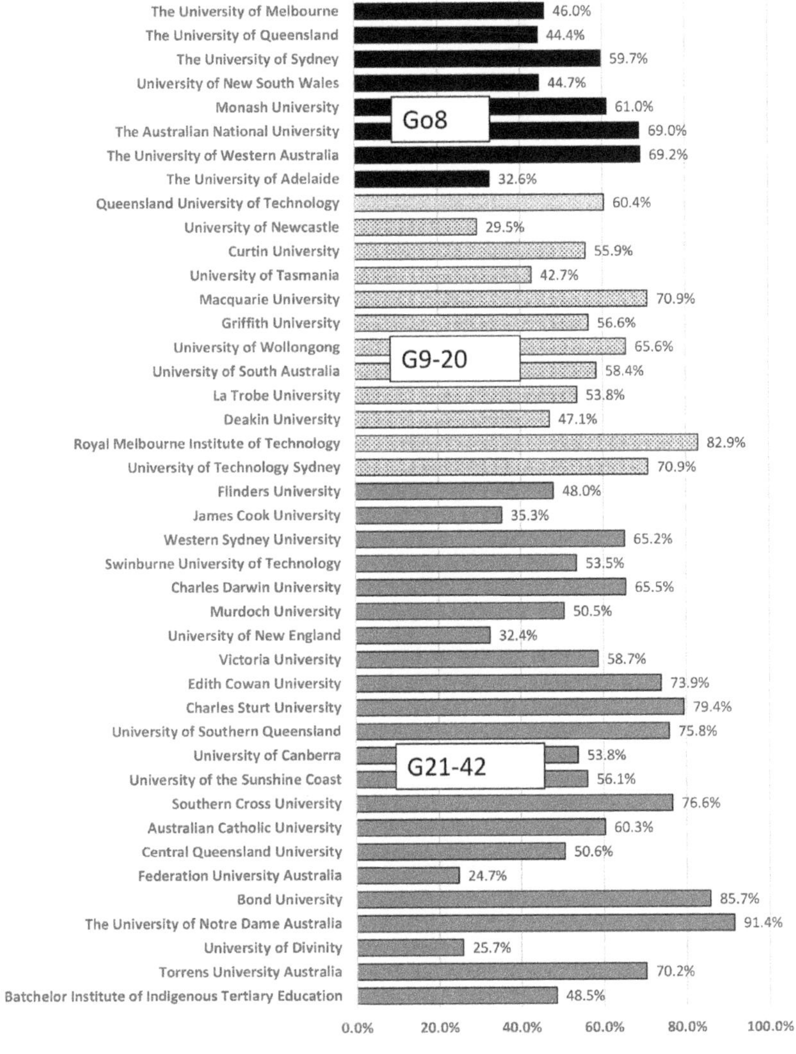

Figure 12.2 General University Funds as a percentage of total expenditure on research in 2018.

Table 12.3 Total International Student Fee Income.

International Student Fees	Go8		G9–20		G21–42	
	2000	**2019**	**2000**	**2019**	**2000**	**2019**
Total International Student Fees $B	0.35	5.15	0.38	3.06	0.21	1.77
% of Total International Student Fees	37.3	51.6	40.4	30.7	22.3	17.7

candidates. Total income received from international student fees across the sector has increased dramatically from $0.95 billion in 2000 to $9.98 billion in 2019, with two thirds of this growth occurring in the period 2012–19. The data for the three groups of universities ranked by RBG in 2020 are summarised in Table 12.3.[11] Whilst all universities have benefited from growth in international student fee income, there has been more significant growth in the Go8 universities across this period.

The relationship between the growth in international student fee income (ISFEE) and expenditure of internal General University Funds on research (GUF) over the period 2004–18 is illustrated in Figure 12.3. The dashed line in the figure shows the "line of equivalence" between these two measures and the data points represent the respective totals for each of the university groups.

For the Go8 group of universities, the data indicate that from 2004 to 2016 the equivalent of the group's total ISFEE income plus some other internally sourced funds have been allocated to internal expenditure on research. Over the same period, the relationship between ISFEE income and internal expenditure on research across both the G9–20 and G21–42 groups of universities is almost equivalent (the data points dots are close to the dashed line). In other words, all three groups of universities show a consistent relationship between increasing level of ISFEE income and internal expenditure on research.

In all three groups of universities the relationship between ISFEE income and internal General University Funds expenditure on research "flattens" after 2016. This indicates that a proportion of the increased

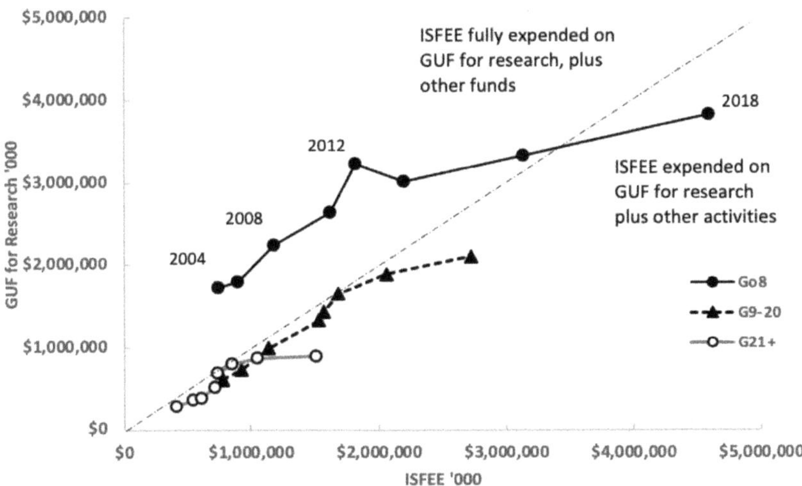

Figure 12.3 Total ISFEE vs Total GUF by group.

ISFEE income at this time has been directed to supporting other functions in addition to research. This "flattening" has occurred during the period of the steepest increase in the number of international students and ISFEE income. One interpretation of this observation is that in the period from 2004 to 2016 the numbers of international students could be absorbed into the cost structures of universities, leaving their fees available to support research. However, after 2016, extra resources were required to support the education and other support services of the rapidly increasing international student cohort.

These broad observations are based on group data and it is recognised that the circumstances at each university at each time point are different. However, the strength of the general relationship between ISFEE income and General University Funds for research is striking.

The scope and excellence of university research

Having examined some of the income and expenditure aspects of research that reveal the diversity in *scale* of activity in Australia's university sector, it is also important to consider the *scope* and quality of that research activity.

In the late 2000s, the Australian Research Council (ARC), in consultation with external advisers, government stakeholders and the universities, designed and implemented the Excellence in Research for Australia program (ERA). Under the ERA, research outputs submitted by universities are assessed by the ARC across 22 major disciplines and 158 sub-disciplines.[12]

The broad outcomes of the ERA for each of the three main rounds conducted so far at the major discipline level show that over the period 2012–18, while the number of disciplines assessed per university did not change significantly, the incidence amongst universities of disciplines assessed as being "below world standard" declined. As identified by the ARC, the quality of research across the sector as assessed by the ERA improved over the period.[13]

However, when considered against the scale of research activity as measured by the RBG, there is a clearer picture of a relationship between scale and scope of research across the sector. Thus, the number of major disciplines per university that were assessed declined with lower levels of RBG[14] and the average percentage of disciplines assessed as being below world standard increased.[15] This relationship was also apparent at the sub-discipline level, especially for the number of disciplines assessed in the G21–42 group of universities (lower scale and scope).[16] However, the incidence of discipline assessments below world standard in this group was lower than in the major discipline category.[17]

Conclusions, and looking ahead

Overall, the RBG data combined with the ERA data for the three groupings of Go8, G9–10 and G21–42 universities reveal considerable diversity across the sector. It is founded on consistent correlations between research scale – which is determined largely by success in winning external income, substantial levels of investment in research from General University Funds, numbers of research active staff and the proportion of research-only staff – and capacity to produce research of world standard or above in a wider range of disciplines.

The data on research activity presented here suggests that the often-stated notion that Australia's universities are almost uniformly comprehensive in terms of education offerings is not matched in terms of the scale or scope of their research. Questions arise for current and future governments as to the suitability of this picture for the quality and capacity of Australia's future education and research system at university level, as well as the contribution that our universities make to the broader economic, fiscal, demographic and socio-political future that we face.

Research in Australia's universities faces several threats. In current economically challenged times both universities and government research funding policies need to address these threats if Australia is to retain its current high international standing in research, as well as retain adequate sovereign research capacity and preparedness to serve the country's interests. The strong correlation between ISFEE income and General University Funds expenditure on research shows how exposed Australia's university research sector is to any reduction in international student fee income. Given the universal predominance across the sector of General University Funds expenditure on research salaries and operating costs, and the impact of COVID on international student fee income, we can expect some significant changes in staff profiles and operations that are likely to affect research output from our universities. Will governments take seriously the need to bridge the gap between current funding levels and the real costs of research? If they fail to do so, then by implication they will have shifted the burden of research funding further to fee-paying students, and if there is a continued downturn in that source of income it is research that will suffer.

Questions arise therefore as to the sustainability of the current model of funding for university research in both the short and longer term, and the alternative strategies that are required to stabilise, let alone enhance, the productivity, excellence and international profile across the breadth of Australia's university sector.

There are several current policy settings that have an impact on future levels of research activity in universities that are additional to the impact of any reduction in ISFEE income. An obvious challenge for Australia's new (2022) government will be to address stagnation in the real growth of funding for Research Block Grants and competitive research grant funding for basic and applied research across all research disciplines. This is distinct from the rapid and significant growth in funds that have been made available in recent years from the Medical Research Future Fund (MRFF) for medical and clinical research. MRFF funding is directed towards chosen priorities and is of course welcome, as is the lift in other government priority-directed funding (Category 2). However, without a broad base of fundamental and exploratory research supported through Commonwealth competitive grant funding (Category 1), outcomes from the MRFF and other categories of funding will eventually suffer.

Further, some aspects of the previous government's Job-ready Graduates Package contain implications for research that have largely been ignored in the public commentary on this reform. These include the removal of research funding from the Commonwealth Grant Scheme (CGS) base funding for domestic student enrolments, adjustments in student-related funding for discipline clusters, diversion of some Commonwealth funding for undergraduate education to encourage PhD placements in industry, and removal of the safety-net provisions in the RBG allocations since the changes following the Watt Review of the RBG system were implemented in 2017.[18]

If these settings continue, university leaders will be challenged on how best to ensure adequate research and innovation across the disciplines they regard as essential to their mission and purpose as a university. Care will be required in balancing available resources between the two fundamentals of quality education and quality research.

The uncertainty of the financial position faced by universities today prompts consideration now of the potential future long-term scale and scope of both education and research in our universities. What options are there to address the issues of diversity in discipline strength and scale of research activity and performance across a university sector that is both widely dispersed geographically and universally under challenge? The imperative is to understand and view the current sector as a whole-of-Australia asset and make a unified plan for its future.

Notes

1 See Department of Education, Skills and Employment (2015). *Review of Research Policy and Funding Arrangements – Report November 2015*, https://bit.ly/3IBzwQd.
2 Data from https://www.dese.gov.au/research-block-grants. The analysis reported here was completed on data available up to the time of writing in 2021. RBG and related data for later years is currently being analysed.
3 Data from https://www.dese.gov.au/research-block-grants/higher-education-research-data-collection-herdc.
4 Data from https://www.dese.gov.au/research-block-grants/resources/hdr-completions-time-series.
5 An alternative method would be to adopt the common lobby group distinctions – Go8, IRU, ITN, RUN and non-aligned. However, the relative performance in RBG outcomes across each of these groups is more variable.
6 The difference in timing in the columns is related to the lag in data used to determine the RBG.
7 Data from https://www.dese.gov.au/higher-education-statistics/ucube-higher-education-data-cube.
8 The ratio for the Batchelor Institute of Indigenous Tertiary Education is an outlier in this group with a ratio of 3.00 and was excluded from the average of the group G21–42 group.
9 Data from https://www.dese.gov.au/research-block-grants/resources/higher-education-expenditure-rd-herd-university.
10 HERD data are reported every two years and the most recent available data as at May 2022 covers the period 2004 to 2018.
11 Data are from https://www.dese.gov.au/higher-education-publications/finance-publication/2008-2019-finance-publications-and-tables.
12 See https://www.arc.gov.au/excellence-research-australia.
13 See https://www.arc.gov.au/ERA/NationalReport/2018/pages/content/ceo-foreword.
14 Maximum is 22; averages for the three ranked groups of universities are Go8 = 21.5; G9–20 = 19.3; G21–42 = 13.7.
15 Go8 = 0.6%, G9–20 = 5.1%, G21–42 = 40.5%.
16 Maximum is 158; Go8 = 87.0, G9–20 = 57.7, G21–42 = 28.1.
17 Go8 = 0.4%, G9–20 = 4.6%, G21–42 = 23.1%.
18 Department of Education, Skills and Employment (2015) Review of Research Policy and Funding Arrangements, https://bit.ly/3IBzwQd. The safety-net provision was that no university would receive less than 95 per cent of its RBG in the previous year; the provision was originally for three years to 2019 but was extended to the allocation in 2021 due to COVID-19, except for the additional Research Support Program funding allocated in that year.

Part 4

Revisiting the public good

13

Let us have more scientists, and more humanists

Michael A. Goodman

> As parents we clamour more and more that our sons and daughters shall be taught things at school which will enable them to earn money after they have left school, and nothing else. Again, I say plainly that that is a pitiful conception of education.
>
> Robert Menzies, Opposition Leader,
> House of Representatives, Parliament of Australia, 1945.[1]

> Our nation has faced adversity before and we have risen to the challenge – we have done so by looking after each other and backing ourselves … It's common sense. If Australia needs more educators, more health professionals and more engineers then we should incentivise students to pursue those careers … When Australia was rebuilding after World War II, then Prime Minister, Sir Robert Menzies, recognised the important role of universities in educating Australians to power our economic recovery.
>
> Dan Tehan, Minister for Education,
> National Press Club address, 19 June 2020.[2]

Former Australian Minister for Education Dan Tehan's statement in 2020 launched a new federal education policy for Australia. The aim of this policy was to reduce university costs for students undertaking courses thought to "educate the next generation of Australians to get a job".[3]

To pay for these reductions, university fees for study in disciplines not considered essential to the nation, notably in the humanities, would be raised. Whether this policy was designed to encourage students to enrol in "job-ready" courses or dissuade students from entering into humanities disciplines, it certainly has the potential to accomplish the latter.[4] In the midst of the COVID-19 pandemic, the announcement of these new policies was met with widespread alarm, particularly among university academics, scholars and administrators.[5] Set in a larger history, however, Tehan's argument for prioritising specific occupational categories highlights a longstanding conflict between the idea of the university as an institution generally protected from government or other interference, especially regarding disciplinary offerings, and the responsibility of higher education to the economic wellbeing of the nation.[6] These seemingly disparate notions, between institutional autonomy and the demands upon institutions to contribute to the national welfare, are often pitted against each other; and often appear most in opposition during periods of significant economic disruption and social transformation.[7] Both conceptions have been claimed to be essential public goods that must be guarded and promoted by national governments. This chapter takes an historical viewpoint to examine federal government interventions into universities as acts in support of the national welfare. I examine two pivotal – and historically connected – examples of such interventions in mid-20th century Australia, both appealing to urgent national needs. The first was during the Second World War and involved the then federal Labor government's intrusion into university independence to meet wartime "manpower" demand. The second, in the 1950s, was the federal Liberal government's policy to significantly expand the university system following the recommendations of the 1957 *Report of the Committee on Australian Universities*.

The university problem

The roots of Australian Commonwealth funding for universities can be located in the provisional measures to prioritise specific fields of study to meet immediate wartime requirements. On 19 January 1942, in the midst of the Second World War, John J. Dedman, the Labor government's Minister for War Organisation of Industry, called a conference between his department and Australian universities. In his opening remarks, Dedman observed that "the problem of University policy as viewed by the government is a much broader one than that of adjusting the Universities to the calling up of men for service with armed forces".[8] The "problem" was that universities were not devoting enough of their resources to the war, at least not in the way the wartime government thought best.

At the conference held at the University of Melbourne, Dedman told those in attendance, including the Australian Vice-Chancellors' Committee members as well as representatives from the Department of War, the Army, the Technical Training Division of the Department of Labour and National Service, and the Man Power Priorities Board, that in a time of war no institution could remain "sheltered". All must be willing to act, and adapt, to serve the needs of the nation. He continued:

> It is not necessary for me to spend any time in emphasising the great danger in which Australia stands at the present time … the present situation demands the reorganisation of our whole national life; and that no section of the community, and no institution, however sheltered it may have been in the past, can stand aside, and avoid sharing in these changes… That goes for industry; for commerce, for scientific research, and for education; and I am sure that Universities recognise that it is their new tasks and new responsibilities, rather than their old privileges, that count.[9]

Universities "must be willing to do untraditional things", Dedman announced.[10] The core tenets of university independence, the "old privileges", must be suspended.[11] Nothing was sacred in a time of war, Dedman insisted; all parts of the country must participate to meet these "essential" needs of the nation.[12] To address this, he called upon universities to make significant changes, including: altering the composition and management of research activities to meet wartime demands; changing the courses of study offered; and, most critically, adopting new entry requirements and placing restrictions on the number of students enrolling in selected courses of study. This last item was already a significant issue in 1942. The government had previously established "reserved" courses that protected some students from being called up into service while in the midst of their studies at university.[13] These selected courses were considered essential to the wartime effort – they included: physics, chemistry, dentistry, medicine, metallurgy, engineering, bacteriology, biochemistry, geology, botany and agriculture.

An unintended consequence of this new policy, however, was the government's understanding that a far larger number of students enrolled in the reserved courses in order to avoid military service, using these courses as "havens of refuge" and thus overwhelming universities' resources to meet increased demand.[14] Responding to this perception, the government created quotas for the reserved courses based on merit – although the interpretation of merit was defined by individual universities. This quota system was formally established through the National Security Act, Production Executive Minute dated 29 January 1942, known as Regulation 16.[15] This decree, however, generated new problems for universities and brought into question the extent of the constitutional powers of the Commonwealth to intervene in university affairs. According to the Australian Constitution, education is the responsibility of individual states (with the exception of the Australian Capital Territory). In order to establish the quota system, the wartime government had largely relied on a broad interpretation of Section 96 of the Australian Constitution which allows for the Commonwealth to direct funding, with "terms and conditions", to the states.[16]

These restrictions on courses provoked a legal challenge that made its way up to the High Court of Australia. In the 1943 decision for *The King against the University of Sydney*, the court ruled against the Commonwealth's ability to regulate admission to specific university courses. Even given the expansive wartime powers of the government, the course quotas went beyond what the High Court deemed to be constitutional and so declared Regulation 16 invalid.[17] Justice George Rich's opinion in support of the decision was far-reaching:

> [I]t is outside the power of the Commonwealth Parliament to exercise general control of education in the schools or universities

> of Australia, prescribe what children, and how many of them, shall attend the schools, the method of qualification for entrance, regulate the number of students entitled to matriculate, discriminate between faculties and restrict the number of students to be admitted to or enrolled in any faculty, determine the course of study and curricula in the various faculties of the universities, the nature and subjects of examinations, and set the standards for passing the examinations.[18]

The court's decision highlights the difference between national good, what the Commonwealth government considered a priority for the nation's needs – in this case, training essential to the war efforts – and the public good, the constitutional separation of powers that deemed education as best guided by the states. The High Court determined that the rights of the Australian states to determine their own educational priorities outweighed the Commonwealth government's claim that higher education was a national concern.

While the government sought to find ways to work around the High Court's decision through incentive-based scholarships and other measures, the end of the war made the argument for the Commonwealth's power to control university admissions no longer pertinent. Dedman announced that "after the cessation of hostilities" the government would end its policies to manage enrolment and course selection. Nonetheless, tertiary education in Australia would not return to being exclusively a concern of the states as it was before the war.

Grasping the important role universities would play in postwar reconstruction in the training and research required as part of its vision for Australia's role in the new global economy, the federal Labor government retained much of the institutional infrastructure connected to its wartime higher-educational efforts. On 26 July 1945, only weeks away from the official end to the war, Dedman, now Minister for Postwar Reconstruction, announced the government's postwar policy for higher education in Australia: it retained the recently established Universities Commission, set up the Commonwealth Office of Education which would house the Commission, and committed to the establishment of the Australian National University in Canberra.[19] Commonwealth grants would continue to go to universities, at least in the short term, for facilities and other expenses to support the Commonwealth Reconstruction Training Scheme, an initiative to assist the repatriation of servicemen and women by financially supported opportunities to retrain. The scheme also included a significant investment in the university education of returned personnel.

Supply and demand

Even so, the federal government's expansion into higher education provision was still limited. Universities and state governments were lobbying for far greater Commonwealth financial support for the underfunded and overstretched universities in this postwar period – although there were also concerns at the time that new funding would come with increased scrutiny and could give the federal government greater leverage to intervene in university matters.[20] In 1957, under the leadership of the Menzies Liberal government, the recommendations of the *Report of the Committee on Australian Universities*, commonly referred to as the Murray Report after its chairman, Sir Keith Murray, would radically rewrite the higher education system throughout Australia.[21] One of the Murray Committee's central goals was to respond to the pressing national need for greater tertiary technological education – citing the severe shortage of graduates in meeting industrial demand. This need was considered as a national good, for the good of the Australian economy. The report noted, for example, that in Melbourne alone the industrial demand in 1956 for graduates in engineering, chemistry and physics "exceeded by nine to fifteen times the supply".[22]

By the mid-1950s, there was widespread concern that Australia was falling far behind when compared to the growth in science and technology education in the USA, UK and Soviet Union.[23] Leaving the choice of study up to students, the committee contended, was not working to meet the current needs of industry: "there is little sign that a greater proportion of the able young men of to-day are turning towards the pure and applied sciences in the choice of their careers than was the case in the generation before the war".[24] The responsibility for solving this problem, the committee continued, rested with the government and Australian universities, amongst other institutions:

> It is difficult to resist the conclusions that some such diversion in the flow of talent is necessary, and that steps ought to be taken to present to the public, and not least boys and girls in the schools, as true a picture as is possible of what the future holds in store for Australia. We believe that active steps to do this should be taken without avoidable delay by governments, universities, industries and schools.[25]

The Murray Report decisively highlighted the role of technology for Australia's future, noting the "vital importance of science and technology to the life and progress not only of industry but of the nation". However, this was not to be at the expense of humanities. Even with the explicit priority for technological education, and the need for a "diversion in the flow of talent", which might sound familiar today, the authors of the Murray Report also maintained that there must be a role for the humanities. These were not mutually exclusive efforts. Wartime had highlighted the importance of technology for the postwar world economy, but wartime and fear of fascism (and later communism) had also highlighted the importance of a broadly educated and critical citizenship. The Murray Committee were explicit in connecting these two priorities:

> It has been becoming more and more clearly, and widely, recognised of recent years that the world simply cannot afford that its highly specialised professional men, technologists and scientists should not also be fully educated as rounded human beings … Many of the most serious problems in the world to-day are moral problems and are problems of human relationships. The need for the study of humanities is therefore greater and not less than in the past.[26]

The Murray Committee in their recommendations attempted to align the national good with the public good – the economic future of the nation with the societal.

Although throughout the Murray Report, the Murray Committee refers to both "men and women" when referring to potential university students and the future Australian workforce, it is important to note that in prioritising technical education, the Australian government was prioritising occupations that were dominated at the time by men. The Australian 1961 Census enumerates this disparity in technical and professional occupations. For example, the Census category of "Architects, Engineers and Surveyors" lists 29,776 Males and 170 Females.[27] Under the category "Chemists, Physicists, Geologists and Other Physical Scientists" are totalled 8,014 Males, 637 Females.[28] And for "Biologists, Veterinarians, Agronomists and Related Scientists", the results are 3,955 males, 342 females.[29] To add further context, the total number of men and women enrolled in Australian universities in 1961 was more than three to one, 44,264 men and 13,408 women.[30] Even with almost twice as many men in the workforce as women at the time, greater support of technical education would predominantly serve Australian men. More women, however, were entering into higher education, steadily increasing throughout the post-Murray Report years.[31]

Without fear or favour

In his introduction to the 1957 bill that would enact the recommendations of the Murray Report, Prime Minister Menzies further underscored the value that the humanities had as part of the new attention to the role of universities for Australia. Speaking to the House of Representatives, Menzies stated:

> I hope that we will not, under current pressures of emotions, be tempted to ignore the basic fact that civilisation in the true sense requires a close and growing attention, not only to science in all its branches, but also to those studies of the mind and spirit of man, of history and literature and language and mental and moral philosophy, of human relations in society and industry, of international understanding, the relative neglect of which has left a gruesome mark on this century. Let us have more scientists, and

> more humanists. Let the scientists be touched and informed by the humanities. Let the humanists be touched and informed by science.[32]

The "gruesome mark on this century", as Menzies put it, was war. The cautionary tale of the rise of German fascism, as many had attributed at least in part, was that an over-reliance on technocrats had helped to foster the Nazi rise to power. Menzies was warning the parliament that too great a reliance on science and technology at the expense of "studies of the mind and spirit of man" was not the path forward for Australia.[33] The important role of university in teaching liberal values through the humanities was also of a piece with another argument for the importance of academic and university independence.[34]

The humanities in this period were understood and expected to accomplish a variety of functions. As normative disciplines, their inclusion was considered as especially needed amongst concerns for the resulting societal ills of technological advancement, which in itself was considered as lacking any inherent normative values, being a potential for good or evil. The humanities were also defined by their role in "preserving culture", at a time when many considered cultural fragmentation as a threat to social cohesion.[35] And, lastly, and as a combination of these expectations, the humanities, as well as the social sciences, were understood as essential to good citizenship – in the understanding and teaching of skills and knowledge for a healthy democracy.[36]

The Murray Committee made clear from the outset its understanding that universities could not function as they were meant to without retaining a core tenet of the idea of the university – "the unchangeable value in their work and nature", university independence.[37] "Even in time of war and national danger", they stated in the report, Western nations were attempting to uphold the essential liberal nature of the university: "the right and duty of the universities to pursue new knowledge without fear or favour and to educate in a liberal spirit and with integrity; and even in times of economic depression they have shown increasing signs of seeking to maintain the life and work of universities in full vigour".[38] The Murray Committee argued that society needed "good" universities, operating without their "essential liberal nature" being altered: "Both governments and the public have come to be aware that the national community of our age cannot flourish without good universities."[39] This was the "function of the university" as the Murray Committee understood it, one in which the public good they provide is understood beyond the instructional value of specific disciplines. To sever or significantly alter these institutional components, even considering the importance of technical training for Australia, the report determined, would come at a significant cost to the nation:

> The technical and specialist requirements are without doubt in themselves no less than a matter of life and death to the nation; but they are not the end of the affair. It is the function of the university to offer not merely a technical or specialist training but a full and true education, befitting a free man, and, the citizen of a free country.[40]

The Murray Report marked for Menzies a moment of recognition for the essential place of universities for the new Australia. Education, including university education, was the key to the political, social and economic future of the nation. A future that should include, according to Menzies, more than solely material success:

> We must, on a broad basis, become a more and more educated democracy if we are to raise our spiritual, intellectual, and material living standards. Viewed in this way, our universities are to be regarded not as a home of privilege for a few, but as something essential to the lives of millions of people who may never enter their doors.[41]

A zero-sum game

Minister Tehan, in announcing his government's new policies to prioritise "the jobs that will be in demand in the future", recalled that this was not such a radical departure for a Commonwealth government.[42] Former Prime Minister Menzies, he stated, had also "recognised the important role of universities in educating Australians to power our economic recovery".[43] Certainly Menzies' adoption of the Murray Report's recommendations almost as a whole demonstrated his commitment to Australian universities and the importance of, as he put it in his invitation to Sir Keith Murray to chair his committee, the "economic development of the nation".[44] By strategically reframing Menzies' commitment to the importance of universities for Australia's economic future – omitting his corresponding commitment to the liberal notions of the university – Tehan's statement was meant to convey that there was a long-held acceptance that universities should primarily be in service to the Australian economy. This ignores the other role that Menzies assigned to Keith Murray – to report on how universities must "serve" Australia to further the nation's "social development" alongside its economic development.[45]

The mid-20th century interventions by governments into the realm of universities discussed in this chapter demonstrate the broadly changing role of universities in the 20th century – especially underscoring new responsibilities assigned to universities during times of economic and social disruption. These interventions also highlight the specific ways that governments sought to define the university's institutional boundaries. By insisting on the value of the teaching of the humanities in Australian universities combined with a significant focus on technological education, Menzies and the Murray Committee did not simply reproduce a key idea of the university but tried actively to *shape* it, to apply it to present needs. The intervention called for by Murray, in turn, was made possible by how the federal government had brought tertiary education within its ambit as a response to wartime and new national needs.

Tehan's strategic evocation of Menzies in 2020 failed to recognise Menzies' involvement in the development of the "dual purpose" institution.[46] The pressure to increase more instrumental training at universities is understood by some as a zero-sum game in which the liberal, often represented by the humanities, should be sacrificed to the more immediate economic needs (as they understood them) of the nation. However, Menzies had desired an idea of the university that would contain both notions, "more scientists and more humanists", for the good of an Australia that required more than merely economic gain.

This idea, it was hoped, would contain both concepts of the public good – the good brought about by safeguarding the liberal nature of universities and the societal good fostered by the work of humanist scholarship; combined with the more tangible good of the economic results brought about by an increased and better trained workforce. Tehan, on the other hand, in establishing new policies favouring "educating Australians for the jobs that will be in demand in the future", at the expense of the humanities, wanted to engage in this zero-sum game with universities, one with winners and losers.[47] Unless the humanities, the independence of universities, and the liberal ideal of the university are protected, as the Murray Committee had endeavoured to do, the humanities will not survive this contest.

Notes

1 Commonwealth, Parliamentary Debates, House of Representatives, 26 July 1945, 4616–4617.
2 Tehan, Dan (2020). "Minister for Education Dan Tehan National Press Club address," speech delivered 19 June 2020, https://bit.ly/3yHnd0r.
3 Tehan, "Press Club Address".
4 In the short time in which this policy has been initiated, it seems that student preferences are a more important factor in course selection than the degree costs. Data collected by the Universities Admissions Centre shows no significant change in year 12 first-preferences to the "Society and Culture" fields of study for their undergraduate course. https://bit.ly/3RBtrr3.
5 Baker, Nick and Matt Connellan (2020). Shock and dismay over 'short-sighted' policy that will double the cost of arts degrees. *SBS News*, 19 June. https://bit.ly/3RCYGlw; Khadem, Nassim (2020). Government's university fee changes mean humanities students will pay the entire cost of their degrees. *ABC News*, 20 June. https://ab.co/3RF9pwa.
6 Cardinal John Newman's *The idea of a university* presented a similar case in 1853. Newman, John Henry (1919). *The idea of a university: defined and illustrated*. New York: Longmans, Green and Co., 167.
7 Grant Harmon described this struggle between "accountability and autonomy" as an "inherent tension in the relationship between higher education and government". Harmon, Grant (1983). The erosion of university independence: recent Australian experience. *Higher Education* 12(5): 502–03.
8 National Archives of Australia: Commonwealth Office of Education, Central Office; A1361, ID 202479 1/17/17 PART 1, 1 "The Conference between the Department of War Organisation of Industry and The Universities".

9 National Archives of Australia, "The Conference between the Department of War Organisation of Industry and The Universities," 2.
10 National Archives of Australia, "The Conference between the Department of War Organisation of Industry and The Universities," 3.
11 National Archives of Australia, "The Conference between the Department of War Organisation of Industry and The Universities," 3.
12 National Archives of Australia, "The Conference between the Department of War Organisation of Industry and The Universities," 2.
13 National Archives of Australia: Commonwealth Office of Education, Central Office; A1361, ID 202479 1/17/17 PART 1, 2 "Control of Universities", undated, approximately early 1942.
14 National Archives of Australia: Commonwealth Office of Education, Central Office; A1361, ID 202479, "Production Executive Minute", Canberra, 24 September 1942, Decision No. 137, Agendum No. 105/1942.
15 National Archives of Australia: Commonwealth Office of Education, Central Office; National Security Act, A1361, ID 202479 1/17/17 PART 1, 1 "Production Executive Minute", 29 January 1942, Decision No. 11, Agendum No. 2/1942.
16 Section 96 of the Australian Constitution is generally referred to as being so capacious as to give constitutional licence to allow the Commonwealth the broad power to fund universities. It states: "During a period of ten years after the establishment of the Commonwealth and thereafter until the Parliament otherwise provides, the Parliament may grant financial assistance to any State on such terms and conditions as the Parliament thinks fit." *Commonwealth of Australia Constitution*, s 96.
17 *The King v University of Sydney; Ex parte Drummond* ((1943) 67 CLR 95 at 105).
18 *The King v University of Sydney*. The ruling placed a limit on interpretation of Section 96 powers of the Australian Constitution.
19 "This scheme for granting financial assistance to students has been administered by the Universities Commission, which was set up under National Security Regulations. The government has decided to introduce legislation to provide for a continuance of that commission, and that legislation will give to it a much more permanent status than it has at present." Dedman, *Debates*, House of Representatives, 26 July 1945, 4627.
20 Australian Vice-Chancellors' Committee (1952). *A crisis in the finances and development of the Australian universities*. Melbourne: Melbourne University Press.
21 With the implementation of the Murray Report recommendations, Australia went from nearly 0 per cent (there was funding going through CSIRO for research grants) of university income coming from the Commonwealth in 1939 to 43.9 per cent by 1961. The peak of Commonwealth funding was reached in 1981 with 89.3 per cent of university income coming from the Commonwealth; by 2014 this was down to 41 per cent. Department of Employment, Education and Training, Higher Education Division (1993).

National report on Australia's higher education sector. Canberra: Australian Government Publishing Service, 75; Department of Education and Training (2015). *Higher Education Funding in Australia*. Canberra: Department of Education and Training, 7.

22 Murray, Keith, Ian Clunies Ross, Charles R. Morris, Alex Reid, and J. C. Richards (1957) *Report of the Committee on Australian Universities* [Murray Report], Canberra: Government Printer, 18.

23 Murray Report, 8 and 17. With the launch of the first artificial satellite in October 1957, the Soviet Union would shift the focus on science education dramatically just a few weeks after the Murray Report was submitted. Menzies, however, would remain resolute in his belief that the humanities not be sacrificed to increased support towards science and technology education. Clark, Jennifer (2017). In the shadow of sputnik: a transnational approach to Menzies' support for science education in Australia, 1957–1964. *Paedagogica Historica* 53(5): 623–39.

24 Murray Report, 28.

25 Murray Report, 28.

26 Murray Report, 8–9.

27 Australian Bureau of Statistics (1961). *Census Bulletin No. 32, Occupations of the Population, Australia, States and Territories*, 30 June 1961.

28 Australian Bureau of Statistics, *Census Bulletin No. 32*.

29 Australian Bureau of Statistics, *Census Bulletin No. 32*. Note, all of these data are listed with the phrase "Exclusive of full-blood Aboriginals", this is a reference to Section 127 of the Australian Constitution, "In reckoning the numbers of the people of the Commonwealth, or of a State or other part of the Commonwealth, aboriginal natives shall not be counted," which was repealed by the 1967 Australian Referendum. "The 1967 Referendum", National Library of Australia, https://www.nla.gov.au/research-guides/the-1967-referendum.

30 Department of Education, Training and Youth Affairs, *Higher Education Students Time Series Tables*, Selected Higher Education Statistics, 2000, Commonwealth of Australia 2001, 6.

31 The number of women listed as "full-time" students enrolled in higher education institutions in Australia would finally equal, then surpass men in 1986. Department of Education, Training and Youth Affairs, *Higher Education Students Time Series Tables*, 6–7.

32 "Universities Committee Report", *Debates*, House of Representatives, 28 November 1945, 2696.

33 For example, see Spaeth, J. Duncan (1944). The humanities in peace and war. *Bulletin of the American Association of University Professors* 30(4): 581–88; Neureiter, Paul R. (1934). Hitlerism and the German universities. *Journal of Higher Education* 5(5): 510–16.

34 Murray Report, 11.

35 Hollinger, David A. ed. (2006). *The humanities and the dynamics of inclusion since World War II*. Baltimore, MD: Johns Hopkins University Press.

36 Small, Helen (2013). *The value of the humanities*. Oxford: Oxford University Press.
37 Murray Report, 7.
38 Murray Report, 7.
39 Murray Report, 7.
40 Murray Report, 8.
41 Commonwealth, Parliamentary Debates, House of Representatives, "Universities Committee Report", 28 November 1957, 2701, https://bit.ly/3IDb3u3.
42 Tehan, "Press Club Address".
43 Tehan, "Press Club Address".
44 Murray Report, 127, Appendix A.
45 Murray Report, 127, Appendix A.
46 Murray Report, 79. I use this term differently than in the Murray Report that critiqued this notion of the "dual purpose" institution, one which attempted to combine the more basic training of "craftsmen and technicians" with the more advanced training, as they saw it, of "professional engineers and technologists". The Murray Committee was specifically referring to the recently established New South Wales University of Technology, which they considered would suffer under this problematic combination of interests.
47 Tehan, "Press Club Address".

14

Building a university culture fit for purpose

Tim Soutphommasane and Stephanie Wood

"Culture eats strategy for breakfast." Often attributed to the management guru Peter Drucker, the quote has become axiomatic. Few would dispute that success depends as much on the quality of the people in an organisation as it does on its strategy. Even the most compelling or cunning strategy will fail if the people involved are not up to executing it. An organisation's strategic plans can unravel if its culture is not fit for purpose.

In one sense, there should be little cause to find this confounding or even curious. Drucker's original insight has been perhaps misunderstood over the years, coming to signify an essential incompatibility between culture and strategy. Yet, within successful organisations, culture and strategy – far from existing in conflict – reinforce one another. Understood in this way, culture reaches well beyond the usual concerns of human resources departments; it is not confined to the realm of diversity, equity and inclusion, important though those matters are. Rather, culture sits at the heart of performance and success. A good culture injects into people a sense of trust and collective purpose: it says something about who a group of people are, how they conduct themselves, and what motivates them.

How exactly, though, have such ideas translated into a university setting? In this chapter, we reflect on the meaning of institutional culture and the public purpose of universities. We then consider efforts in building an institutional culture at the University of Sydney. Whereas in the past, a sense of mission in the place has been implicit and local – embedded in the practice of doing academic work, and in the membership of a disciplinary community of scholarship – the development of a Culture Strategy at the University of Sydney has reflected the contemporary need for a renewed sense of mission and purpose within a large, public university. As we argue, this imperative highlights a challenge for universities at large, given the role they must play in the public conversation. At a time when the very mission of Australian universities is being scrutinised and contested, what kind of culture does a public university need in order to be fit for purpose?

What is institutional culture?

We speak about culture in a very particular sense. We are not referring to an ethnic, societal or national culture, the kind of culture typically studied by anthropologists, sociologists, historians and philosophers. Culture, as we discuss it, is not referring to "a whole way of life" or "societal culture" that covers a comprehensive range of human activities.[1] Rather, we are referring to organisational or institutional culture. By this we mean the habitual way that groups behave within an organisation or institution. As Schein and Schein explain, culture in this sense means "the accumulated shared learning" of a group as it "solves its problems of external adaptation and internal integration". It describes a pattern of beliefs, values and norms that are treated as "the correct way to perceive, think, feel, and behave in relation to those problems".[2]

Understood this way, we can point to an institutional culture along the following lines. It can be observed through the social interactions between people when they go about their work, or the formal rituals or customs that mark certain events or milestones. It is also expressed through publicly announced values and principles that guide an organisation's actions, and through the self-image and symbols that define an organisation's identity. It is there, too, in the implicit or unspoken rules that determine how people must get along in an organisation. Taken together, these respectively reflect what has been described as the three levels of institutional culture: artifacts (visible structures and processes, and observed behaviour), espoused beliefs and values (aspirations and ideologies), and basic underlying assumptions (unconscious beliefs, often taken for granted, that determine behaviour and feeling).[3]

The culture of most, if not all, organisations is shaped by their history. An organisation's beliefs, values and behaviours often reflect what contributed to its success at its inception. They also help give it meaning in the present: they are the components that provide an organisation with a sense of depth and stability. Moreover, they cover all aspects of a group's activities and functioning. Contrary to some framings of culture – namely, those that present culture as merely relating to the internal dynamics of a group – an institutional culture, properly understood, covers aspects including strategy, structure and operations. Perhaps most significantly of all, an institutional culture is fundamentally tied to its sense of mission or purpose. Put another way: *how* an organisation does things flows on from *why* it exists.[4]

As organisations, Australian universities come in many forms, each reflecting certain histories and circumstances. Yet all our universities – and arguably all their institutional cultures – share, to some degree, a particular sense of mission, drawn from a certain model of the modern Western university. One thinks here of Cardinal Newman's "idea of a university", which he described as "a place of teaching universal knowledge", free from doctrinal authority.[5] Or the cultural image of universities as institutions of academic freedom, where scholars perform research and experimentation. Within this inherited tradition, the work of universities is one defined by the pursuit of truth and knowledge, and the empowerment of the minds of students.

Yet to what extent does such a story about purpose still resonate? If it still does, it has perhaps been given some modern updating, at least if we look at how university cultures are being given explicit expression. Such modern statements have gone beyond the historical mottos Australian universities have adopted, whether that is to seek truth or wisdom, to know the nature of things, or to cultivate heart and mind. At the University of Sydney, for example, the work of teaching and research has in recent years come to be often described in terms of "leadership for good". In its current strategy, the Australian National

University states an institutional intention to provide the "intellectual leadership and moral courage" to overcome threats to the very fabric of our democracy, strengthen our national mission and meet its unique responsibilities as an institution established with the nation-building purpose of putting education and research at the service of national prosperity and peaceful global development.[6] Meanwhile, King's College London has positioned itself as a university whose goal is to make "the world a better place, going above and beyond what is expected of a university".[7]

The institutional culture of universities, you might say, appears to be showing signs of being defined more and more by a sense of outward-looking purpose concerned with serving the public good. But perhaps they are still just that: merely signs, as opposed to a definitive shift. The idea of culture remains more narrowly defined within universities' thinking than suggested above. For example, while many Australian universities mention institutional culture in their strategic documents (incorporating statements about cultural aspirations and values), they primarily do so in the context of equity, diversity and inclusion. And while some universities have established Deputy Vice-Chancellors or Pro Vice-Chancellors responsible for equity, diversity and inclusion, or Indigenous strategy, none have taken similar steps around "culture". Typically, "culture" remains the remit of Human Resources and Operations portfolios and concerned with internal workplace culture, rather than the remit of senior academic leaders and directed at more strategic concerns.

Public purpose

Any definitive shift towards a more outward-looking institutional culture, underpinned by a sharpened public mission, is also complicated by another factor: the "cultural DNA" of Australian universities themselves. The institutional purposes of Australian universities have arguably been characterised by some measure of complexity, if not tension. While inheritors of a Western tradition of scholarship defined by truth and knowledge, Australian universities have also developed along their own particular path. "The unworldly university", as Glyn Davis observes, "has always been rare".[8] Our universities have been geared towards training students for the professions; our tradition has been more vocational than intellectual. Even so, any pragmatism has still been accompanied by a historical notion of the "liberal arts"; the Australian concept of a university has always been underpinned by a civilising public purpose. In 1957, the Murray Report, regarded by some as the founding document for the modern Australian university, stated:

> No nation in its senses wishes to make itself prone to self-delusion, or to deceit by other nations; and a good university is the best guarantee that mankind can have that somebody, whatever the circumstances, will continue to seek the truth and to make it known. Any free country welcomes this and expects this service of its universities.[9]

In more recent times, the civic dimension of Australian universities has grown more ambivalent. What Davis described as the "pragmatic" cast of universities' mission has perhaps evolved to grow more synonymous with the market. It is there, for example, in the language that has come to dominate higher education. Maybe it's inevitable as our universities have grown larger in size and more complex. Maybe it's to do with the growing reliance of the sector on international student revenue (inextricably linked, of course, with declining government funding). But, as reflected in how people refer to a university degree as a "product", to students as "customers", or to vice-chancellors as "CEOs", something has shifted in the way that we think about universities.[10] Universities have become more business-like, in both their operation and governance. Critics say it has everything to do with corporate capture, characterised by more focus on short-term performance, increasing salary gaps between senior management and university employees. Our universities, the largest of which have annual revenues similar to a publicly listed company in the ASX100, are increasingly being judged as though they are corporations.

Moreover, within the public discourse itself, universities are being redefined. It was once the case that political leaders, whatever their political stripe, would speak in civic terms about the role of universities.

Liberal Prime Minister Robert Menzies argued that universities should not be "mere technical schools", but should include "the preservation of pure learning, bringing in its train not merely riches for the imagination but a comparative sense for the mind, and leading to what we need so badly – the recognition of values which are other than pecuniary".[11] Gough Whitlam, whose Labor government abolished tuition fees for tertiary education, saw universities as engines for social mobility: "we believe that a student's merit rather than a parent's wealth should decide who should benefit from the community's vast financial commitment to tertiary education".[12]

Today, however, the university is being increasingly reduced to an instrument of the national economy. "Research commercialisation" was the declared top priority for then federal education minister Alan Tudge, who argued that universities must "interact with business and generate new ideas, new jobs, and new sources of wealth for Australia".[13] Rather than conduct research for the intrinsic advancement of knowledge, academics should be more motivated by the imperative of "translating research down the commercialisation path". According to Tudge, universities must think more about their impact, though this is primarily commercial, rather than civic in nature: "we want academics to become entrepreneurs, taking their ideas from the lab to the market". It remains to be seen what the newly elected Labor government will prioritise for the higher education sector.

To be fair, a shift from the civic to the commercial has not happened overnight; it can be traced to developments in the 1980s when reforms underlined the role of universities as drivers of economic growth and productivity.[14] The evolution of universities' mission may also reflect broader ideological shifts in society. The rise of neoliberalism, and the enthusiastic embrace of the market across all spheres of society, has made it more challenging to speak about any compelling sense of civic or public purpose. The late historian Tony Judt put it best when he observed that Western democracies suffer from a "linguistic disability".[15] We no longer know how to speak about a sense of collective purpose. And we seem to believe that economic aspiration is now the only sentiment worth appealing to. Public conversations are increasingly dictated by the needs of the market, as opposed to the needs of society.

Against such developments, it is understandable then if the mission or purpose of a university has grown ambiguous. While speaking about teaching and research, or about truth and knowledge, may still move many academic colleagues instilled in the ethos of a university, it may not have the same effect on other colleagues. Equally, it may not translate to citizens outside the university world. The noble credo of truth and knowledge might not be enough to capture the public imagination.

It is revealing, for example, that the federal government changed the rules of its 2020 JobKeeper COVID-19 stimulus subsidy three times in order to exclude public universities from claiming it – the only sector to be targeted in this way. Yet it did so without, we would argue, feeling any significant political consequence. There was no widespread public outrage, beyond the anger within the sector. The Australian public does not appreciate what universities contribute to society in the same way that they do other sectors. Not even in the midst of a pandemic when official public health responses rely on advice and vaccines grounded in science and research.

This, by no means, amounts to repudiation of universities serving a public good or civic purpose. It is only to say that any task of connecting universities' identities and cultures with a civic purpose or public good feels more urgent than ever.

And not only out of sectoral self-interest. Liberal democracies today are growing polarised. Populism and post-truth politics have disoriented our debates. Marked by profound, if not irreconcilable, disagreements that are increasingly defined by identity, liberal democracies find it hard now even to define what is common ground among their citizens. It is possible that the market may only grow more powerful in filling this civic vacuum. If anything, then, current circumstances warrant redoubled efforts within universities to articulate a public good – not a retreat from it. If liberal democracy is coming under challenge, surely universities have a fundamental role to play in defending that order.

A Culture Strategy: the case of the University of Sydney

As Australia's oldest university, the University of Sydney is associated with a certain idea of continuity. Yet it has experienced significant change during the past 30 years, change many would say has accelerated during the past decade. Its main campus on the Camperdown-Darlington fringe of Sydney's central business district, for one, looks rather different to the campus of the past, with its blend of Gothic sandstone and modern architecture.

Organisationally, too, the institution has grown to be very different. Whereas a decade ago, the university comprised 16 faculties, there are now five faculties and three university schools.[16] The central Education and Research portfolios have also been joined by others relating to Indigenous Strategy and Services, Operations, Advancement and External Relations. Once largely a collection of autonomous academic departments, over time the university has developed a stronger central identity for an institution that consists of more than 60,000 students and 8,500 staff positions.[17]

The development of a Culture Strategy reflects these changes. Introduced in the university's 2016–2020 Strategic Plan, the Culture Strategy formed one of the three strategic pillars for the university alongside research and education. It was assigned three clear goals, tied to the university's pursuit of excellence in research and education: (1) the creation of a university culture based on a set of values, (2) the development of leadership at all levels, and (3) the breaking down of institutional barriers.[18] Led by an academic director, and reporting directly to the Vice-Chancellor, the Culture Strategy focuses institutional attention on culture as a dedicated university-level strategy.

This attention reflects, in part, the cultural history of the University of Sydney. Unlike newer institutions that have emerged with a clear mission or identity, the university has a historically fragmented or decentralised character. It can be more accurate to say that there are many cultures within the university, rather than just one. Returning to the idea of institutional culture as a pattern of beliefs, values and norms learned by a group as it solved its problems of external adaptation and internal integration, we might say that the University of Sydney's culture has been a centrifugal one. The prevailing basic assumptions at the University of Sydney over time have been that an academic's discipline or department is a more decisive affiliation than the academic's membership of the university at large, often leading to perennial tensions between its faculties and "the centre".

As part of a push for a more cohesive institutional identity, the Culture Strategy has established a set of shared values that would define a culture enabling every member of the university to realise their full potential.[19] The values – codified in the four couplets of "courage and creativity", "respect and integrity", "openness and engagement" and "diversity and inclusion" – include a commitment to intellectual and ethical independence of mind, the equal treatment of colleagues, and the aspiration to orient the university outwardly towards the communities around it. The values have been embedded in leadership expectations, and measured through the annual performance review process for staff.[20] A revised Code of Conduct for staff and affiliates now contains explicit references to the values.[21] There have also been dedicated leadership development programs for emerging and established managers and leaders, as well as bespoke executive education-style workshops, which have sought to embed practices relating to excellence, collegiality and inclusion.

A values-based culture is still in the early stages of maturity. Based on a consultation exercise in early 2020, staff reported back that their ideal university culture is one defined by collaboration, multidisciplinary research, a sense of purpose and values, transparency, and altruistic support for staff, students and the community. This is an ideal not yet fully realised. While staff believed the current culture was defined by a sense of educational purpose, they also believed it was defined by history and legacy, elements of social disconnection, and political and bureaucratic complexity. Many believed that existing hierarchies and structures did not always encourage creativity and innovation, especially when work cannot be contained within traditional academic or administrative boundaries. Staff also identified that they desired more behavioural guidance on the university's values – that is, on how the university community could "live" its espoused values.

These different elements of the cultural aspirations of staff, in turn, reflect how the work of institutional culture-building must be multidimensional. It is not only about how people must conduct themselves, but also how people think of who they are and why it is that they conduct their work. Put another way, institutional culture-building is about values, people and purpose.

Returning to our earlier reflections, the ideas of "service" and the "public good" have been especially powerful in getting people to reflect on how they model their values and collegiality, and the purpose behind their work. Often this latter task has challenged academics to think beyond the usual strictures of "teaching and research", and to tell a bigger story about how their endeavours connect with society. For example, during the course of COVID-19, as part of the Culture Strategy, colleagues were invited to speak about how their work contributes to community responses to the pandemic, whether that is connected to work within the Faculty of Medicine and Health or elsewhere.

Such a focus on culture and purpose could easily be regarded as a soft exercise relating to morale – or, in the language of human resources, "staff engagement". Yet we would contend a cultural sense of mission is paramount. The most successful organisations are frequently those imbued with a clear collective purpose. For example, filmmakers Pixar, frequently cited as an exemplar of organisational culture, famously inducts its staff by bringing them into the theatre where screenings are held. There, new staff – whether directors or café baristas or janitors – are asked to sit in the fifth row, where the directors sit, and are told: "Whatever you were before, you are a filmmaker now. We need you to help us make our films better."[22] How many academics and higher education professionals can articulate a purpose behind their work, beyond their own individual motivation? How many could make sense of how their individual efforts belong to a broader institutional effort?

With such questions in mind, the university has embarked on one institutional experiment aimed at generating public impact. The Culture Strategy team in conjunction with colleagues at the Sydney Policy Lab, one of the university's multidisciplinary initiatives that brings together researchers from across faculties, convened in late 2020 an independent taskforce to inquire into how Australia could re-engage with the world and rebuild from the pandemic. The taskforce, which brought together leaders from business, law, the arts, civil society and higher education, delivered a report in May 2021 providing a roadmap for Australia reopening its borders, with recommendations on how it could strengthen social bonds.[23] This was followed by an online summit of leaders from a range of sectors in August 2021. Along with creating a coalition with non-university partners, the exercise mobilised the university's academic expertise. In addition to the taskforce basing its recommendations on expert advice from infectious diseases specialists, we convened discussions that brought together academics from a range of disciplines and faculties to help shape the taskforce's deliberations. This was an exercise in getting the university as an institution to shape public discourse on one of the pressing public policy challenges of our time – and doing so in a way distinct from the traditional delivery of education in the classroom or research through peer-reviewed publications.

Such purpose-oriented projects have, it must be said, stretched both thinking and practice in the university. They have, among other things, underlined that institutional purpose can only be realised if backed by institutional capability. Getting academics and higher education professionals to see their work as part of a broader institutional mission or purpose is itself a challenge. More than this, it remains sometimes difficult to direct colleagues' efforts to a public purpose. Academic colleagues can sometimes struggle to reframe their work for purposes other than peer-reviewed research. Professional colleagues can similarly be constrained by their specialised operational expertise. The cultural goals around "values" and "people" have, in many ways, come naturally. Defining our "purpose", by contrast, has not perhaps come as easily.

Fit for purpose?

It is natural to view programs on institutional culture as fundamentally inward-looking, focused on improving the internal dimensions of a university. Indeed, work at the University of Sydney emerged from historical efforts within the university to generate a more cohesive institutional identity, one that transcends the university of years past which may have resembled a collection of local fiefdoms operating under a nominal university title. Yet, initiatives under the university's Culture Strategy have a dual focus, reflecting the importance of institutional culture to organisational strategy. It is not enough to foster a culture where academic and professional colleagues see themselves as part of a united whole, guided by shared values and a sense of collegiality. Any such culture must also be connected with an institutional mission or purpose.

While a reflection of the University of Sydney's particular history, this work touches on some of the challenges facing universities at large. For, while universities have traditionally understood their purpose as concerned with teaching and research, it is unclear that this alone will be enough to carry universities into a post-pandemic world. It is time for universities to consider, reflect and reorient themselves for a reality in which society may not regard their institutional value as self-evident. In a polarised, fragmented political culture, we cannot take for granted that people appreciate the pursuit of truth and the advancement of knowledge as virtues.

One path universities can take is to reaffirm our civic or public purposes.[24] We need to be present in people's minds, by ensuring we communicate the tangible benefits we bring to their lives. While many of these benefits come in the form of education and research, they are not exhausted by education and research. Universities serve a public purpose beyond these traditional functions – and it is time that we are more articulate about that purpose.

But, if universities are to succeed in such purposes, they will require cultural change. Institutional purpose can only be realised with capability. And if universities are to embrace a more explicit civic purpose, it will not be enough to assert it; rather, it will need to be embedded in their cultures. So can universities build cultures that are fit for purpose?

Notes

1 Williams, Raymond (1958). *Culture and society, 1780–1950*. London: Chatto & Windus; Kymlicka, Will (1995). *Multicultural citizenship: a liberal theory of minority rights*. Oxford: Oxford University Press.
2 Schein Edgar H. and Peter Schein (2017). *Organizational culture and leadership*, 5th ed. Hoboken, NJ: Wiley, 6.
3 Schein and Schein, *Organizational culture and leadership*, 17–29.
4 See Coyle, Daniel (2018). *The culture code: the secrets of highly successful groups*. New York: Bantam Books.
5 Newman, John Henry (1888). *The idea of a university, 8th ed.* New York: Longmans, Green and Co.
6 Australian National University. *ANU by 2025: Strategic Plan 2021–2025*, 8. https://bit.ly/3OafIF1.
7 King's College London, *King's Strategic Vision* (2019), 1. https://bit.ly/3uQM9kK.
8 Davis, Glyn (2013). The Australian idea of a university. *Meanjin* 72(3): 32.
9 Murray, Keith, Ian Clunies Ross, Charles R. Morris, Alex Reid, and J. C. Richards (1957) *Report of the Committee on Australian Universities* [Murray Report], Canberra: Government Printer.
10 See, for example, Connell, Raewyn (2019). *The good university: what universities actually do and why it's time for radical change*. Melbourne: Monash University Publishing.
11 Robert Menzies (1942). "The Forgotten People", speech, delivered 22 May 1942.
12 Gough Whitlam (1972). Election speech delivered at Blacktown, NSW, 13 November 1972.
13 Alan Tudge (2021). "Lifting the impact of universities to strengthen Australia's future". Speech delivered at the University of Melbourne, 26 February 2021. https://bit.ly/3o9Zhh2.
14 Dawkins, John (1988). *Higher education: a policy statement*. Canberra: AGPS, 3; see also Bell, Sharon (2017). *Perspectives on education for the public good: charting uncertainty*. Penrith: Western Sydney University. DOI: 10.4225/35/5967fc20faa09.
15 Judt, Tony (2010). *Ill fares the land*. London: Penguin.
16 The University of Sydney, *Strategic Plan, 2016–2020*, 15. https://bit.ly/3PomE20.
17 The University of Sydney, *Annual Report 2020*, 14, 29. https://bit.ly/3OaFBEC.
18 The University of Sydney, *Strategic Plan, 2016–2020*, 7.
19 The University of Sydney, *Strategic Plan, 2016–2020*, 43–44.
20 The University of Sydney, *Strategic Plan, 2016–2020*, 44–45.
21 The University of Sydney, *Staff and Affiliates Code of Conduct 2021*, 2. https://bit.ly/3yJPR0U.

22 Coyle, *The culture code*, 86.
23 Open Society, Common Purpose Taskforce (2021). *A roadmap to reopening*. Sydney: Sydney Policy Lab. https://bit.ly/3Ob6cRI.
24 Grant, Jonathan (2021). *The new power university: the social purpose of higher education in the 21st century*. London: Pearson Education; Marginson, Simon (2016). *Higher education and the common good*. Melbourne: Melbourne University Publishing.

15

Teaching and learning at Australian universities in uncertain times

Matthew A.M. Thomas, John Iromea, Remy Low, Victoria Rawlings and Susan Banki

Introduction

Teaching and learning have always been among the most important activities of universities. These vital educational processes have historically demanded adaption in response to social, cultural, and technological developments. The emergence of the world wide web, for instance, ushered in a new era of teaching and learning for universities as they transitioned toward online learning management sites, "electronic mail", and new forms of knowledge engagement and dissemination. While this pedagogical transition occurred over many years – and in some cases decades – the COVID-19 pandemic spurred significant changes to teaching and learning, seemingly overnight. This chapter draws on the lived experiences of four university academics and one international PhD student who worked to smoothly – though imperfectly – transition toward the "new normal" across undergraduate, post-graduate, and research education. In presenting these narrative reflections, it chronicles the immense challenges faced by those involved in teaching and learning at universities in recent years, imparting important lessons. Implicit in these accounts, too, are policy implications as well as insights into the ways that teaching and learning may be (re-)envisioned in the future.

Reflection 1: Teaching a first-year undergraduate unit during COVID-19

Remy Low and Victoria Rawlings

Together, we usually coordinate a first-year foundational unit of study in education called Education, Teachers and Teaching, which seeks to call into question many of the taken-for-granted assumptions that students (and also teachers) may have about education: What is "education"? Who are "teachers"? Who and what are we "teaching"? Each year we get around 500 eager undergraduates sitting in front of us on day one and, given that it's usually timetabled at 9 am on a Monday morning, charged with nervous excitement for their first ever university lecture. Of course, the Monday morning zeal diminishes significantly as the semester wears on – both for the students and for us as their teachers – especially for those who have to travel some distance to get to campus. Yet for the most part, students do persist in attending, even though attendance isn't taken. And we as their teachers continue to infuse intrigue and energy into our lectures to make it worth their while, as best we can, through discussion activities and Oprah-style audience interaction. Student feedback about this unit over the years has indicated to us that the lectures make for consistently positive learning experiences, although a few souls each year also make wry mention of the 9 am start times.

Embodied excitement. Timetable inflexibility. Collective energy. Attendance fatigue. The Monday morning lecture for our unit of study is perhaps emblematic of what has been gained and lost in teaching since the outbreak of COVID-19 in Australia in early 2020. While having hundreds of students crammed into a lecture theatre may have once been a given in university life not that long ago, it bespeaks the impact that the pandemic has had on our shared consciousness that we find it difficult to imagine it happening again anytime soon.

In the years leading up to 2020, one of the key challenges we have faced in teaching this unit is overcoming what Gramsci might call the "common sense" of what education, teaching, and learning entails.[1] While many of us would prefer to live in a society that allows for radical reforms of institutional arrangements like education without the need for a disaster to induce it, sadly for us – students and teachers –

our sedimented, habitual ways of seeing and doing exert a compelling conservative force. In many ways, COVID-19 has done the job of shattering common sense educational arrangements for us.

As we caught a glance of the pandemic approaching (Remy was in East and Southeast Asia when it first started to make headlines), we knew that many students would not be able to join us due to border closures. During early meetings to consider how we could best cater for those who could not join us, a host of conditions for learning that we had taken for granted suddenly became visible to us: borders, language, internet access, home environments, support services, even the policies that guide how students are assessed. All that was solid, to cite a well-known bearded thinker (i.e., Marx), began to melt into air[2]. Everything we had presumed about pedagogy, curriculum, assessment, and welfare (not to mention our own job security) began to look a lot less certain.

Plenty has been said about this or that platform, the virtues and vices of this or that pedagogical method, the ways and means of VPNs and plug-in enhancements. No doubt much more will be said in our scholarly circles about "pandemic pedagogy" or "COVID curriculum" – such is the opportunistic nature of academic publishing these days. We do not wish to rehearse what others may have already said or are eager to say. Like everyone else teaching through this period, we too had to experiment with platforms, change our curriculum and pedagogy, and get very familiar with that clunky meeting app called "Zoom". What we wish to focus on is the overarching ethic that guided all the decisions we made, even if it was unclear to us at the time what the outcomes might be: *care*. As Nel Noddings points out, teaching led by an ethic of care entails attentiveness and "motivational displacement" – that is, shifting energy toward the needs and objectives of the students we care for.[3]

So, in terms of curriculum, for instance, we consolidated the content of our course into a series of key questions that related to the recorded lectures and readings of each week, which were clearly arranged into a sequence of tasks. While this may seem like a lot of detail – some might even argue that we were "babying" our first-year students – we wanted to respond to their sense of confusion about navigating what was required of them. This forced us to make even more explicit what was conventionally assumed that students should know (e.g., "Before the lecture, complete this required reading"; "As you watch the lecture, make a note of the concepts that you do not understand. You can bring these to your tutor for further discussion in your tutorial class"). This practice of scaffolding was perhaps overdue, especially as it plots a clearer path to academic success for first-year students who may not have the family background – the " cultural capital" – to intuitively know how.[4] Finicky? Maybe. Caring? We think so.

Another example is in the way we communicated with our students. Aware of the stresses, anxieties, and grief experienced by many of our students as the world seemed to be upended, we made it imperative that our whole teaching team regularly "checked in" with struggling students as indicated by data from the learning management system, sharing with colleagues ways of crafting personalised messages so that students knew we were there for them. We also produced multiple video messages during critical times of their learning and worked with them to respond to their preferences for how classes should be run. One of us (Victoria) opened a WeChat account so that students could get in touch about their concerns in this period, which was particularly helpful to students in China who had not ever set foot on the University campus. The software and platforms we used were circumstantial; technology trends are second only to pandemic spikes in their unpredictability. The point was that we used what was at hand to compensate for the absence of physical presence, even if we seemed over-persistent with messaging and awkward on video. Too much? Maybe. Caring? We hope so.

Most importantly, and without any over-egged sentimentality, we cared deeply for one another as a teaching team. Whether expressed through short messages of kindness, assistance with technology troubles, making time to listen to one another, celebrating the small successes of each tutor – this mutual care sustained us through the most uncertain of days.

If nothing else, surely a global pandemic has made this much clear: life depends on care. So too does education.

Reflection 2: Simulation in a pandemic? Insights from the MA in Human Rights

Susan Banki

A typical class during my post-graduate Human Rights Simulation unit is lecture-light and experience-heavy. I might stand in front of the room discussing a philosophical ethic of justice or a particular social justice approach only about one-fifth of the time. The rest would be spent illuminating those concepts through practical, hands-on exercises that I designed over many years. Thus, prior to COVID-19, a visitor to my classroom might find students moving between huddled group meetings and paired role-plays, brainstorming data collection one moment and depicting power relationships pictorially the next. Coloured highlighters and bright post-it notes exchanged hands frequently. Different parts of the room might represent different countries or different thematic approaches to addressing human rights violations. Friendships were formed in the intimacy of emotionally and intellectually challenging face-to-face exercises.

You know what I will say next: this is not a unit that lends itself to Zoom-ification.

I have written about the principles underlying the unit,[5] and I have been awarded university and national-level prizes for its design and implementation. I have partnered with several other universities in Australia to develop innovative social justice models, one of whom modified it for distance learning.[6] Thus, I already understood that simulated activities could be adapted for use with online learners. But while I tinkered with changes to the unit every year, responding always to constructive student feedback, I had never myself had to envision how to create an engaging, intellectually rich, and emotionally safe space online until March 2020, when my students and I were plunged into the change from face-to-face to online learning between weeks 3 and 4 of a 13-week unit. In the lines that follow, I summarise the rapid changes I undertook to continue to create meaning in the Zoom-room. These are concerned with attention to emotional, logistical, and substantive challenges.

The Human Rights Simulation unit relies on a certain level of trust among the students. A series of " fishbowl" exercises allows students to observe each other under situations of (manufactured) pressure, whether emotional, temporal, or intellectual. This, combined with significant group work, demands a teaching environment in which students feel safe trying out different approaches to addressing human rights violations. When COVID-19 unexpectedly meant that we could not meet in person, I created the temporal space to allow students to express the difficulties – emotional, financial, logistical – that they were experiencing. A simple student check-in may not seem like a key strategy for a postgraduate unit, but it proved critical in developing strong online relationships.[7] These relationships strengthened student learning as group members supported one another in research and strategic analysis (both key components of the unit). The support also operated on a meta-level, projecting for students how they might offer care for one another in future work environments. To be clear, the relationship-building aspect of the unit is something I have always tried to incorporate, but in the context of COVID-19, students learned how to enact and perform trust and care via virtual channels, in and of itself an approach that has become increasingly important.[8]

Another key aspect of the simulation that required radical rethinking was the creative use of classroom space. How, I wondered as a technological novice, could I mimic virtually the movement of desks and chairs into different formations, suggesting different government or intergovernmental meetings? How might I permit students to move fluidly between different themes, that, in the past, I assigned to different sections of the classroom? I confess here that my efforts were less than 100 per cent successful. Certainly, the use of different Zoom screens can offer nearly infinite virtual backgrounds to call to mind, for example, a conference at the United Nations or a lobbying meeting at Parliament House. But these can also serve as a distraction from the task at hand: to focus on the work done at such meetings. Chat rooms on Zoom, with which we all became intimately familiar within a few weeks of teaching, provided some possibilities for dividing students into groups, although the technology was slow and clunky for creating pre-determined groups. Further, switching between chat rooms to facilitate and guide small group conversation is abrupt and disruptive compared to the quiet visit to a group of students sitting around a few desks pushed together. Other platforms not available institutionally may have offered speed and flexibility, but with little time to adopt and train for these, I relied on Zoom, with imperfect results.

Finally, I considered carefully how much substantive change I should make to the human rights topics covered in the semester. Soberingly, COVID-19 has created a great many new avenues for the exacerbation of human rights violations, from increasing restrictions on migrants and refugees to increased justifications for control and surveillance, to grave issues of inequity in health and education made far worse by COVID-19. Was there such a thing as COVID-overload? Might highly topical human rights issues serve as too much of a trigger to students who were currently experiencing anxiety themselves? I chose a middle path here. I retained the overarching human rights themes of the semester (political conflict and asylum seeker rights) and, within each of these topics, added content about the effects of COVID-19. Students therefore considered these impacts, but were not expected to use every conceptual and practical tool at their disposal to respond to COVID-related injustices exclusively.

At the close of this exceptionally challenging semester, I was pleased to see that my students remained committed and engaged. I received, in fact, the highest scores for this unit I had ever received, a testimony, perhaps to the strength of spirit of students who want to continue to learn, and address human rights violations, under the toughest of conditions.

Reflection 3: Teaching and learning to do research

John Iromea and Matthew A.M. Thomas

Completing a doctoral program is challenging in the best of times. The experience typically involves wrestling with difficult questions about the nature of knowledge and what can be known; honing research questions, exploring methodological approaches, and applying data collection and analysis strategies; pondering the implications and long-term impact of one's research; and so much reading, writing, and revising. Ideally, this process is aided by a strong relationship between the PhD student and supervisor, who is charged with ensuring successful (and timely) completion of the degree. As the COVID-19 pandemic began to unfold, it quickly became clear that these relationships were more important than ever before, as PhD students experienced a whole host of additional challenges on top of those generally associated with completing a higher degree by research (HDR). In what follows we discuss several key issues and affordances that emerged in our relationship as an international PhD student (John) and his supervisor (Matthew).

To begin, we'd like to acknowledge the immense sacrifices that many international HDR students make to study abroad. In John's case, he was fortunate enough to receive a full scholarship from the government of the Solomon Islands to complete his PhD studies. This meant, however, leaving behind his wife, children, and broader extended family to move to Australia. It also meant transitioning – culturally, financially, socially, physically – to a new environment at the University of Sydney. The different foods and 'cold' winter season felt particularly challenging to him, though obviously missing his family remained the biggest challenge of the move. Quickly, though, he established new communities in Sydney, including at the university.

COVID-19 changed John's circumstances in several ways. First, the initial fear and uncertainty associated with the pandemic caused him to wonder how it would affect his research, his degree, his family in the Solomon Islands, etc. Fortunately, John's research data was collected in 2019 before the pandemic, and therefore his progress was not affected as badly as some of his peers. For many other PhD students – including some of Matthew's other supervisees – significant adaptations to data collection were necessary, such as cancelling in-country fieldwork, revising research methods like participant observation, conducting interviews over Zoom, and requesting documents, policies, and curricula to be scanned and emailed rather than gathered in-person. Nonetheless, the additional concern and worry for John was layered on top of the normal angst experienced by many PhD students while completing their studies. Second, John stopped his regular trips to campus due to safety and public health regulations. This meant he was no longer able to meet face-to-face with his supervisor (Matthew) or his peers, with whom he enjoyed regular informal chats in the corridors and at research seminars and events.

Indeed, Matthew and other research supervisors also faced new challenges. Gone were the face-to-face discussions about data collected in the field, or the opportunities to walk together to get coffee before or after a meeting. Whilst personal connections were perhaps less fluid and non-verbal cues more difficult to read, Zoom meetings were scheduled more regularly to stay in touch, affording a more frequent check-in. Alternate approaches for providing feedback were also explored – some with better results than others – including sharing documents on-screen during supervision meetings or pre-recording feedback using a screen capture application like Loom. These somewhat unnatural options did have their affordances, however, such as built-in capabilities to record meetings such that John could revisit key feedback from supervision sessions. Others included an arguably more honest and vulnerable depiction of our respective lives. A few times John's flatmates walked past in the background; Matthew occasionally held or entertained his baby during a meeting due to limited childcare; we all saw the decorations (or lack thereof) of people's houses and flats; and we built solidarity by discussing and lamenting the pandemic, the challenges of teaching and learning virtually, and the loss of research communities based on campus.

Indeed, both John and Matthew missed desperately the many research seminars and workshops offered on campus. Following an initial lull due to confusions at the start of the pandemic, these eventually re-emerged in an online fashion, including the very seminar series upon which this book grew. In a sometimes schmick, sometimes clunky manner, these now virtual seminars were able to be attended by staff, HDR students, and others off-location, from Beijing to Brisbane. This increased accessibility notwithstanding, what was lost was the caring conversations about family members whilst grabbing a muffin before a seminar, or the ability to walk out the door with the presenter and ask one or two more follow-up questions, or simply the opportunity to sit physically near others with similar research interests and know that we, as researchers, are part of a shared community. This, it turns out, is much more challenging to implement in virtual spaces.

But thankfully, John has submitted his PhD. He is now back in the Solomon Islands and reunited with his family. He has completed one of the most challenging academic achievements, and under some of the most unusual of circumstances. His relationship with his supervisor – and indeed the entire way he worked and lived in Sydney – changed drastically as a result of the pandemic. Yet together, John and Matthew worked ardently though imperfectly to ensure successful and timely completion, and together they learned how to navigate the unknown world of teaching and learning to do research before and during a pandemic.

Conclusion

Much has been learned in recent years about how to navigate the complex dynamics of a pandemic, on societal, institutional, and individual levels. The reflective accounts above highlight just a few of the many ways in which teaching and learning were adapted by university workers and students in Australia. Increased emphases on care and communication, addressing quandaries about creativity and content, and coming to terms with the new realities of campus culture – or lack thereof – all emerged as core changes to pedagogical business as usual. Little is known about whether or how much teaching and learning will return to normal, but one thing is certain: we have all learned an immense amount along the way about how to adapt these vital educational processes in uncertain times.

Notes

1 Coben, Diana C. (2002). Metaphors for an educative politics: "common sense", "good sense" and educating adults. In Borg, Carmel, Joseph A. Buttigieg and Peter Mayo, (eds) *Gramsci and education*, 275–304. Lanham, MD: Rowman & Littlefield.
2 Marx, Karl (2000 [1848]). *Manifesto of the Communist Party*. https://bit.ly/3AWCP2V.
3 Noddings, Nel (2012). The caring relation in teaching. *Oxford Review of Education, 38(6)*, 771–81.
4 Wolfgramm-Foliaki, Ema, and Santamaría, Lorri J. (2018). Excavating stories of first generation students in Aotearoa New Zealand. In Bell, Amani, Lorri J. Santamaría (eds), *Understanding Experiences of First Generation University Students: Culturally Responsive and Sustaining Methodologies*, 27–46. London: Bloomsbury.
5 Banki, Susan, Elisabeth Valiente-Riedl and Paul Duffill (2013). Teaching human rights at the tertiary level: addressing the "knowing–doing gap"

through a role-based simulation approach, *Journal of Human Rights Practice*, 5(2), 318–36.

6 Mcgaughey, Fiona, Lisa Hartley, Susan Banki, Paul Duffill, Matthew Stubbs, Phil Orchard, Simon Rice, Laurie Berg and Paghona Peggy Kerdo (2019). "Finally an academic approach that prepares you for the real world": simulations for human rights skills development in higher education, *Human Rights Education Review* 2(1), 70–93.

7 Banki, Susan (2021). "Learning alone-a with Corona": two challenges and four principles of tertiary teaching, *Journal of Research in Innovative Teaching & Learning* 14(1), 65–74.

8 Rose, Ellen and Catherine Adams (2014). "Will I ever connect with the students?": online teaching and the pedagogy of care, *Phenomenology & Practice* 8(1) 5–16.

16

Universities, their publics, and climate change

Tamson Pietsch

Nearly 100 years ago, the American educational philosopher John Dewey wrote a book about how publics might work in a democratic society coming to grips with the implications of increasingly specialised knowledge. Publics, according to Dewey, have no pre-existence or a priori cause. Rather, they are called into being when three factors are in place: first, when the impacts of any situation or set of events are intellectually and emotionally appreciated by the various people they affect; second, when a shared interest is generated among different groups; who, third, then take action to address and regulate and attend to those impacts. "The public", Dewey wrote, "consists of all those who are affected by the indirect consequences of transactions to such an extent that it is deemed necessary to have those consequences systematically cared for." And when circumstances change, so too do those publics and their demands.[1]

In this chapter I argue that Dewey's notion of the public (or publics) might offer a way of thinking about and pressing for the purpose of universities in the context of the new historical circumstances arising from the impacts of climate change. More specifically, it might help clarify problems that universities confront, identify the public interest they share, and point to avenues for possible action. Doing so offers the possibility of renewing the public purpose underpinning the social contract, or settlement, between knowledge institutions, publics and the state.

John Dewey was not, of course, an advocate of classical social contract theory. He thought that seeing society as an aggregation of isolated individuals failed to attend to the actual historical origins of social and political institutions. There are, however, other ways of understanding the social contract as it pertains to universities, that are more compatible with Dewey's notion of society as an organism and his commitment to human beings as fundamentally social creatures constituted by and within common habits and institutions.[2] The higher education system that we have in Australia today reflects what, in Dewey's terms, might be thought of as the social arrangements for the care of knowledge that have arisen in response to the social and economic conditions of the last 40 years.

But these conditions have changed, and new arrangements are needed if the shared interest is to be served. The notion of a social contract, together with Dewey's concept of publics, pushes those who care about higher education to think more seriously about what the public purpose of universities is and who their constituencies are in these, our times. It pushes them to ask what shared interest they address, how it is perceived, and what mechanisms and agencies might be instituted to care for it.[3]

Universities are dynamic and vital institutions that across time have repeatedly adapted to changing contexts and reinvented themselves to meet the needs of new masters, new conditions and new publics.[4] How the social contract is redrawn at the start of the 21st century is of vital public importance. It is embedded in questions of power, democratic mandate and, ultimately, the ability of our societies to adapt to the profound and far-reaching challenges presented by climate change.

Universities, public good, and the social contract

As a concept in political theory the notion of a "social contract" has a deep genealogy that includes many contemporary approaches and critics.[5] But at its broadest and in the context of higher education, it might be understood, in Peter Maassen's words, as "the relationship between the state and its institutions, [which holds] that in order to form a social order there has to be a mutual understanding of, trust in, and commitment to the roles and responsibilities of all partners involved".[6] Rather than a formal treaty, a social contract in this sense is a largely unstated agreement about the distribution of obligations, benefits, content and purpose, which is negotiated and renegotiated in different eras under the pressures of new political and economic conditions: war, the ambitions of a monarch, religious rupture, technological change, nationalism, democratic society, economic imperatives.

Maassen is among the writers on higher education who, in the last two decades, have taken up this notion of the social contract as a way of redrawing the line between the university and the political realm. These scholars argue that for much of the 20th century, in return for public funding, universities created knowledge for the benefit of society. In addition, they trained new generations of scientists and professionals, most of whom would go to work in industry. Both these roles were seen as public goods, which benefited all members of society, and universities received status as well as funding in return for providing them. Industrial research, which was located outside the universities, took up the research discoveries made in the universities and translated them into the innovations on which economic growth was thought to depend. In between the two sat government science which, in Michael Gibbons' words, "fill[ed] the gap between the public good of the university science and the private good of industry".[7]

By the turn of the millennium, however, the economic, social, political and policy environment that underpinned this settlement shifted. The marketisation of higher education, the deindustrialisation of Western economies, the European Bologna integration process, and the growing biotechnology industry which saw the emergence of new sites of knowledge formation and new kinds of collaboration, all put pressure on the old arrangement. Universities, which increasingly looked like large corporations whose marketing documents emphasised the private, individual benefit of a degree, began to feel both public and political pressure to demonstrate their "impact" and value to society. Thinking in terms of a social contract that needed renewing proved attractive to many education scholars reflecting on these changes.

Two decades into the 21st century, the terms on which universities operate have shifted even more profoundly. The emergence of linked and granulated big data supercharged by digital platforms, the effects of COVID-19 and political responses to it, and above all the profound implications of climate change, have eroded the old arrangement that underlay universities' relationship to society on one hand, and the state on the other. For some time in Australia it has been evident that government higher education policy settings instituted at the end of the 1980s were no longer fit for purpose, and since the turn of the century, universities have increasingly relied on international student fees to supplement their income and fund research.[8] But both the pandemic-induced collapse of the international student market and lack of subsequent state support have significantly changed the terms on which universities in Australia operate and left many within the sector floundering.[9] The 2020 Job-ready Graduates Package (discussed in detail elsewhere in this collection) introduces a new operating environment for universities. In many ways it increases the focus on private value, whilst mapping out an even more utilitarian vision for higher education. Reduced public funding for tuition is linked more closely to government designated employment sectors, and the burden of tuition debt is carried more heavily by individuals. Research support, meanwhile, is predicated upon anticipated economic and social impact. On one view these changes reflect the former Coalition government's response to labour market pressures and the need to foster the nation's scientific and technical capacity, combined with its desire to reduce the public cost of the higher education system. But are they changes fit for purpose? Do they help address the common problems of our time?

Taking the long view on universities reveals big shifts in their relationship with the state on the one hand and their publics on the other. In Dewey's terms, it helps render the causes of their predicament intellectually and emotionally legible. When seen in the long view, universities are far from ivory towers. They are, and always have been, institutions that are intimately connected to economies and political processes, that have courted different constituencies in different contexts. This view enables those who care about universities to move beyond a defensive and oppositional position, towards acknowledgement of the need to change, and a preparedness to fight for the terms on which it will take place.

Universities in a climate changed world

Thinking about how publics are constituted helps us reckon with the societal demands of our era and points to the ways institutions like universities might help fashion a future that can meet these challenges. One set of imperatives will of course flow from the economic and social effects of COVID-19. But even more pressing for our generation and the generations that follow is climate change, the systems of social and ecological extraction that drive it, and the forms of adaptation and mitigation that it will require. Like the wars and ambitions of states and religious ruptures of the past, these processes are already fundamentally altering the conditions in which human society operates. They are reshaping what communities want and need and increasingly demand. They are making questions of distribution and access an urgent political imperative. This is not an imperative that the current policy settings for universities address, yet it is one that publics will increasingly insist is met.

Where does that leave universities? According to Dewey, governments alone do not set the terms in which institutions operate. Rather, both governments and institutions are constituted by publics to care for and meet a shared interest. If circumstances change and the arrangements put in place are no longer effective, then new arrangements will be required. Facing the implications of climate change presents universities with an opportunity (and indeed obligation) to rethink and reframe the way they understand and express their role and purpose and the source of their legitimacy. If during the 19th century, the public purpose of the university was to fashion a governing class, and during the 20th century it was, variously, to produce trusted knowledge, train professionals, fashion citizens and produce workers for a deregulated economy, then in the 21st century it might be to anchor communities in a climate changed world. Confronting the profound societal implications of the environmental crisis has the potential to open a new orientation and public purpose for the university.

What might publics demand of universities as our societies struggle to meet the consequences of the climate crisis? First, universities will be called on to become more sustainable. Where they invest their funds, who they partner with, what they consume, how they use their physical assets, and what they teach will increasingly be judged in terms of impact on the planet. Many institutions are already taking steps in this direction, with divestment action and the production of renewable energy key initiatives. But much more can and must be done when it comes to contracting and partnerships and curricula, and at a speed to match the urgency of the crisis. Moreover, teaching and research in all discipline areas must begin to engage with these imperatives.

Second, universities will be required to generate the knowledge and skills required to enable a positive societal transition to a lower emissions economy.[10] But producing expertise and technical advice will be only one aspect of this contribution, not least because university research is itself vulnerable to climate change. Expensive investments in certain infrastructure and equipment risks becoming stranded assets, as do some skills and competences.[11] Expertise that is not embedded in society – expertise that understands itself as telling people what they need or offering silver bullet solutions – is likely to fail. Serving communities confronting climate change will mean training those who care for and maintain human society. School teachers, nurses and medical professionals, social workers, biologists and librarians are just some of those who are explicitly charged with undertaking this work of caring and nurturing social as well as physical life systems. They will be key workers in a warming world: equally important, if not more, as those who strive to produce new technical solutions.

Third, universities will be asked to serve as holding environments for a society in flux.[12] They will be required to be institutions able to "handle coming contingencies and [help] . . . others do the same".[13] This means embracing their role as homes of meaning making, where stories are told and retold, uncertainty is named, and the norms of discussion, analysis and action are fostered – not only for those directly enrolled in university courses, but with and alongside the whole of society. As the effects of climate change reshape our cities and economies, support for, distribution of, and access to higher education will become political questions not only for individuals, but for the whole community.

This is not the vision for universities that is currently guiding higher education policy in Australia and universities alone cannot bring about a new settlement. But they can attend much more fully to the public that is already forming to demand a new set of arrangements that will better serve the common interest. Although governments have been slow to institute these arrangements, universities can themselves begin the work of drawing together the public who will demand them, by clearly articulating our society's shared predicament and identifying alternative pathways. As Wendy Steele and Lauren Rickards show in their recent book on the Sustainable Development Goals (SDGs) in higher education, this means recognising that universities have contributed to the systems that produce unsustainable development, and understanding that they have a crucial role to play in the maintenance, repair and regeneration required to support human society on this planet.[14] This has the capacity to renew their public purpose and help bring about a new social contract for higher education better suited to the needs of our time.

Renewing the social contract

The arrangements that were put in place to care for the consequences of late 20th century post industrial economies are no longer fit for purpose. New conditions, as Dewey wrote, "make the consequences of associated action and the knowledge of them different" in every age. New conditions demand new forms of organisation.[15] The terms on which universities will operate in the 21st century are not yet set, and that is because the most recent reforms do not acknowledge, let alone engage with, the existential challenge that is currently confronting human societies across the world.

This country is our common home. For better or for worse, we must live in it together. What kind of Australia do we want? How about a society which sustains and cares for each of us in our individual and collective joys and hardships, because together we sustain and care for it?

How about an economy that serves society and the planet rather than the other way round? Confronting the profound implications that climate change will have for all dimensions of our social and economic life has the capacity to renew the public legitimacy and purpose of universities in Australia. As these implications intensify, action is something that the many constituents of our higher education system will not just seek, but demand.

Notes

1 Dewey, John and Mervin L. Rogers (2016 [1927]). *The public and its problems: an essay in political inquiry*. Athens: Ohio University Press, 69, 77–82.
2 Dewey, John (1929). *Experience and nature*. London: George Allen & Unwin.
3 Dewey, *The public and its problems: an essay in political inquiry*, 78.
4 On publics, see Huber, Valeska and Jürgen Osterhammel, eds (2020). *Global publics: their power and their limits, 1870–1990, Studies of the German Historical Institute, London*. Oxford, New York: Oxford University Press.
5 For an overview see D'Agostino, Fred, Gerald Gaus and John Thrasher (1996). Contemporary approaches to the social contract. *Stanford Encyclopedia of Philosophy*. https://stanford.io/3AOOJM7.
6 Maassen, Peter (2014). A new social contract for higher education?. In Gaële Goastellec and France Picard eds. *Higher education in societies*. Rotterdam: Sense Publishers, 36.
7 Gibbons, Michael (2005). Engagement with the community: the emergence of a new social contract between society and science. Community Engagement Workshop, Griffith University, 4 March 2005, 2.
8 Pietsch, Tamson (2020). A history of university income in the United Kingdom and Australia, 1922–2017. *History of Education Review* 49(2): 229–48.
9 Department of Education, Skills and Employment (2020). Job-ready Graduates Package Higher Education Reforms. Canberra: Department of Education, Skills and Employment. https://bit.ly/3ARyj5p.
10 Rickards, Lauren and Tamson Pietsch (2020). Climate change is the most important mission for universities of the 21st century. *The Conversation*, 4 June. https://bit.ly/3On8kGt.
11 Rickards, Lauren and James Watson (2020). Research is not immune to climate change. *Nature Climate Change* 10(3): 180–83.
12 For development of the notion of "public things" as holding environments, see Honig, Bonnie (2017). *Public things: democracy in disrepair*. New York: Fordham University Press.

13 Rickards and Pietsch, Climate change is the most important mission for universities of the 21st century.
14 Steele, Wendy and Lauren Rickards (2021). *The sustainable development goals in higher education: a transformative agenda?* Cham, Switzerland: Palgrave Macmillan.
15 Dewey, *The public and its problems: an essay in political inquiry*, 80, 82.

Continuing the conversation

Julia Horne and Matthew A.M. Thomas

The introduction to this volume opened with a narrative about a conversation held over dinner. Conversations themselves are ubiquitous, but our hope in this volume is to help inspire and jumpstart a more robust and reflective conversation about higher education in Australia. The conversations highlighted within this volume are immensely important, and reconsidering the past, present and future, we believe, may lead to new ways of understanding and advancing the public good in Australia and beyond.

Efforts to advance and improve Australian universities must continue, and we encourage public discussions about what universities are, or what they should be. As highly influential social institutions, we contend that public universities should belong to the public, where mutual respect and admiration help support a thriving public good that benefits all.

The time is ripe for fresh conversations, and we are cautiously optimistic about the possibility for new forms of engagement between universities, governments, and their publics.

After the change in government in May 2022, the federal government quickly sought dialogue with Australia's public universities. In July 2022, to an audience that included many vice-chancellors, the Minister for Education Jason Clare described the ALP's higher education policy – the Australian Universities Accord – as a "reset". In Clare's words, it is "an opportunity to build a long-term plan for our universities ... I want this to be a bipartisan effort. I want [us] to come up with reforms that last longer than the inevitable political cycle."[1] In his first 100 days, Clare spoke of other higher education challenges that needed fixing. Echoing the 2008 Bradley Review, he reaffirmed that education should not be limited to those who can afford it: for example, the current 30 per cent gap between those young people who have university degrees and those Aboriginal and Torres Strait Islander young people who don't is appalling and insupportable.[2] He also outlined investigations to wind back some of the more constraining aspects of ARC research funding. And perhaps most innovatively, he re-introduced the idea that international students who graduate with an Australian degree could be desirable residents. Only 16 per cent of international students stay in Australia after their studies end. "Wouldn't it be great", Clare observed, "if they stayed on and helped us fill some of the chronic skills gaps we have got?"[3]

We welcome this renewed dialogue and the Minister's commitment to be guided by wide-ranging advice from universities themselves including, as Clare stated "staff, unions, business, students, parents, and all political parties".[4] But inspired by the essayists in this volume, we would add to this mix a broad representation of young people from all walks of life, including Aboriginal and Torres Strait Islander peoples, those from culturally diverse background, international students and women. Whether they are university students or not, their thoughts on higher education are surely essential to reform, particularly as informed members of the public. We would also add educationalists with expertise in closing the gap at schools. To take the next steps in broadening social access to higher education, we need to appreciate the nature of educational disadvantage and how its entrenchment at an early age becomes the major barrier to higher education later.[5]

In sum, provisionally these are all good signs that the current government wants to have a meaningful "accord" with universities that at the very least allows constructive, if imperfect, dialogue. To sustain the conversation in various ways we welcome ongoing dialogue with politicians, policymakers, and other key stakeholders. We encourage publications about Australian universities across a wide range of mediums, including in popular and non-academic outlets. We also seek to engage students, parents and community members in informal chats at the café, on and beyond campus, and out in the community. We see this volume as the beginning of a host of conversations about Australian universities and their future.

Finally, if you are interested in learning more about the origin of these conversations, or many of the topics examined in this volume, we would encourage you to explore the original History of University Life webinars recorded in 2020–21 online at "History of University Life Series Youtube".[6] Available webinars include:

- "University education is a pathway to employment", with speakers Susan Goodwin, Ariadne Vromen, and Julia Horne.
- "International students and Australian universities", with speakers Julia Horne, Gaby Ramia, and Matthew A.M. Thomas.
- "Higher education reform – where to now?", with speakers Glyn Davis, Tamson Pietsch, Ren-Hao Xu, and Matthew A.M. Thomas.
- "Can the humanities and social sciences survive the COVID crisis?", with speakers Joy Damousi, Michael Goodman, Jane Hall, and Julia Horne.
- "The current crisis in perspective – let's focus on equity", with speakers Tim Payne, Gwilym Croucher, Samantha McMahon, and Julia Horne.
- "Archiving university life in the age of COVID-19", with speakers Nyree Morrison, Jennifer Stanton, Richard Neville, and Julia Horne.
- "Universities are back in the news", with speakers Helen Proctor, Gwilym Croucher, James Waghorne, Alan Pettigrew, and Julia Horne.

Notes

1 Clare, Jason (2022). Minister for Education, "Reset, rebuild and reform", Speech delivered to the Universities Australia 2022 Gala Dinner, 6 July 2022. https://bit.ly/3QHqBPC.
2 Clare, Jason (2022), Minister for Education, Speech to the Australian Indigenous Education Foundation, 10 August 2022. https://bit.ly/3daHV1N.
3 Clare, Jason (2022), Minister for Education, Keynote Speech to the Australian Financial Review Higher Education Summit, 30 August 2022. https://bit.ly/3LdYR4j.

4 Clare, "Reset, rebuild and reform."

5 Horne, Julia (2022). A new accord: restoring good relations between government and universities. *Australian Book Review* July (444): 26–27.

6 Horne, Julia and Matthew A. M. Thomas, "History of University Life Series," produced with the assistance of the School of Humanities, University of Sydney, uploaded 18 April 2022, University of Sydney Faculty of Arts and Social Sciences YouTube Channel, videos, https://bit.ly/3a1xWdw.

Contributors

Julia Horne is Professor of History at the University of Sydney. She works on the history and politics of Australian higher education, and her publications include *Sydney: the making of a public university* (Miegunyah Press, 2012, co-authored with Geoffrey Sherington) and *Preserving the Past: the University of Sydney and the Unified National System of Higher Education 1987–96* (Melbourne University Publishing, 2017, co-authored with Stephen Garton). From 1996 to 2002 she ran the UNSW Oral History Program during which she created a substantial collection of interviews and in-depth surveys about student life, with an emphasis on the international student experience in the 1950s–1970s.

Matthew A.M. Thomas is a currently a lecturer in International and Comparative Education at the University of Glasgow, though this project commenced whilst holding his position as a senior lecturer in Comparative Education and Sociology of Education at the University of Sydney. His research examines educational policies, pedagogical practices, and teacher and higher education. Most recently, Matthew is the co-editor of *Examining Teach for All* (Routledge, 2021) and the *Handbook of Theory in Comparative and International Education* (Bloomsbury, 2021).

Susan Banki is a senior lecturer in the Department of Sociology and Social Policy at the University of Sydney. Her research is focused on human rights, social justice, and political activism. She has published in the *Journal of Refugee Studies*, *Third World Quarterly*, and the *Journal of Human Rights Practice*. Her latest book project is an examination of the exile politics of refugees.

Jennifer Barrett is Pro Vice-Chancellor Indigenous (Academic) (PVC-I) and Director of the National Centre for Cultural Competence (NCCC) at the University of Sydney. She has worked at the University of Sydney since 2000, becoming Professor of Museum and Heritage Studies in January 2020. Professor Barrett was the Director of the University's Culture Strategy (2016–2019), and Pro Dean, Academic in the Faculty of Arts and Social Sciences (2010–2016). Core to her professional history has been involvement with Aboriginal and Torres Strait Islander communities, colleagues and leaders, in teaching and learning, research, external engagement and leadership roles in the arts and cultural sectors. Professor Barrett's work supports the development of cultural protocols, repatriation issues, and contributes to a comprehensive approach to curriculum. Jennifer Barrett is a Dunghutti woman with cultural connections to the Macleay River region in northern NSW.

Gareth Bryant is an Australian Research Council DECRA Fellow at the University of Sydney, where he is senior lecturer in the Department of Political Economy and economist-in-residence with the Sydney Policy Lab. Gareth is a political economist who researches how public policy and public finance can create more sustainable, equal and democratic economies. His research has focused on issues including climate finance, renewable energy, higher education, housing, labour and Indigenous justice.

Gwilym Croucher is a researcher and lecturer in the Melbourne Centre for the Study of Higher Education at the University of Melbourne. A higher education analyst, he was a 2017–18 Fulbright Scholar and has been a Chief Investigator on Australian Research Council and Office for Learning and Teaching funded projects. His recent book (with James Waghorne) is *Australian Universities: a history of common cause* (UNSW Press, 2020).

Glyn Davis AC is Secretary of the Department of Prime Minister and Cabinet and Head of the Australian Public Service. This essay reflects his previous role as Vice-Chancellor at the University of Melbourne (2005–18), and develops themes from his 2017 book *The Australian Idea of a University* (Melbourne University Publishing, 2017). Glyn Davis is a public policy specialist, and remains Visiting Professor at the Blavatnik School of Government, and Visiting Fellow at Exeter College, Oxford.

Michelle Dickson is a Darkinjung/Ngarigu academic in the Sydney School of Public Health, and lives and works on Gadigal land. An Associate Professor, Dickson has worked in Aboriginal and Torres Strait Islander health and wellbeing service delivery and health professions education for 27 years. She is Deputy Head of School and former Academic Program Director of the Graduate Diploma in Indigenous Health Promotion. In 2021 the Public Health Association of Australia (PHAA) awarded her for contributions to Aboriginal and Torres Strait Islander public health. Dickson focuses on privileging First Nations ways of knowing, being and doing in education, research, health and wellness.

Michael Goodman has worked in a variety of university and NGO settings, including as the Associate Director of the Center for the Humanities at the University of Wisconsin-Madison and the Associate Director of Programs at the Wisconsin Academy of Science, Arts and Letters. His current scholarship focuses on the history of higher education and national education policies, institutional history, and the history of the humanities and technology education.

Susan Goodwin is Professor of Policy Studies at the University of Sydney. She undertakes research on social policy and social change. Her recent books include *Working Across Difference: social work, social policy and social justice* (2019), *Higher Education, Pedagogy and Social Justice* (Palgrave Macmillan, 2019) and *Poststructural Policy Analysis* (Palgrave Macmillan, 2016, co-authored with Carol Bacchi). Her current ARC Discovery Project with Helen Proctor (University of Sydney) and Jessica Gerrard (University of Melbourne) explores community organising in Australian education policy in the 1970s and 1980s.

Peta Greenfield holds a PhD in Classics and Ancient History. Her work includes over a decade of teaching and learning in secondary English. She is a co-host of the popular Ancient Roman podcast *The Partial Historians*. Her publications span diverse platforms from *Byteside* to *Ancient World Magazine*. Within the Office of Deputy Vice-Chancellor Indigenous Strategy and Services she supports innovative research work across disciplinary lines.

Valerie Harwood is a Professor of Sociology and Anthropology of Education at the University of Sydney. Valerie's research is centred on a social and cultural analysis of participation in educational futures. This work involves learning about collaborative approaches and in-depth fieldwork on educational justice with young people, families and communities.

John Iromea is an international student who completed his PhD, specialising in Educational Leadership, within the Sydney School of Education and Social Work, University of Sydney. His research focuses on school leaders' and teachers' perceptions of leadership, cultural knowledge, and school effectiveness in the Solomon Islands, where he worked previously as a deputy principal in secondary schools. His recent publications include: Educational leadership in the Solomon Islands: Training principals for quality schooling (*Journal of Leadership, Accountability and Ethics*, 2020) and Access, ethical leadership and action in Solomon Islands education: A tok stori (*International Education Journal: Comparative Perspectives*, 2021).

Lisa Jackson Pulver AM is a Koori woman who has family connections to south western NSW, the northern coast of NSW, South Australia, as well as to people in Wales, Scotland and Norway. Today, she is the Deputy Vice-Chancellor, Indigenous Strategy, and Services at the University of Sydney. She is a Professor of Public Health, an epidemiologist and medical educator. Her career in the academy has spanned decades and she spends her spare time serving our nation in the Royal Australian Air Force. Professor Jackson Pulver was made a member in the General Division of the Order of Australia in 2011, and is an academic leader, recognised expert in public health, prominent researcher, visionary, and tireless advocate for health and education.

Remy Low is a senior lecturer in the Sydney School of Education and Social Work, University of Sydney. He is committed to cultivating culturally responsive educators who can work in diverse contexts. This informs his research in the history and philosophy of education, which flows in two broad directions. First, he examines the social, cultural and religious factors that have shaped education in the present. Second, he explores how educator responsiveness may be fostered and sustained through contemplative practices from different traditions. Remy is the author of *The Mind and Teachers in the Classroom: exploring definitions of mindfulness* (Palgrave, 2021).

Samantha McMahon is the Learning Manager at the Bundanon Trust and a senior lecturer in Education Foundation Studies at the University of Sydney. Her research interests include sociology of education, inclusive education and widening university participation. Her work explores how teachers' engagement with multiple knowledges affects the equity of student experience and how students' lived experiences impact their understandings of education.

Tim Payne is Director, Higher Education Policy and Projects, in the Office of the Vice-Chancellor and Principal, the University of Sydney. He is an expert on Australian higher education policy and an adjunct senior lecturer in the Sydney School of Education and Social Work. Tim received the Vice-Chancellor's Award for Outstanding Contribution to the University Community in 2020.

Alan Pettigrew is a neuroscientist with a long career in medical research. Since the 1990s he has held senior appointments at various Australian universities including as Vice-Chancellor and CEO of the University of New England (2006–09) and was the inaugural CEO of the National Health and Medical Research Council (NHMRC) (2001–05). He is currently an expert advisor to the Tertiary Education Quality Standards Agency (TEQSA) and an external Fellow of Senate at the University of Sydney, Pro-Chancellor and Chair of the Senate's People and Culture Committee.

Tamson Pietsch is Associate Professor in Social and Political Sciences and Director of the Australian Centre for Public History at the University of Technology Sydney. Her research focuses on the history and politics of higher education and ideas. Tamson is the author of *Empire of Scholars: universities, networks and the British academic world* (Manchester University Press, 2013) and *The Floating University: experience, empire and the politics of knowledge* (Chicago University Press, 2023). In 2020, Tamson was host of The New Social Contract podcast, which examined how the relationship between universities, the state and the public might be reshaped under the pressures of both COVID-19 and climate change.

Gaby Ramia is Professor of Policy and Society in the Public Policy Program, Department of Government and International Relations, School of Social and Political Sciences at the University of Sydney. His books include *Governing Social Protection in the Long Term* (Palgrave Macmillan, 2020) and *Regulating International Students' Wellbeing* (Policy Press, 2013, co-authored with Simon Marginson and Erlenawati Sawir). Gaby is currently one of three Chief Investigators on an Australian Research Council funded study on international student housing precarity.

Victoria Rawlings is a lecturer in the University of Sydney School of Education and Social Work. She has conducted research with young people for more than a decade, with a focus on gender, sexuality and their social and cultural influences across education, health and sporting institutional contexts. Vic is an Australian Research Council DECRA Fellow, now conducting community-led research with school communities about how to understand and improve school cultures, especially in relation to gender and sexuality. Her publications include *Gender Regulation, Violence and Social Hierarchies in School: 'sluts', 'gays' and 'scrubs'* (Palgrave Macmillan, 2017) and the edited collection *Community-Led Research: walking new pathways together* (Sydney University Press, 2021).

Tim Soutphommasane is Director, Culture Strategy and Professor of Practice (Sociology and Political Theory) at the University of Sydney. He was Australia's Race Discrimination Commissioner from 2013 to 2018. His research in political theory has primarily concerned patriotism, national identity, multiculturalism and race. He is the author of five books, the most recent being *On Hate* (Hachette, 2019).

Ariadne Vromen is Professor at the Crawford School of Public Policy at ANU, and Deputy Dean (Research) at ANZSOG. She has long-term research interests in the social and political participation of young people, and two current collaborative ARC projects on young women's working futures. Her books include *Digital Citizenship and Political Engagement* ((Palgrave Macmillan, 2017) and *The Networked Young Citizen* (Routledge, 2014).

Stephanie Wood is the Program Manager for the University of Sydney's Culture Strategy. Her interest in organisational culture led her to study environments conducive to breakthrough scientific research, such as the discoveries that win Nobel Prizes, at the Nobel Museum in Stockholm. She previously spent ten years as an immunologist at the University of Queensland and Karolinska Institute in Sweden.

Ren-Hao (Leo) Xu is an advanced PhD candidate at the University of Sydney, and a Visiting Fellow at Sciences Po, France. A winner of the prestigious Taiwan Government Scholarship, Ren-Hao worked previously in a variety of educational reform and policy settings, including facilitating the 12-Year Basic Education Reform for the Department of Education, Taipei City Government. His research focuses on educational policies and higher education, particularly enrolment policies in Australia and Taiwan, and can be found in the *Journal of Education Policy*, *Australian Universities* (Sydney University Press, 2022) and *Using Theory in Higher Education* (Springer Nature, 2023). He tweets at @Leo_RenHao.

Index

Aboriginal and Torres Strait Islander students in higher education 17, 36, 160, 168, 172
  enrolments 69, 71, 168
  history 68–70
Aboriginal Study Grants Scheme (ABSTUDY) 32–33, 36, 70, 74, 172
Aboriginal Teachers' Aide program 70
Abschol 69
academic merit 3, 32, 43, 161, 202, 220
academic staff
  female 185
  number of 4, 45, 48, 184–185
Acknowledgement of Country 18, 19–21, 81
affordability 87
assumptions 30, 35, 91, 114, 153, 217, 230
Australian Labor Party (ALP) 5, 62, 156, 163
Australian Research Council (ARC) 192, 252
Australian Taxation Office (ATO) 138
Australian Vice-Chancellors' Committee 153, 156, 201
Austudy 33, 90

bachelor's degree, growth in 134
Behrendt Review *(Review of Higher Education Access and Outcomes for Aboriginal and Torres Strait Islander People)* 76–77
beliefs 216–217
big data 244
Bradley Review (*Review of Australian Higher Education*) 56, 75–77, 252
Brennan, H.G. 153

caring *see* pastoral support services
Chapman, Bruce 155, 157
China 3, 51, 104–106, 123, 126, 232
Clare, Jason 251–252
climate change 9, 11, 241–248
Closing the Gap 75–76
code of conduct 223
Colombo Plan 108–109, 112

Commonwealth Grant Scheme (CGS) 194
Commonwealth scholarships 32, 111, 152
Commonwealth-supported place (CSP) 164, 166, 169–170, 172
Control or Colour Bar? 110
COVID-19 pandemic, effects on tertiary education 29, 44, 121, 133–135, 164, 221, 229
CSIRO 155
cultural artifacts 217
cultural capital 232
cultural competence 74, 75, 81
cultural safety 77
Culture Strategy 216, 222–224, 224, 226

data collection 167, 233, 235
Dawkins, John 42
Dawkins reforms, the (*Higher Education Funding Act*) 4, 11, 56, 133, 134, 177
Dedman 201, 201
Dewey, John 241–242, 244, 245, 247
diversity, equity and inclusion 9, 89, 215, 218
doctoral education 48, 178, 235
Drucker, Peter 215

economic growth 56, 139, 220
economic rights 30
Education Services for Overseas Students 124–127
educational disadvantage 8, 10, 87–89, 91, 96, 98, 252
entrepreneurs, academics as 220
Excellence in Research for Australia (ERA) 192
exclusion, culture of 38, 69–70, 121
expertise and technical advice 246

A Fair Chance for All 9, 73–75, 158–159
fascism 205, 207
FEE-HELP assistance 169
fishbowl exercises 233
Friedman, Milton 151
funding 41, 50
  demand-driven 142, 172
  higher education 2, 4–6, 42, 45, 135–139, 164, 173, 200, 204
  research 2, 47, 127, 166, 178, 179–184, 186, 193

Gadigal country 22–23
General University Funds 186–191, 192
Gillard, Julia 33, 142
government scholarship schemes *see* Commonwealth scholarships
graduate tax 155, 157
Griff, Stirling 164
Group of Eight (Go8) 45, 179, 182, 185–190, 192

Hanson, Pauline 164
Hawke, Bob 10, 33, 140, 154, 157
Henderson Poverty Line 36
High Court of Australia 202–203
higher degree by research (HDR) 236
  completion 178, 179, 182, 236
  students 236–237
Higher Education Contribution Scheme (HECS) 10, 89–90, 94, 138–146, 151–161, 167–169
Higher Education Loans Program (HELP) 89–90, 151, 157–158, 169
Higher Education Participation and Partnership Program (HEPPP) 77, 89, 172
History of University Life seminar series 7–8, 253

Howard, John 33, 140–141
human resources 215, 218, 224
human rights 233–235
humanities 3, 94, 133, 141, 145, 165, 167, 173, 200, 205–207, 209–210, 253

Indigenous, Regional and Low SES Attainment Fund (IRLSAF) 172
Indigenous Strategy 17, 79, 218, 222
industrial research 243
institutional autonomy 200
institutional culture 71, 74, 75, 215–218, 222, 224–226
international student fee income (ISFEE) 190–191, 193, 194
international students 190
  comparisons with France, UK, USA 125, 126, 159
  fees 9, 127, 134, 144, 190, 244
  government policy 109, 112
  history 104–107
  welfare rights 122

JobKeeper scheme 1, 51, 119
Job-ready Graduate Higher Education Reform Package (JRG) 163–174
Jonas, Bill 69
Justice George Rich 202

Keating, Paul 33, 140, 156

labour market 31, 34, 36, 137, 153
"leadership for good" 217
lectures 230–231
Lewis, Irwin 68, 69
liberal democracy 221
loans, student 89, 138, 157; *see also* Higher Education Contribution Scheme (HECS)
  default and doubtful debts 144, 155
  repayment schedule 138, 140, 157
Loom 237

Macquarie University 42
Marshall, Thomas 122
massification of higher education 60–62, 88, 96
masters and doctoral degrees 178
Medical Research Future Fund (MRFF) 194
Menzies, Robert 32, 199, 204, 206–209
military service 202
Moodie, Gavin 44
Morrison government 2, 51, 145–146, 158, 163–165, 168, 171–172
Morrison, Scott 41, 44, 51, 120, 121
multidisciplinary 223–224
Murray Report, the (*Report of the Committee on Australian Universities*) 204–209, 219

Napthine Review, the (*National Regional, Rural and Remote Education Strategy*) 170
National Aboriginal and Torres Strait Islander Education Policy 72–73, 75, 78
National Apology to the Stolen Generations 20
national interest 8, 108, 114, 164
National Security Act 202
National Tertiary Education Union, the (NTEU) 36, 143
National Union of Australian University Students, the (NUAUS) 69
national welfare 200
neoliberalism 220
NSW Department of Education 168

One Nation Party 164
online teaching 10, 44, 173, 233
organisational strategy 226

pastoral support services 77, 169
Penny, Geoffrey 68, 69
Penrith, Luke 22
performance review 223
Perkins, Charles 68–69
Pixar 224
populism 221
price signals 165, 173
Private Overseas Student Programme 109
private value 244
public good 6, 38, 139, 143, 200, 208, 221, 243, 251
public policy 157, 225

racism 106, 121, 124
Research Block Grant (RBG) 178–190, 192, 194
research-only staff 193
research 2, 46, 182, 184, 193, 194
  commercialisation 220, 220, 243
  funding *see* funding: research
  impact 185, 192, 220, 235

school leavers 5, 163, 168–171, 174
Second World War 68, 107, 154, 200–201
soft diplomacy, international education as 108, 114
student fees 42, 46, 135, 136, 139–142
  abolition 152
students
  Aboriginal and Torres Strait Islander *see* Aboriginal and Torres Strait Islander students in higher education
  anxiety and stress 169, 174
  disadvantaged backgrounds 10, 61, 88, 142, 155, 170; *see also* educational disadvantage
  life 37, 91, 97
  regional and remote 88
  support services 124, 169, 191
sustainability 193
Sustainable Development Goals (SDGs) 247
Sydney Policy Lab 224

Taiwan
  410 Civic Education Reform 56–58, 60
  comparisons with Australia 11, 56, 60, 61, 62
  higher education sector 55–61
teacher education 104
Tehan, Dan 44, 164–166, 199–200, 208–210
Tertiary Access Payment (TAP) 171–172
Tertiary Education Allowance Scheme (TEAS) 32, 152
Tudge, Alan 51, 126, 168, 220

United Nations 234
universities
  barriers to entry 8, 89, 94, 156, 168, 252
  corporatisation 219, 243
  operations 45, 47, 48, 193, 219, 244
  size 45, 49
  workforce 48
universal student income 36, 39
Universities Admissions Centre (UAC) 168, 169
Universities Australia (UA) 79
University of Melbourne 45, 68, 69, 201

University of Sydney 5, 18, 23, 27, 45, 68, 69, 99, 104–105
University of Technology Sydney (UTS) 42
UNSW 42, 99, 110–111, 137

vice-chancellors 166, 218–219, 251
Vocational and Educational Training (VET) 123, 144, 160

Watt Review 194
Welcome to Country 20
White Australia Policy 106, 107, 110
Whitlam, Gough 32, 41, 107, 134, 152–153, 154, 220
widening university participation 88–89, 96, 160
Williams, Margaret 68, 69
Williams, Peter Gary 69
women 4, 68, 134, 140, 154, 168, 169, 185–186, 206
Wran, Neville 155–156

Youth Allowance 33, 33–37, 90, 172
youth welfare citizenship 30, 31, 35, 38, 39

Zoom 231–237

www.ingramcontent.com/pod-product-compliance
Lightning Source LLC
LaVergne TN
LVHW051937100826
845154LV00002B/9

* 9 7 8 1 7 6 1 5 4 0 3 0 1 *